THE GUI GUIDE

International Terminology for the Windows™ Interface

European Edition

Microsoft PRESS

PUBLISHED BY
Microsoft Press
A Division of Microsoft Corporation
One Microsoft Way
Redmond, Washington 98052-6399

Library of Congress Cataloging-in-Publication Data
The GUI Guide / Microsoft Corporation.
    p. cm.
   Includes bibliographical references and index.
   ISBN 1-55615-538-7
   1. User interfaces (Computer systems)   2. Computer graphics.
 I. Microsoft Corporation.
 QA76.9.U83G84   1993
 005.4'3--dc20   92-41060
                                   CIP

Printed and bound in the United States of America.

1 2 3 4 5 6 7 8 9   FGFG   8 7 6 5 4 3

Distributed to the book trade in Canada by Macmillan of Canada, a division of Canada Publishing Corporation.

Distributed to the book trade outside the United States and Canada by Penguin Books Ltd.

Penguin Books Ltd., Harmondsworth, Middlesex, England
Penguin Books Australia Ltd., Ringwood, Victoria, Australia
Penguin Books N.Z. Ltd., 182–190 Wairau Road, Auckland 10, New Zealand

British Cataloging-in-Publication Data available.

Microsoft Worldwide Product Group, Ireland
Italian Language Specialists: Licia Corbolante, Sergio Pelino
Swedish Language Specialists: Christina Theander, Henrik Hult
Dutch Language Specialists: Caroline den Os, Johan van Trappen
Finnish Language Specialist: Olavi Hiukka
Danish Language Specialist: Helle Christensen
Norwegian Language Specialist: Knut Utsi
Polish Localizer: Ewa Orlowska
Hungarian Localizer: Gabor Varga
Lingua Manager: Liesbeth van Bijsterveld
Production Editor: Jacqui Gallagher
Production Team Lead: Tom McManamon
Production Trainer: Carole Devaney
Print Production Manager: Patrick Coleman
Localization Services Manager: Gunnie Jacobsson

This book was produced using Microsoft Word.

Microsoft Lingua Redmond
German Terminologist: Irene Scheck
French Terminologist: Jean Marcel Leblon
Portuguese Terminologist: Gerson Stumpf
Spanish Terminologist: José Luis Riesco
Group Language Manager: Anil Singh-Molares
Group Language Manager: Maria Henriksen
Group Language Manager: Diana Ryesky

Microsoft Windows Developer Relations
Consultants: Marjan Plager and Sherry Richardson

WASSER Communication Services
Writer: Annie Pearson
Production Specialist: Dennis Thompson

Microsoft Press
Project Editor: Casey D. Doyle
Technical Manager: David Rygmyr

Contents

Part 2   GUI Terminology Translations

Appendixes

Introduction

Welcome to *The GUI Guide,* a concise handbook for understanding and localizing the terms related to the elements of the graphical user interface (GUI) used in the Microsoft® Windows™ operating system and in Windows-based applications. This introduction presents the following topics:

- Goals for the graphical user interface
- Purpose of *The GUI Guide*
- Contents of *The GUI Guide*
- Companion disk
- Document conventions

Goals for the Graphical User Interface

Microsoft has always been a strong believer in the idea that a graphical user interface is the most intuitive way for people to interact with their computers. Microsoft was among the first companies to make a major commitment to developing graphical applications for computers running the MS-DOS® operating system, from introducing the Microsoft Mouse to implementing the industry-standard operating system, Microsoft Windows.

Graphical user interfaces are now a reality for many users, becoming more common and more important every day. Computer users are benefiting from a single, consistent application interface because the movement of users and files among multiple computers is easier and the need for training and support is reduced.

A principal goal of the GUI in Microsoft Windows is to establish common, consistent communication between the user and the application. Such consistency helps ensure that a user who can use one Windows-based application can use them all. Vital elements of the GUI in Windows include the following:

- Consistent keyboard commands
- Consistent menus for identical actions
- Consistent use of terminology in supported languages

The following illustration shows some of the key elements of the Microsoft Windows graphical user interface discussed in Part 1 of *The GUI Guide*.

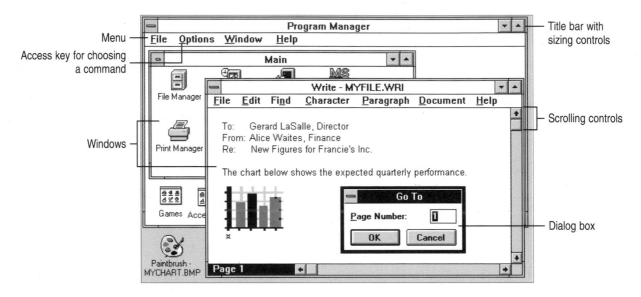

Purpose of *The GUI Guide*

The purpose of this handbook is to provide guidelines for everyone involved in the development or localization of GUI software that runs under Microsoft Windows. *The GUI Guide* provides the following:

- An overview of common terms for which Microsoft has standard translations
- Guidelines for localizing menus and menu commands
- Guidelines for assigning access keys and shortcut keys
- Standard translations for essential GUI elements in 14 European languages

Because Microsoft is constantly updating and attempting to improve terminology, the translations in this handbook are subject to change without notice.

The information presented in *The GUI Guide* is provided to ensure visual and functional consistency in the development and localization of Windows-based applications. You may choose to adopt any recommended or suggested guideline in the user interface design or localization at your own discretion; there is no requirement for conformance expressed or implied in these guidelines. These terms and definitions are used at Microsoft in localized products, and application designers at Microsoft are committed to following the recommendations.

Contents of *The GUI Guide*

The GUI Guide consists of two parts plus an appendix section:

- Part 1, "GUI Terminology Definitions," describes the main components of the Microsoft Windows graphical user interface.

- Part 2, "GUI Terminology Translations," provides recommended translations for GUI components, both by category and alphabetically, in Czech, Danish, Dutch, Finnish, French, German, Hungarian, Italian, Norwegian, Polish, Portuguese, Russian, Spanish, and Swedish.

  Terms that appear in *italic* in Part 1 are translated in Part 2, but more terms are included in Part 2 than are defined and used in Part 1. The terminology lists in Part 2, however, do not provide translations for every term you might encounter in a Windows-based application.

The appendixes include representations of keyboard layouts, tables of national standards for time format and other items, and tables of various character sets.

A bibliography lists relevant literature. The index provides a guide to finding examples and definitions in Part 1 as well as the terminology lists by language in Part 2.

Companion Disk

The terms in Part 2, "GUI Terminology Translations," are included in electronic form as a companion disk to *The GUI Guide*. The companion disk includes files in Microsoft® Windows™ Write tab-delimited format, which lists the terms with their recommended translations. This information can be imported into a spreadsheet, database, or word processor file for easy electronic access to the translated terms. In addition, the disk contains the same lists of terms in Microsoft® Excel format.

For more information about the content and use of the companion disk, please see the license agreement and the README.TXT file that appears on the disk as online documentation.

Document Conventions

The document conventions described in the following table are used throughout *The GUI Guide:*

Convention	Used for
ALL CAPITALS	Filenames, directory names, and acronyms; for example, C:\WINDOWS.
italic	Terms that are translated in Part 2; for example, *application window*.
SMALL CAPITALS	Names of keys on the keyboard; for example, SHIFT, ALT, or CTRL.
KEY+KEY	Key combinations for which the user must press and hold down one key and then press another; for example, CTRL+P or ALT+F4.
KEY, KEY	Key sequences for which the user must press and release one key and then press and release another; for example, ALT, SPACEBAR.

GUI Terminology Definitions

C H A P T E R   1

The GUI Window

This chapter describes the basic elements of windows in the Windows graphical user interface. The following topics are presented:

- Main window elements
- Window arrangements
- Icons
- Pointers and the focus
- Sizing controls
- Scrolling and splitting controls

Main Window Elements

The most characteristic feature of the Microsoft Windows graphical user interface is that applications and their files are presented in *windows* on a background called the *desktop*. The desktop can be blank or can include a design called *wallpaper*.

Each window has a *title bar,* showing the name of the application and/or document. Each movable window also has its own *Control-menu box*, and each sizable window has sizing controls in the title bar. (For more information, see "Sizing Controls" later in this chapter.)

The boundary of a window is defined by a *window frame*. Each side of the window frame is called a *window border*. Note, however, that a window that has been maximized fills the entire screen and does not have a frame.

Although the desktop can contain many windows, only one window at a time can be active, that is, can receive user input. The *active window* has a differently colored title bar from the *inactive windows* that might be open on the desktop.

The user can maximize, *size, move,* and *close* the active window by either choosing a command or performing a mouse action. In some applications, a window can also be *split* into a number of *panes,* allowing the user to *view* various document contents simultaneously.

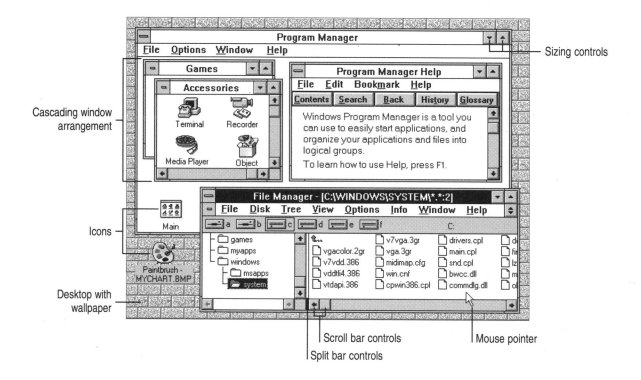

There are two types of windows: *application windows* and *document windows.* An application window appears when an application is started. Document windows are created by an application and usually appear within the application window.

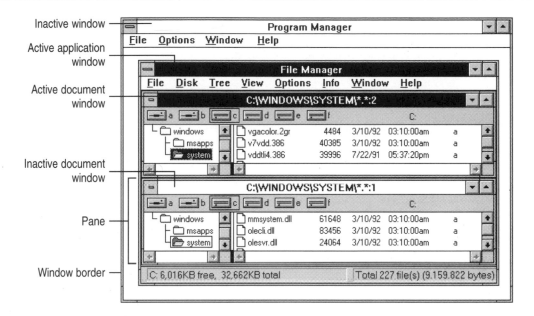

Inactive window
Active application window
Active document window
Inactive document window
Pane
Window border

Window Arrangements

When several windows are open at the same time, they can often be rearranged in two ways, as *cascading windows* or as *tiled windows.* Cascading windows are overlapped so that the title bar of each is visible; tiled windows are *arranged* so that all the open windows are simultaneously visible on the desktop.

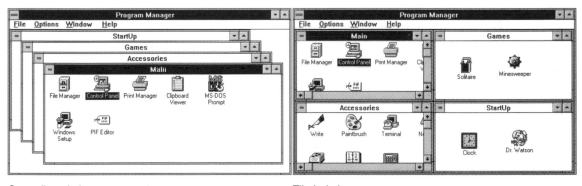

Cascading windows

Tiled windows

For example, *Program Manager* can contain *group windows,* which display the applications and files in a *program group.* A user can arrange the group windows by choosing a command from the *Window menu* or by *dragging* the title bar of a window to place it anywhere within the Program Manager application window.

Icons

As a GUI environment, Microsoft Windows makes extensive use of *icons*. The term "icon" is usually reserved for describing a graphical representation of an item that can be selected or opened, such as a drive, directory, document, or application.

Some icons in Microsoft Windows have specific names or uses, as shown in the following table:

Icon	Icon description
StartUp	A *group icon* appears in the Program Manager window, representing a group window that has been minimized.
Readme	A *program-item icon* appears in a program group in Program Manager, representing an application and/or its associated document.
File Manager	An *application icon* appears on the desktop, representing an application that is running but has been minimized on the desktop.
C:*.*:1	A *document icon* appears in an application window, representing a document window that has been minimized. The appearance of a specific document icon depends on the application that it belongs to. This illustration shows a document icon in *File Manager.*
b c	*Drive icons* and *disk icons* appear in File Manager, representing floppy disk drives and hard disk drives.
	Directory icons, application icons, and *document file icons* appear in File Manager, representing directories and files.

Pointers and the Focus

A pointing device such as a mouse or a roller ball makes it easy to navigate and manipulate items in a GUI environment. A *mouse pointer* on the screen represents the pointing device. Depending on the application and the screen location, the pointer can take different shapes. The most common pointers are shown in the following table. For more examples of pointers, see "Sizing Controls" later in this chapter.

Pointer	Type	Pointer	Type
	Arrow pointer		*Cross-hair pointer*
	Hourglass pointer		Context-sensitive Help pointer
	I-beam pointer (not the same as the selection cursor)		Top-of-table pointer
	Pointers for vertical and horizontal sizing of rows and columns		Pointers for vertical and horizontal *split bars*
	Magnifying glass pointer for *zooming*		No-drop pointer

The focus represents the part of the interface that will receive the next input if no navigation occurs before the input is generated. For mouse input, the focus always coincides with the pointer location after the mouse button has been pressed. For keyboard input, the focus depends on the context:

- In windows, *menus,* and *dialog boxes,* the focus appears as a *selection cursor,* which identifies the item that will be affected next by *clicking* or typing. The selection cursor can appear as a highlighted object, a dotted rectangle around text, or a set of sizing handles.

- In text, the focus is shown by an *insertion point,* which indicates where text will next appear that the user types or pastes. The insertion point usually appears as a blinking vertical bar.

- In spreadsheets, the focus is shown by a highlighted cell border to indicate the cell that will receive typed input and be affected by commands.

Sizing Controls

The size and location of an application window or document window on the screen can be controlled in a number of ways: by using the *Control menu*, by using the sizing controls, or by dragging the window border.

Sizing with the Control Menu

Windows usually have a Control-menu box, which appears in the top left corner of each window. The Control-menu box provides access to the Control menu, which contains commands for window manipulation, such as resizing, moving, and closing the window. Other commands might also be available, depending on the application.

The application window's Control menu can be activated by pressing ALT+SPACEBAR

The document window's Control menu can be activated by pressing ALT+HYPHEN (-)

Sizing with the Sizing Controls

Windows that can be sized usually have sizing controls at the right end of the title bar. Users can click these buttons to size an application window or a document window. The action has the same effect as choosing the related command name from the Control menu. The following table describes the sizing controls:

Sizing control	Name and description
▲	*Maximize button.* Clicking this button enlarges a window to its largest possible size, usually that of the whole desktop or *workspace*.
⬍	*Restore button.* Clicking this button returns the window to the size it was before it was maximized.
▼	*Minimize button.* Clicking this button reduces a window to an icon.

Sizing with the Window Border

A window can also be sized by dragging the window border or *window corner*. When located over a window border or window corner, the mouse pointer appears as a two-headed arrow, indicating the directions in which the border can be dragged.

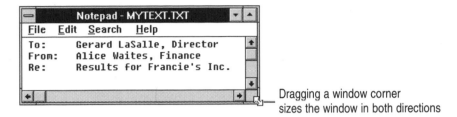

Dragging a window corner
sizes the window in both directions

Alternatively, when the user chooses the *Size* command on the Control menu, the mouse pointer appears as a four-headed arrow, indicating that the user can press any arrow key to resize the window in the related direction.

Scrolling and Splitting Controls

If a document contains more information than can fit inside the window, the user can use scroll bars and split bars to see more data.

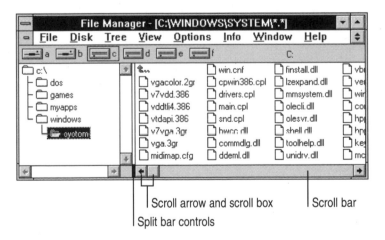

Scroll arrow and scroll box | Scroll bar

Split bar controls

Scroll Bar Controls

Most document windows can display a *vertical scroll bar* and often also a *horizontal scroll bar*. The scroll bar contains two *scroll arrows* and a *scroll box*. The user can drag the scroll box and click the scroll arrows or scroll bar to *scroll* the contents of a window, moving parts of a document into view.

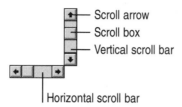

Scroll arrow
Scroll box
Vertical scroll bar

Horizontal scroll bar

The scroll box also provides a visual clue as to the part of the document shown in the current view. For example, if the scroll box is in the middle of the scroll bar, the view shows the middle of the document.

Split Bar Controls

If the application allows the user to *split* the window, each part of the window (also called a pane) usually gets its own scroll bars so that each pane can be scrolled independently.

A *horizontal* or *vertical split bar* indicates where the window has been split. The window split can be changed by dragging the *split box* between the two scroll bars to a new position. When the user points to a split box, the pointer changes shape to show the direction in which the user can drag to split the window. The pointer is shown in the table in "Pointers and the Focus" earlier in this chapter.

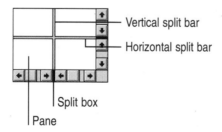

Vertical split bar
Horizontal split bar

Split box
Pane

In some applications, it is possible to *freeze* the panes by locking the split bar in a chosen position. The split bar then becomes a single line, and only one pane can be scrolled at a time. *Unfreezing* reverses the situation.

CHAPTER 2

The GUI Menu

This chapter describes the terms and conventions for menus in Windows-based applications. The following topics are presented:

- Menu elements
- Menu commands
- Guidelines for localizing menu names and menu commands

Menu Elements

Most Windows-based applications have a *menu bar* with at least one menu. A menu has a title called the *menu name* that indicates the purpose of the commands on the menu.

Menus can appear as *drop-down menus* or as *cascading menus*. A drop-down menu opens when a menu name is chosen; a cascading menu (also called a *submenu*) appears when a menu command includes a right-pointing triangle.

Some applications display pop-up, or contextual, menus, which appear in the window near the current mouse pointer location when the user clicks mouse button 2 (usually the right mouse button). Pop-up menus look like and work in the same way as drop-down menus. The items displayed on the menu depend on where the pointer was located when the button was pressed. Pop-up menus provide an efficient way to access commands without using a menu bar or *toolbar*.

When a menu is open, it shows a number of *commands*. Command names can describe actions (such as Replace), style options (such as *Underline*), graphics settings (such as patterns, lines, and colors), program groups or document names (such as GAMES in Program Manager), or document window names (such as C:\MYFILES:2 in File Manager).

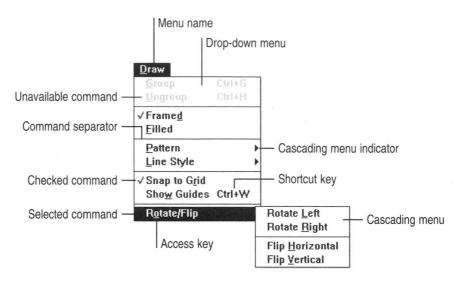

Choosing a menu name in the menu bar opens the menu, which contains at least one command or option. Most applications have a Control menu and the menus *File, Edit,* and *Help*. These menu names appear in standard positions on the menu bar. Many other applications also have *Format, Macro, Options, Utilities, View,* or *Window* menus.

Many of these common menus and the command names they contain have recommended names and a set translation, as described in the "Terminology by Category" sections for each language in Part 2.

Menu Commands

Menu commands can appear on a menu in different modes: normal, selected, unavailable, or with alternating names or special symbols. The different appearances of menu commands are described below. Groups of related commands are usually separated from other commands by a *command separator,* a horizontal line in the menu, as shown in the preceding illustration.

Close   Alt+F4   Menus and commands in Windows-based applications are commonly activated by clicking a name with the mouse. Users can also choose a menu or command from the keyboard, either by using a unique ALT+key combination called an *access key* (underlined in the name), or by pressing the *shortcut key* designated for the command. For more information, see Chapter 6, "GUI Shortcut and Access Keys."

Contents   When a user chooses a command by pointing to it with the mouse or by pressing an arrow key, the name of the *selected command* is highlighted on the menu.

Restore

A command can be either available or unavailable. An unavailable (or disabled) command appears dimmed on the menu.

√ **T**oolbar
• **N**ormal

Some commands are "toggles." That is, they can be switched on or off. When a toggle command is active, its name is preceded by a *check mark* or a dot on the menu. An active toggle command is sometimes called a *checked command.*

Ruler On
Ruler Off

Toggle commands can also appear in pairs of alternating command names, indicating alternative states. Choosing one command causes the other command name to replace it on the menu.

Searc**h**...

An *ellipsis* (...) after a command name indicates that when the user chooses that item a dialog box will appear, requesting more information.

Line St**y**le ▶

A right-pointing triangle following a command name indicates that this choice leads to a new list of items that will appear as a cascading menu or submenu.

Menu commands can also appear as graphical items. These appear most often in cascading menus that provide choices for specifying a line style, pattern, color, or other graphical element.

Guidelines for Localizing Menu Names and Menu Commands

If a new menu name is to be created or translated, it is important to choose a short name, but one that will still make sense to users.

Window
Insert

If the available space on the menu bar is limited, try to avoid using the letters "W" and "M" as the first characters of a menu name, because they each take up the space of two characters.

Both menu names have six letters, but the first one takes 30 percent more space on the menu bar.

Menu names can be made up of a compound name, but no spaces between words are allowed in a menu name.

Menu command names can be made up of more than one word, but the general rule is: the shorter, the better.

To save space on the menu bar, the Help menu name is sometimes replaced by a question mark in localized software.

C H A P T E R 3

The GUI Dialog Box

This chapter describes the items that can appear in a dialog box. The following topics are presented:

- Dialog box elements
- Command buttons
- Dialog box controls
- Edit controls
- Elements of a Font dialog box

Dialog Box Elements

Label Disk...

When the user chooses a menu command that includes an ellipsis (...) in the command name, a dialog box appears in the window. Dialog boxes present choices so the user can give information to the application. The user confirms the choices by choosing the *OK* button, or cancels the dialog box by choosing the *Cancel* button or by double-clicking the Control-menu box.

Dialog boxes have a title bar with a Control menu and a *dialog box title* that describes the command that displayed the dialog box. Dialog boxes can be moved in the window by dragging the title bar or by choosing the *Move* command from the Control menu.

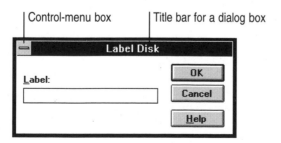

Control-menu box   Title bar for a dialog box

A dialog box cannot be sized. In some cases, however, the dialog box is expandable, initially showing a small number of choices, with more options available when the user chooses a special button.

The following basic elements are used to present the items in a dialog box:

- The focus appears in a dialog box as a dotted rectangle around an option's label or as a highlight in a text box or list box.

File Name:

- *Labels* identify the command buttons, controls, text boxes, and other options in a dialog box, informing the user of their purpose. Labels can consist of text or graphics.

    If an option in a dialog box is not available, its label appears dimmed.

- *Group boxes* are used to present a set of related dialog box controls in a logical way. A group box usually has a descriptive label.

- An access key is usually identified in a control's text label as an underlined character. The user can use the access key to select the option by pressing ALT+key. For more information, see Chapter 6, "GUI Shortcut and Access Keys."

Command Buttons

Every dialog box contains at least one *command button,* which carries out an action, such as confirming the choices in the dialog box, canceling the dialog box, or displaying another dialog box. The OK and Cancel buttons are the most common.

Clicking a command button activates the related command. Pressing ENTER activates the default command button, which has a heavier border than other buttons in the dialog box. Pressing ESC has the same effect as choosing the Cancel button.

An ellipsis (...) after the label on the button means that this choice leads to another dialog box. This type of button is also referred to as a *Goto* or *Gosub button.* A Goto button closes the current dialog box and opens a related one. A Gosub button leaves the current dialog box open and opens a related one, allowing the user to return to the previous dialog box after closing the current one.

Greater-than signs (>>), or *chevrons,* in the label of the command button indicate that the choice expands the current dialog box. This type of button is sometimes called an unfold button.

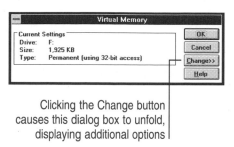

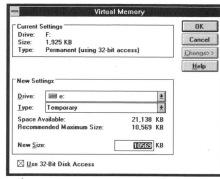

Clicking the Change button
causes this dialog box to unfold,
displaying additional options

Dialog Box Controls

Besides command buttons, the principal dialog box controls include check boxes, option buttons, sliders, and value sets. For descriptions of text boxes and list boxes, see the next section, "Edit Controls."

Check Boxes

Check boxes can exist alone or in a group box. Each check box can be selected independently of other check boxes. An "X" appears in the check box when it is selected. In some applications, check boxes can also be filled with a color, indicating that the current selection in the document contains a mixture of settings.

Option Buttons

Option buttons (sometimes called radio buttons) usually appear in a group box of related options. Only one option button in a group can be selected at a time. Clicking another option button in the same group switches off the previous selection automatically. The selected option button contains a dot.

Sliders

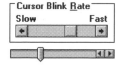

A *slider* is used to display and adjust continuous attributes, such as volume, brightness, or speed. The *slider indicator* is a marker that shows the present value and can be dragged along the bar to set a new value. Some sliders are similar to scroll bars.

Value Sets

A *value set* is a group of related buttons with either graphics or text labels. When an item in a value set is selected, a highlight appears around the button. Only one item in a value set can be selected at a time.

Other controls in a dialog box may also appear as graphical items as shown below:

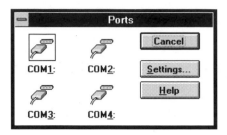

Edit Controls

Edit controls are used to specify text or numbers in a dialog box. These controls include text boxes, list boxes, combo boxes, linked text and list boxes, and spin boxes.

Text Boxes

The user can type text in a *text box* (sometimes referred to as an entry field). Text boxes can appear alone or in a group. The application defines the required and accepted user input for a text box, such as a filename, a number, or text.

List Boxes

List boxes show a list of items the user can select. A scroll bar appears when the list is too long to display in the box without scrolling. To save space, some dialog boxes contain *drop-down list boxes*. Clicking the drop-down arrow opens the list box to show the available options.

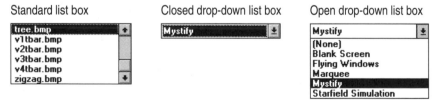

Combo Boxes

Text boxes and list boxes are sometimes combined in a *combo box* or a *drop-down combo box*. A combo box allows the user to select from a list or type data directly in the text box. A standard combo box is always open; a drop-down combo box can be opened by clicking the drop-down arrow.

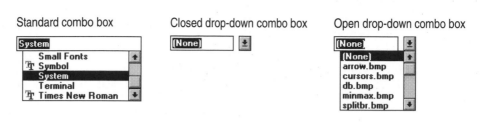

Standard combo box   Closed drop-down combo box   Open drop-down combo box

Linked Text and List Boxes

A text box and one or more list boxes can appear together as a *linked text and list box.* This makes it possible to combine choices from multiple list boxes into one entry in a text box. For example, the recommended *Open* and *Save As* dialog boxes use linked text and list boxes. In these dialog boxes, the choices in the *Drives, Directories,* and *List Files of Type* boxes combine as one entry in the *File Name* text box.

Linked text and list boxes often allow the use of *wildcards* in the text box to limit the number of choices in the list box. For example, dialog boxes that require a filename and dialog boxes for searching text usually allow wildcards. When wildcards are allowed, the question mark (?) can be used to represent any single character, and the asterisk (*) can be used to represent any number of characters.

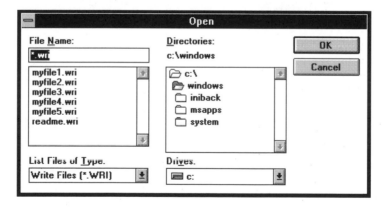

Spin Boxes

A *spin box* controls a cycle of values. The user clicks an arrow to raise or lower the value. Often the user can also type a value in the text box.

Elements of a Font Dialog Box

In Microsoft Windows, a *font* is the name of a typeface. Many applications present a standard dialog box for the user to select a font and its size and style; other applications allow more aspects of a character's appearance to be defined.

The following table describes the dialog box controls that are commonly available for defining the appearance of text in Windows-based applications:

Control	Description
Font box	A list of all the typefaces installed on the computer.
Font Style box	A list of the styles such as *bold, italic,* or regular that are available for the typeface selected in the Font box.
Size box	A list of the point sizes available for the typeface selected in the Font box.

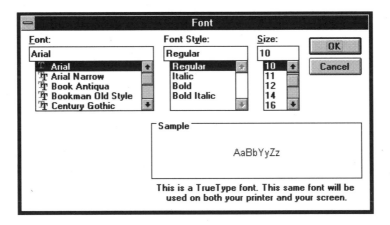

C H A P T E R   4

Other GUI Visual Elements

This chapter describes several special GUI elements that often appear in application windows. The following topics are presented:

- Toolbars and rulers
- Sizing handles
- Text frames
- Toolboxes and other graphical options
- Multimedia controls

Toolbars and Rulers

Many applications show options graphically as *rulers* or *tools* on a toolbar. A user can, for example, set margins or tabs by dragging a marker on a ruler. The ruler usually appears horizontally beneath the menu bar or toolbar at the top of the window, but it might also appear along the window's vertical border.

A toolbar appears as a horizontal bar at the top of the window and contains buttons, drop-down list boxes, and sometimes status areas. By clicking a button on the toolbar, the user can choose the related command or start an action.

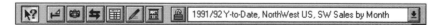

An application might define its own buttons in a toolbar, or it might use any of nine standard buttons. The standard buttons are described in the following table:

Button	Command	Button	Command
✂	Cut	🖨	Print
📋	Copy	💾	Save
📋	Paste	❓	Help
📄	New	⬆❓	Context-sensitive Help
📂	Open		

Sizing Handles

Sizing handles (also called resizing handles) appear on the border of a selected object. The recommended number of sizing handles is usually four or eight. The user can change the object's appearance by cropping or sizing with the sizing handles. *Cropping* means that parts of the object's visual content are cut off by dragging the sizing handles. *Sizing* means that the *scale* of the object is changed by dragging one of the sizing handles in the appropriate direction. Sizing keeps the object's visual content intact but reduces or enlarges the object.

Sizing handles also show which object has the focus and will therefore receive the next action.

Text Frames

Text frames (not to be confused with *text boxes*) are sizable fields in which the user can type text. Clicking the text frame causes border sizing handles to appear. Text frames can also be moved to a new location.

$84,600	$28,200	$23,400	$25,900
2250	Target for FY94:		10000
600	Increase market share		2000
2400	by 25%		2700
2460			8200
7500	2500	3000	3000

— Text frame in a spreadsheet

Toolboxes and Other Graphical Options

Many applications present a collection of options in easy-to-use graphical views such as *toolboxes, palettes,* and *galleries.* Depending on the purpose the option serves, graphical options might present measures, colors, patterns, or presentation formats. For each of these graphical options, clicking an item carries out an operation such as changing an object's appearance or switching a toggle command on or off.

Toolboxes might appear in fixed positions along the border of the application window or as a "floating" palette that includes a title bar and Control-menu box for moving or closing the toolbox. A toolbox is used in the same way as a toolbar.

Galleries are a collection of graphical options that can appear as options on a floating palette or in a dialog box.

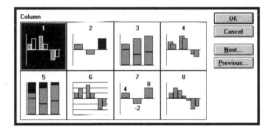

Multimedia Controls

For applications that have multimedia capabilities, special controls may be provided to control a media player such as a CD-ROM audio player, MIDI *device,* or sound recorder.

Common visual controls resemble the buttons on an audiotape or videotape player, with arrows indicating the direction for playing or rewinding the media, plus a slider for controlling the timing, volume, or other elements. The user chooses these controls like any other button, by clicking or dragging.

For a list of common menu and command names used for multimedia applications, see the "Terminology by Category" sections for each language in Part 2.

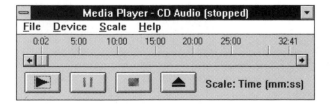

C H A P T E R   5

GUI Messages and Status Indicators

This chapter describes various elements of the Microsoft Windows graphical user interface that provide feedback to the user about current activities in an application. The following topics are presented:

- Message boxes
- Status bars
- Progress indicators

Message Boxes

Message boxes provide feedback to the user in the form of status information or a warning. Message boxes can be moved, but not sized. They usually have one or more command buttons, allowing the user to respond to the message.

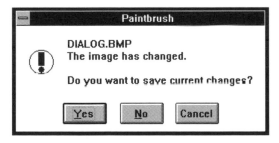

Three types of messages can appear, each with a distinctive symbol that emphasizes the nature of the message, as described in the following table:

Symbol	Type of message
![info]	A *message* provides information from the application or system software. No action is required; the user must acknowledge the message by choosing the OK button.
![warning]	A *warning message* indicates that an error has occurred or that a potentially destructive action is impending that requires user action. The user must make a choice before proceeding. The most common answers are OK, Cancel, *Yes,* and *No.*
![stop]	A *critical message* indicates that a serious system-related or application problem has occurred that must be corrected before the user can continue to work on any application. The user must make a choice before proceeding. The most common answers are OK, *Retry,* and Cancel.

Status Bars

Many applications display a *status bar* at the bottom of the application window to provide information for the user. The status bar can be used to communicate the following kinds of information:

- Clarify the purpose of a selected menu command
- Give instructions for performing a task
- Show the coordinates of the selection cursor
- Indicate the state of a toggle command

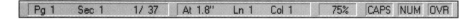

Some applications display a *message line* in the status bar. For example, while saving a file, some applications show the percentage completed of the action. Other applications also use the status bar to display context-sensitive Help when the user points to menu names or menu commands.

Several *status-bar indicators* are suggested for use in Windows-based applications. Suggested abbreviations are also provided, but complete words are preferred wherever possible. In the following list, the mode indicators are shown in the order in which they should appear (from left to right) in the status bar:

Indicator	Mode
EXT	*Extend selection*
CAPS	*Caps Lock on*
NUM	*Num Lock on*
SCRL	*Scroll Lock on*
OVR	*Overtype on*
REC	*Macro Recorder on*

Other abbreviations that might appear in the status bar of a text-oriented application include the following:

Abbreviation	Indicator
Pg	*Page*
Sec	*Section*
Ln	*Line*
Col	*Column*

Translations for status bar indicators and the other abbreviations appear in Part 2.

Progress Indicators

Usually an application displays the hourglass pointer when an action takes some time. A *progress indicator* in a message box can also be used to keep the user informed of the status of a complex, time-consuming action such as formatting a disk or copying a large number of files. The rectangle is gradually filled with color from left to right as the action proceeds.

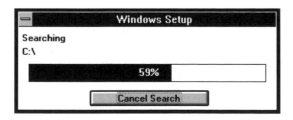

C H A P T E R   6

GUI Shortcut and Access Keys

This chapter describes how shortcut and access keys are defined in Windows-based applications. The following topics are presented:

- Shortcut keys
- Access keys

Shortcut Keys

Undo   Ctrl+Z

A user interface should provide consistent shortcut keys for frequently used commands. A shortcut key can be used to activate a command without first opening the menu containing the command. Shortcut keys are often listed beside command names in menus as reminders. A shortcut key usually consists of one of the following:

- A CTRL+key combination (such as CTRL+Z for Undo)
- A function key (such as pressing F1 to get Help)
- A modified function key (such as ALT+F4 for Exit, or CTRL+F12 for Open)

A large number of shortcut keys are mnemonic and therefore require localization. But some shortcut keys are commonly used among various language versions of localized products. For example, the following shortcut keys are recommended for common menu commands:

Command name	Shortcut key
Clear	DEL
Copy	CTRL+C (also CTRL+INS)
Cut	CTRL+X (also SHIFT+DEL)
Paste	CTRL+V (also SHIFT+INS)
Undo	CTRL+Z (also ALT+BACKSPACE)

The following common menu commands have shortcut keys that use mnemonic keys related to the localized command name:

Command name	Recommended shortcut key before localization
New	CTRL+N
Open	CTRL+O
Print	CTRL+P
Save	CTRL+S
Bold	CTRL+B
Italic	CTRL+I
Underline	CTRL+U

Translations for common shortcut keys and command names appear in Part 2.

In some applications, commands for formatting text can also be activated by clicking an icon. If the icon contains a mnemonic letter, this should be the same letter as used for the corresponding access key or mnemonic shortcut key.

The following guidelines will help in assigning shortcut keys:

- Assign single keys for frequently performed or small-scale actions.
- Assign SHIFT+key combinations for actions that complement another key combination.
- Assign CTRL+key combinations for infrequent or large-scale actions.
- Avoid assigning ALT+letter combinations because these are used for access keys.
- Avoid assigning function keys as the first choice for shortcuts. Although function keys are easier to localize, they might seem to be arbitrary compared to modifier keys such as a mnemonic CTRL+key combination.

Access Keys

Often, the user can choose menu names, menu commands, dialog box options, and command buttons by pressing access keys. Access keys are usually a combination of the ALT key plus a character, where the character is the under-lined letter in the menu name or other item; for example, ALT, F, O chooses the Open command from the File menu.

Recommended access keys have been defined for many common menus and commands. In Part 2, the recommended access keys for localized versions appear in parentheses after the menu or command name in the listings for a specific language.

The following guidelines describe how to assign a unique access key if no recommended access key is defined.

Guidelines for Access Keys for Menu Names or Command Buttons

Open...

Exit

1. Use the first letter of the name.

2. Use a distinctive consonant.

3. Use any other unique letter.

Guidelines for Access Keys for Menu Commands or Dialog Box Labels

Assign to Key...
Assign to Menu...

1. Use the first letter of the most important word.

   The example in the margin shows a pair of similar command names that appear together on the same menu. For alternating command names such as Ruler On and Ruler Off where only one command appears on the menu at any moment, use the first letter of the shared word (for example, the "R" in Ruler).

2. Use the first letter of the first word.

3. Use any other unique letter.

CHAPTER 7

User Actions

This chapter presents definitions for common terms describing user actions in Windows-based applications. The following topics are presented:

- Keyboard actions
- Mouse actions
- Manipulating window appearance
- Selecting options or content
- Viewing document content
- Removing document content
- Linking, embedding, and manipulating objects

Keyboard Actions

The user can communicate with the application by using the keyboard. The most commonly used keyboard actions are shown in the following table:

Term	Definition
Press and hold down	Press a key, and leave the key depressed while performing another action.
Type	Type a text string, which appears on the screen as each key is pressed.

Mouse Actions

The user can communicate with the application by using the mouse. Most Windows-based applications define actions for a two-button mouse. Mouse button 1 (usually the left mouse button) is the selection button and is used for most mouse actions. Applications define how mouse button 2 (the right mouse button) is reserved for context-specific actions. The most common mouse actions are shown in the following table:

Term	Definition
Click	Quickly press and release the mouse button without moving the mouse. The insertion point moves to the position of the mouse pointer. Clicking an item in a menu, dialog box, toolbar, or scroll bar usually results in an action. Clicking mouse button 1 selects an item or activates a window or control.
Double-click	Click the mouse button twice in rapid succession without moving the mouse. The insertion point moves to the position of the mouse pointer. Double-clicking with mouse button 1 usually selects data in a document, or selects an option and carries out a command in a dialog box.
Drag	Hold down the mouse button while moving the mouse, and then release the mouse button at the end of the operation. Data is selected between the starting and ending points of the drag. Dragging the scroll box in a scroll bar scrolls the document contents in the window. Dragging while holding down mouse button 1 identifies a range of objects, or moves or resizes items.
Drop	Release the mouse button when dragging an object in an application that has *drag-and-drop* capabilities.
Point	Move the arrow pointer to the desired location on the screen. The insertion point stays at its current location.

Manipulating Window Appearance

The user can change the size and appearance of a window. The following list explains the most common actions for manipulating windows:

Term	Definition
Arrange	Rearrange windows or icons so that they all become visible.
Close	Close the window, including all subordinate windows if applicable.
Freeze	Lock the split bar, making only one pane scrollable.
Hide	Make the window temporarily invisible.
Move	Drag the window to a new location on the screen.
Resize	Same as Size.
Restore	Return the window to the size it was before it was minimized or maximized.
Select	Make a window the active window.
Size	Change the size of the window.
Split	Split the window into panes.
Switch	Activate the next open window or next icon.
Unfreeze	Undo Freeze.

Selecting Options or Content

The philosophy behind the "intuitive interface" has resulted in many new terms that are often closely related, but do not always have the same meaning. The following list explains the most common terms that describe selecting and manipulating window contents:

Term	Definition
Cancel	Close a drop-down menu or dialog box, or cancel the current selection.
Check	Turn on a toggle command in a drop-down menu, or select a check box option in a dialog box.
Choose	Choose a menu command or command button.
Clear	Undo selection of check box or option button.
Extend selection	Make the current selection larger.
Reduce selection	Make the current selection smaller.
Select	1. Mark data in the window for further manipulation. Selected text or objects appear highlighted or outlined.
	2. Open a drop-down menu.
	3. Click a drop-down arrow to open a list box.
	4. Turn on an option button or check box in a dialog box.

Viewing Document Content

There are various ways to move around a document and view its content. The following list describes related terms:

Term	Definition
Autoscroll	Automatically display the next part of the document when required. For example, if the user is selecting text and reaches the bottom of the window, the application automatically scrolls to display the next screenful of text.
Browse	Show a document in increments, usually screenful by screenful.
Collapse	Hide subtext (in Outline mode).
Expand	Display subtext (in Outline mode).
Print Preview	Show on screen how the printed document will look.
Scroll	Move the document contents through the active window.
Scroll Lock	Scroll in a document with the SCROLL LOCK key on, so that the cursor position or selection is not changed when the user navigates with the mouse or keyboard.
View	Look at a document in a certain mode, such as Draft mode or Outline mode.
Zoom in	View an enlarged image of a document.
Zoom out	View a reduced image of the document, or undo zoom in.

Removing Document Content

The contents of a document can be removed in a number of ways. The following list describes the options:

Term	Definition
Clear	Discard the current selection without placing it on the Clipboard. Or remove the contents of a selected object (such as a cell or text), but leave the object intact.
Copy	Copy the current selection to the Clipboard.
Cut	Remove the current selection, and copy it to the Clipboard.
Delete	Remove the current selection; if an object is selected, remove both object and contents.
Paste	Place the contents of the Clipboard at the insertion point.

Linking, Embedding, and Manipulating Objects

An *object* is a single block of data (for example, text or graphics). Objects can be sized, edited, moved within a document, imported from an external source, and permanently linked with that source. The following terms are related to object manipulation:

Term	Definition
Arrange	Move selected objects into a regular, evenly spaced array.
Crop	Adjust the content of an object by cutting parts of it.
Group	Make one object from a collection of selected objects.
Size	Adjust the dimensions of an object by *scaling* its width and/or height.

In *object linking and embedding* (OLE), the *source document* furnishes information as a *linked object* that is displayed in the *destination document*. An *embedded object* is placed in a *container document* (the destination document), but it has no source document. An embedded or linked object can also be placed in a destination document as a *package,* which is an icon that represents the data, command, or file that the object contains. The following terms are related to OLE:

Term	Definition
Embed	Insert an object in a document by creating a new object, by using the *Insert Object* command, or by using copy-and-paste operations. The object appears in its original format and can be edited or, in the case of macros and multimedia objects, can be played or run.
Link	Insert a copy of information from a source document into a destination document by using the *Paste Link* or *Paste Special* command. The linked object maintains a connection between the two documents that the user can examine or change in the Links dialog box. When the information is changed in the source document, the changes appear in the destination document.
Update	Cause the changes made to a linked object to appear in a destination document.

GUI Terminology Translations

CHAPTER 8

Czech

This chapter lists the Czech translations of all terms formatted in *italic* in Part 1. Terminology is listed in two ways: by category and in alphabetical order. The first section includes translations in the following categories: Window Elements, Menus, Dialog Boxes, Message Boxes, Other GUI Screen Elements, Keys, User Actions, and Applications For Microsoft Windows.

Terminology by Category

ENGLISH	CZECH	ENGLISH	CZECH
WINDOW ELEMENTS		window size	velikost okna
Main window elements		window title	titulek okna
active window	aktivní okno	workspace	pracovní prostor
application window	okno aplikace		
border	okraj	**Window controls**	
bottom window border	dolní okraj okna	Control-menu box	políčko ovládací nabídky
cascading windows	kaskáda oken	down scroll arrow	šipka přetáčení dolů
desktop	pracovní plocha	horizontal scroll bar	vodorovný přetáčecí pruh
document window	okno dokumentu	horizontal split bar	vodorovný dělící pruh
group window	okno seskupení	left scroll arrow	šipka přetáčení doleva
Help window	okno nápovědy	Maximize button	maximalizační tlačítko, tlačítko
inactive window	okno, které není aktivní		pro maximalizaci
left window border	levý okraj okna	Minimize button	minimalizační tlačítko, tlačítko
menu bar	nabídkový pruh		pro minimalizaci
pane	podokno	Restore button	obnovovací tlačítko, tlačítko
right window border	pravý okraj okna		(pro) obnovení
ruler	pravítko	right scroll arrow	šipka přetáčení doprava
status bar	stavový pruh	scroll arrow	přetáčecí šipka
tiled windows	dlaždicové uspořádání oken	scroll bar	přetáčecí pruh
title bar	titulkový pruh	scroll box	přetáčecí běžec
toolbar	nástrojový pruh	split bar	dělící pruh
top window border	horní okraj okna	split box	dělící políčko, políčko pro změnu
wallpaper	tapeta		(roz)dělení
window	okno	up scroll arrow	šipka přetáčení vzhůru
window background	pozadí okna	vertical scroll bar	svislý přetáčecí pruh
window border	okraj okna	vertical split bar	svislý dělící pruh
window corner	roh okna		
window frame	rám okna		

ENGLISH	CZECH	ENGLISH	CZECH
Pointers		Size	Změň velikost (v)
arrow	šipka	Minimize	Minimalizuj (n)
arrow pointer	šipka	Maximize	Maximalizuj (x)
cross-hair pointer	nitkový kříž	Next	Další (d)
hourglass pointer	přesýpací hodiny	Close	Zavři (z)
I-beam pointer	I-kurzor	Run...	Spusť... (u)
insertion point	kurzor	Switch to...	Přepni do jiné úlohy... (p)
mouse pointer	ukazovátko myši	Split	Změň rozdělení (r)
pointer	ukazovátko		
selection cursor	kurzor pro provádění výběru	File menu	Soubor (s)
		New...	Nový... (n)
Icons		Open	Otevři (o)
application icon	ikona aplikace	Close	Zavři (z)
directory icon	ikona adresáře	Close All	Zavři vše (v)
disk icon	ikona disku	Save	Ulož (u)
document file icon	ikona souboru s dokumentem	Save As...	Ulož pod jménem... (p)
document icon	ikona dokumentu	Save All	Ulož vše (l)
drive icon	ikona jednotky	Delete	Smaž (m)
group icon	ikona seskupení	Page Setup	Nastavení vzhledu stránky (h)
icon	ikona	Print	Vytiskni (t)
program-item icon	ikona programové položky	Print Preview	Ukázka před tiskem (e)
		Printer Setup	Nastavení tiskárny (s)
General terms		Exit	Konec (k)
access key	přístupová klávesa	Exit and Return to	Konec a návrat do
check mark	označení		(jméno aplikace) (k)
ellipsis	tři tečky	Update	Aktualizuj (a)
font	písmo		
object	objekt	Edit menu	Editace (e)
program group	seskupení programů	Undo	Zpět (z)
program item	programová položka	Repeat	Opakuj (a)
shortcut key	zkratková klávesa	Cut	Vyřízni (v)
sizing handle	úchopný bod pro nastavení	Copy	Kopíruj (k)
	velikosti	Copy Special	Rozšířené kopírování (r)
status-bar indicator	indikátor na stavovém pruhu	Paste	Přilep (p)
tool	nástroj	Paste Link	Přilep propojení (i)
unavailable command	nedostupný povel	Paste Special	Rozšířené přilepení (l)
		Clear	Smaž (s)
MENUS		Clear All	Smaž vše (v)
Menu elements		Find...	Vyhledej... (v)
cascading menu	kaskádová nabídka	Search...	Vyhledej... (v)
checked command	označený povel	Replace...	Zaměň... (z)
command	povel	Go To...	Přejdi na jinou stránku, kartu
command separator	oddělovač povelů		atp.... (p)
drop-down menu	rozbalovací nabídka	Delete...	Smaž... (s)
menu	nabídka	Insert...	Vlož... (v)
menu command	nabídkový povel	Object...	Objekt... (o)
menu name	jméno nabídky	Insert Object...	Vlož objekt... (j)
selected command	vysvícený povel		
submenu	vnořená nabídka	Options menu	Volitelné (v)
		Preferences	Preference (r)
Menus & commands		Full Menus	Plná nabídka (p)
View menu	Zobrazení (z)	Short Menus	Zkrácená nabídka (z)
Insert menu	Vložit (v)		
		Format menu	Formátování (f)
Control menu	Ovládací nabídka	Character...	Znak... (z)
Restore	Obnov (o)	Paragraph...	Odstavec... (o)
Move	Přesuň (s)	Section...	Oddíl... (l)

ENGLISH	CZECH
Document...	Dokument... (d)
Number...	Číslo... (s)
Alignment...	Zarovnání... (r)
Utilities menu	Pomůcky (p)
Tools menu	Nástroje (t)
Customize	Upravte si podle svého (u)
Macro menu	Makro (m)
Record...	Záznam... (z)
Run...	Spusť... (s)
Edit	Editace (e)
Assign to Key	Přiřaď ke klávese (p)
Assign to Menu	Vlož do nabídky (v)
Window menu	Okno (o)
New Window	Nové okno (n)
Cascade	Kaskáda (k)
Tile	Dlaždice (d)
Next Window	Další okno (a)
Arrange All	Uspořádej vše (u)
Hide	Skryj (s)
Unhide...	Zruš skrytí... (s)
Split	Rozděl (r)
Freeze Panes	Zmraz podokna (z)
Remove Split	Zruš rozdělení (r)
Unfreeze Panes	Zruš zmrazení podoken (z)
Zoom...	Lupa... (l)
Help menu	Nápověda (n)
Contents	Obsah (b)
How to use Help	Jak používat nápovědu (j)
Search for Help on	Vyhledej nápovědu (v)
Active Window	Aktivní okno (a)
Keyboard	Klávesnice (k)
Mouse	Myš (m)
Tutorial	Kurs (k)
About	O aplikaci XXX (o)
Device menu	Zařízení (z)
Scale menu	Měřítko (m)
MIDI Sequencer...	Sekvencer MIDI... (m)
Sound...	Zvuky... (z)
Time	Čas (a)
Tracks	Stopy (s)
Effects menu	Efekty (f)
Revert...	Obnov... (b)
Insert File...	Vlož soubor... (v)
Mix with File...	Smíchej se souborem... (s)
Delete Before Current Position	Smaž až do běžného místa (d)
Delete After Current Position	Smaž od běžného místa dál (o)
Increase Volume (by 25%)	Zvyš hlasitost (o 25%) (z)
Decrease Volume	Sniž hlasitost (s)
Increase Speed (by 100%)	Zvyš rychlost (o 100%) (v)
Decrease Speed	Sniž rychlost (n)

ENGLISH	CZECH
Add Echo	Přidej ozvěnu (p)
Reverse	Reverzuj (r)
Help application	
File menu	Soubor (s)
Open	Otevři (o)
Print Topic	Vytiskni heslo (v)
Print Setup...	Nastavení způsobu tisku... (z)
Exit	Konec (k)
Edit menu	Editace (e)
Copy...	Kopíruj... (k)
Annotate...	Komentář... (m)
Bookmark menu	Záložka (l)
Define...	Definice... (d)
Help menu	Nápověda (n)
How to use Help	Jak používat nápovědu (j)
Always on Top	Vždy na vrchu (v)
About Help...	O aplikaci Nápověda... (o)
Buttons	
Contents	Obsah (b)
Search	Hledání (h)
Back	Zpět (p)
History	Historie (t)
Glossary	Slovník (o)
DIALOG BOXES	
dialog box	okno dialogu, dialogové okno
wildcard	znak obecné náhrady
Dialog box elements	
button	ovládací knoflík
check box	políčko k zaškrtnutí
chevrons	dvojitá šipka vpravo (>>)
combo box	kombinovaný seznam
command button	tlačítko povolu, povolové tlačítko, tlačítko s povelem
dialog box title	titulek dialogového okna
drop-down combo box	rozbalovací pole se seznamem, rozbalovací seznam
drop-down list box	titulek dialogového okna
Goto/Gosub button	tlačítko Goto/Gosub
group box	pole skupiny - skupinové pole
label	pojmenování
linked text and list box	sloučené ediční pole se seznamem
list box	pole se seznamem, seznam
option button	tlačítko přepínače, přepínací tlačítko
progress indicator	indikace průběhu, indikátor průběhu
push button	tlačítko

ENGLISH	CZECH
radio button	knoflík
slider	běžec
slider indicator	indikátor polohy běžce
spin box	protáčející se políčko
text box	textové pole
value set	nastavení hodnoty

Dialog box buttons

Add	Přidat
Apply	Použít
Cancel	Zrušit
Change	Změnit
Create	Vytvořit
Default	Standardní
Define	Definovat
Done	Hotovo
Go To	Přechod na jinou stránku
Help	Nápověda
More	Více
No	Ne
OK	OK
Options	Volitelné
Quit	Konec
Redo	Znovu
Reset	Vynulovat
Resume	Obnovit
Retry	Zkusit znovu
Search	Hledat
Set	Nastavit
Setup	Nastavení
Switch to	Přepnout
Yes	Ano

Dialog box labels

All	Vše (v)
Collate Copies	Snášení kopií (s)
Copies	Počet kopií (k)
Direction	Směr (s)
Directories	Adresáře (a)
Down	Dolů (d)
Drives	Diskové jednotky (d)
File Name	Jméno souboru (j)
Find Next	Vyhledat další (v)
Find What	Vyhledat (v)
Font	Písmo (p)
Font Style	Styl písma (s)
From	Odkud (o)
Landscape	Na šířku (k)
List Files of Type	Typ zobrazených souborů (t)
Match Case	Rozlišuj malá a velká písmena (r)
Match Whole Word Only	Pouze celá slova (p)
Orientation	Orientace (o)
Pages	Počet stran (s)
Paper Size	Formát papíru (f)
Portrait	Na výšku (v)
Printer	Tiskárna (t)
Print Quality	Kvalita tisku (v)

ENGLISH	CZECH
Print Range	Vytisknout stránky (s)
Print to File	Tisk do souboru (s)
Read Only	Pouze čtení (p)
Replace All	Zaměnit všude (d)
Replace With	Zaměnit za (z)
Sample	Vzorek (z)
Save File as Type	Tvar uložení souboru (t)
Scaling	Měřítko (m)
Selection	Výběr (v)
Size (font size)	Velikost (v)
Source (paper)	Zdroj (z)
To	Kam (k)
Up	Nahoru (n)

MESSAGE BOXES

critical message	kritická zpráva
message	zpráva
message box	okno se zprávou
message line	řádek pro zobrazení zprávy, řádek se zprávou
warning message	výstražná zpráva

OTHER GUI SCREEN ELEMENTS

Graphical options

gallery	galerie
palette	paleta
text frame	textový rámec
toolbox	nástroje

Status bar abbreviations

Caps Lock on (CAPS)	CAPS
Column (Col)	sl.
Extend selection on (EXT)	EXT
Line (Ln)	ř.
Macro Recorder on (REC)	MAKRO
Num Lock on (NUM)	NUML
Overtype on (OVR)	PŘES
Page (Pg)	str.
Scroll Lock on (SCRL)	SCRL
Section (Sec)	odd.

Character formats

bold	tučně (t)
double underline	dvojité podtržení (d)
italic	kurzíva (k)
small capitals	kapitálky (a)
underline	podtržení (o)

Paragraph formats

centered	vystředěný (e)
justified	zarovnaný do bloku(b)
left aligned	zarovnaný vlevo (l)
right aligned	zarovnaný vpravo (p)

ENGLISH	CZECH	ENGLISH	CZECH
KEYS		**USER ACTIONS**	
Shortcut keys		**Keyboard actions**	
CTRL+B (Bold)	CTRL+T	enter	vložit
CTRL+C (Copy)	CTRL+C	press and hold down	držet (stisknuto)
CTRL+D (Double underline)	CTRL+D	type	zadat, napsat
CTRL+E (Center)	CTRL+E		
CTRL+I (Italics)	CTRL+K	**Mouse actions**	
CTRL+J (Justify)	CTRL+B	click	kliknout
CTRL+L (Left align)	CTRL+L	double-click	dvojitě kliknout
CTRL+R (Right align)	CTRL+P	drag	zatáhnout, zavléknout,
CTRL+U (Underline)	CTRL+O		přesunout
CTRL+V (Paste)	CTRL+V	drag-and-drop	přesunout a umístit
CTRL+W (Word underline)	CTRL+S	drop	umístit
CTRL+X (Cut)	CTRL+X	point	ukázat na
CTRL+Z (Undo)	CTRL+Z		
DEL (Clear)	DEL	**Manipulating window**	
		appearance	
Keynames		arrange	uspořádat
(keypad) *	klávesa * na numerické	close	zavřít
	klávesnici, klávesa num. *	freeze	zmrazit
(keypad) +	klávesa + na numerické	hide	skrýt
	klávesnici, klávesa num. +	move	přesunout
(keypad) -	klávesa - na numerické	resize	změnit velikost
	klávesnici, klávesa num. -	restore	obnovit (velikost)
(kcypad) /	klávcsa / na numcrické	select	vybrat
	klávesnici, klávesa num. /	size	změnit velikost
ALT	klávesa ALT	split	rozdělit
ALT GR	klávesa ALT GR	switch	přepnout
BACKSPACE	klávesa BACKSPACE	unfreeze	zrušit zmrazení
BREAK	klávesa BREAK		
CAPS LOCK	klávesa CAPS LOCK	**Selecting options or**	
CTRL	klávesa CTRL	**content**	
DEL	klávesa DELETE (DEL)	cancel	zrušit
DOWN ARROW	klávesa ŠIPKA DOLŮ	check	potvrdit, zaškrtnout, označit
END	klávesa END	choose	zvolit (si)
ENTER	klávesa ENTER	clear (undo Select)	zrušit (zaškrtnutí)
ENTER (keypad)	klávesa ENTER na numerické	extend selection	rozšířit výběr, vztáhnout
	klávesnici, klávesa num.		výběr i na
	ENTER	reduce selection	(z)redukovat výběr, zúžit výběr
ESC	klávesa ESC	select	vybrat (si), zvolit (si)
HOME	klávesa HOME	select (check box, option button)	zaškrtnout (políčko k zaškrtnutí),
INS	klávesa INSERT (INS)		vybrat si jedno z tlačítek
LEFT ARROW	klávesa ŠIPKA VLEVO	select (data)	vybrat (si), zvolit (si)
NUM LOCK	klávesa NUM LOCK	select (drop-down menu)	vybrat (si), zvolit (si)
PAUSE	klávesa PAUSE	select (list box)	vybrat (si), zvolit (si)
PG DN	klávesa PAGE DOWN		
	(PG DN)	**Viewing content**	
PG UP	klávesa PAGE UP (PG UP)	autoscroll	automatické přetáčení
PRINT SCREEN	klávesa PRINT SCREEN	browse	nalistovat
RIGHT ARROW	klávesa ŠIPKA VPRAVO	collapse	sbalit
SCROLL LOCK	klávesa SCROLL LOCK	expand	rozbalit
SHIFT	klávesa SHIFT	scroll	přetáčet
SPACEBAR	MEZERNÍK	view	zobrazit
SYS RQ	klávesa SYS RQ	zoom in	+ lupa
TAB	klávesa TAB	zoom out	- lupa
UP ARROW	klávesa ŠIPKA NAHORU		

ENGLISH	CZECH	ENGLISH	CZECH
Removing content		size	změnit velikost
clear	smazat	source application	zdrojová aplikace
copy	kopírovat	source document	zdrojový dokument
cut	vyříznout	update	aktualizace
delete	smazat, vypustit, zrušit, vyjmout		
paste	přilepit	**APPLICATIONS FOR MICROSOFT WINDOWS**	
Manipulating objects			
arrange	uspořádat	Accessories	Příslušenství
automatic link	automatické propojení	Applications	Aplikace
Clipboard	Schránka	Calculator	Kalkulačka
container application	přijímající aplikace	Calendar	Diář
container document	přijímající dokument	Cardfile	Kartotéka
copy	kopírovat	Character Map	Mapa znaků
crop	oříznout	Clipboard Viewer	Schránka
destination application	cílová aplikace	Clock	Hodiny
destination document	cílový dokument	Control Panel	Ovládací panel
drag-and-drop	přesunout a umístit	File Manager	Správce souborů
embed	vložit	Games	Hry
embedded object	vložený objekt	Main	Hlavní skupina
group	skupina	Media Player	Přehrávač záznamů
link	propojení	MS-DOS Prompt	Prompt MS-DOS
linked object	propojený objekt	Notepad	Poznámkový blok
main application	hlavní aplikace	Object Packager	Balíčkovač objektů
main document	hlavní dokument	PIF Editor	Editor PIF
manual link	ruční propojení	Print Manager	Správce tisku
object	objekt	Program Manager	Správce programů
object linking & embedding (OLE)	vkládání a propojování objektů (OLE)	Recorder	Makrokamera
OLE (object linking & embedding)	OLE (vkládání a propojování objektů)	Sound Recorder	Záznam zvuku
OLE application	aplikace OLE	StartUp	Spustit při startu
package	balíček	Terminal	Terminál
paste	přilepit	Windows Setup	Instalační program Windows Setup
scale	změnit měřítko		

Terminology by Alphabet

Notes:
1.   All terms formatted in **bold** refer to menu names or command names.
2.   All characters between parentheses are preferred access keys.

ENGLISH	CZECH	ENGLISH	CZECH
(keypad) *	klávesa * na numerické klávesnici, klávesa num. *	CAPS LOCK	klávesa CAPS LOCK
(keypad) +	klávesa + na numerické klávesnici, klávesa num. +	Caps Lock on (CAPS)	CAPS
		Cardfile	Kartotéka
(keypad) -	klávesa - na numerické klávesnici, klávesa num. -	**Cascade**	**Kaskáda (k)**
(keypad) /	klávesa / na numerické klávesnici, klávesa num. /	cascading menu	kaskádová nabídka
		cascading windows	kaskáda oken
		centered	vystředěný (e)
About	**O aplikaci XXX (o)**	Change	Změnit
About Help...	**O aplikaci Nápověda... (o)**	Character Map	Mapa znaků
access key	přístupová klávesa	**Character...**	**Znak... (z)**
Accessories	Příslušenství	check	potvrdit, zaškrtnout, označit
active window	aktivní okno	check box	políčko k zaškrtnutí
Active Window	**Aktivní okno (a)**	checked command	označený povel
Add	Přidat	check mark	označení
Add Echo	**Přidej ozvěnu (p)**	chevrons	dvojitá šipka vpravo (>>)
Alignment...	**Zarovnání... (r)**	choose	zvolit (si)
All	Vše (v)	clear	smazat
ALT	klávesa ALT	**Clear**	**Smaž (s)**
ALT GR	klávesa ALT GR	**Clear All**	**Smaž vše (v)**
Always on Top	**Vždy na vrchu (v)**	clear (undo Select)	zrušit (zaškrtnutí)
Annotate...	**Komentář... (m)**	click	kliknout
application icon	ikona aplikace	Clipboard	Schránka
Applications	Aplikace	Clipboard Viewer	Schránka
application window	okno aplikace	Clock	Hodiny
Apply	Použít	close	zavřít
arrange	uspořádat	**Close**	**Zavři (z)**
Arrange All	**Uspořádej vše (u)**	**Close All**	**Zavři vše (v)**
arrow	šipka	collapse	sbalit
arrow pointer	šipka	Collate Copies	Snášení kopií (s)
Assign to Key	**Přiřaď ke klávese (p)**	Column (Col)	sl.
Assign to Menu	**Vlož do nabídky (v)**	combo box	kombinovaný seznam
automatic link	automatické propojení	command	povel
autoscroll	automatické přetáčení	command button	tlačítko povelu, povelové tlačítko, tlačítko s povelem
Back	Zpět (p)		
BACKSPACE	klávesa BACKSPACE	command separator	oddělovač povelů
bold	tučně (t)	container application	přijímající aplikace
Bookmark menu	**Záložka (l)**	container document	přijímající dokument
border	okraj	**Contents**	**Obsah (b)**
bottom window border	dolní okraj okna	**Control menu**	**Ovládací nabídka**
BREAK	klávesa BREAK	Control-menu box	políčko ovládací nabídky
browse	nalistovat	Control Panel	Ovládací panel
button	ovládací knoflík	Copies	Počet kopií (k)
Calculator	Kalkulačka	copy	kopírovat
Calendar	Diář	**Copy**	**Kopíruj (k)**
Cancel	Zrušit	**Copy...**	**Kopíruj... (k)**
cancel	zrušit	**Copy Special**	**Rozšířené kopírování (r)**
		Create	Vytvořit

ENGLISH	CZECH	ENGLISH	CZECH
critical message	kritická zpráva	drag-and-drop	přesunout a umístit
crop	oříznout	drive icon	ikona jednotky
cross-hair pointer	nitkový kříž	Drives	Diskové jednotky (d)
CTRL	klávesa CTRL	drop	umístit
CTRL+B (Bold)	CTRL+T	drop-down combo box	rozbalovací pole se seznamem,
CTRL+C (Copy)	CTRL+C		rozbalovací seznam
CTRL+D (Double underline)	CTRL+D	drop-down list box	titulek dialogového okna
CTRL+E (Center)	CTRL+E	drop-down menu	rozbalovací nabídka
CTRL+I (Italics)	CTRL+K	**Edit**	**Editace (e)**
CTRL+J (Justify)	CTRL+B	**Edit menu**	**Editace (e)**
CTRL+L (Left align)	CTRL+L	**Effects menu**	**Efekty (f)**
CTRL+R (Right align)	CTRL+P	ellipsis	tři tečky
CTRL+U (Underline)	CTRL+O	embed	vložit
CTRL+V (Paste)	CTRL+V	embedded object	vložený objekt
CTRL+W (Word underline)	CTRL+S	END	klávesa END
CTRL+X (Cut)	CTRL+X	enter	vložit
CTRL+Z (Undo)	CTRL+Z	ENTER	klávesa ENTER
Customize	**Upravte si podle svého (u)**	ENTER (keypad)	klávesa ENTER na numerické
cut	vyříznout		klávesnici, klávesa num. ENTER
Cut	**Vyřízni (v)**	ESC	klávesa ESC
Decrease Speed	**Sniž rychlost (n)**	**Exit**	**Konec (k)**
Decrease Volume	**Sniž hlasitost (s)**	**Exit and Return to**	**Konec a návrat do**
Default	Standardní		**(jméno aplikace) (k)**
Define	Definovat	expand	rozbalit
Define...	**Definice... (d)**	extend selection	rozšířit výběr, vztáhnout výběr i na
DEL	klávesa DELETE (DEL)	Extend selection on (EXT)	EXT
DEL (Clear)	DEL	File Manager	Správce souborů
delete	smazat, vypustit, zrušit,	**File menu**	**Soubor (s)**
	vyjmout	File Name	Jméno souboru (j)
Delete	**Smaž (m)**	**Find...**	**Vyhledej... (v)**
Delete...	**Smaž... (s)**	Find Next	Vyhledat další (v)
Delete After Current Position	**Smaž od běžného místa dál (o)**	Find What	Vyhledat (v)
		font	písmo
Delete Before Current Position	**Smaž až do běžného místa (d)**	Font	Písmo (p)
		Font Style	Styl písma (s)
desktop	pracovní plocha	**Format menu**	**Formátování (f)**
destination application	cílová aplikace	freeze	zmrazit
destination document	cílový dokument	**Freeze Panes**	**Zmraz podokna (z)**
Device menu	**Zařízení (z)**	From	Odkud (o)
dialog box	okno dialogu, dialogové okno	**Full Menus**	**Plná nabídka (p)**
		gallery	galerie
dialog box title	titulek dialogového okna	Games	Hry
Direction	Směr (s)	Glossary	Slovník (o)
Directories	Adresáře (a)	Go To	Přechod na jinou stránku
directory icon	ikona adresáře	**Go To...**	**Přejdi na jinou stránku, kartu atp.... (p)**
disk icon	ikona disku		
Document...	**Dokument... (d)**	Goto/Gosub button	tlačítko Goto/Gosub
document file icon	ikona souboru s dokumentem	group	skupina
		group box	pole skupiny - skupinové pole
document icon	ikona dokumentu	group icon	ikona seskupení
document window	okno dokumentu	group window	okno seskupení
Done	Hotovo	Help	Nápověda
double underline	dvojité podtržení (d)	**Help menu**	**Nápověda (n)**
double-click	dvojitě kliknout	Help window	okno nápovědy
Down	Dolů (d)	hide	skrýt
DOWN ARROW	klávesa ŠIPKA DOLŮ	**Hide**	**Skryj (s)**
down scroll arrow	šipka přetáčení dolů	History	Historie (t)
drag	zatáhnout, zavléknout, přesunout	HOME	klávesa HOME

ENGLISH	CZECH	ENGLISH	CZECH
horizontal scroll bar	vodorovný přetáčecí pruh	mouse pointer	ukazovátko myši
horizontal split bar	vodorovný dělící pruh	move	přesunout
hourglass pointer	přesýpací hodiny	**Move**	**Přesuň (s)**
How to use Help	**Jak používat nápovědu (j)**	MS-DOS Prompt	Prompt MS-DOS
I-beam pointer	I-kurzor	**New...**	**Nový... (n)**
icon	ikona	**New Window**	**Nové okno (n)**
inactive window	okno, které není aktivní	**Next**	**Další (d)**
Increase Speed (by 100%)	**Zvyš rychlost (o 100%) (v)**	**Next Window**	**Další okno (a)**
Increase Volume (by 25%)	**Zvyš hlasitost (o 25%) (z)**	No	Ne
INS	klávesa INSERT (INS)	Notepad	Poznámkový blok
Insert...	**Vlož... (v)**	NUM LOCK	klávesa NUM LOCK
Insert File...	**Vlož soubor... (v)**	Num Lock on (NUM)	NUML
insertion point	kurzor	**Number...**	**Číslo... (s)**
Insert menu	**Vložit (v)**	object	objekt
Insert Object...	**Vlož objekt... (j)**	**Object...**	**Objekt... (o)**
italic	kurzíva (k)	object linking & embedding	vkládání a propojování objektů
justified	zarovnaný do bloku(b)	(OLE)	(OLE)
Keyboard	**Klávesnice (k)**	Object Packager	Balíčkovač objektů
label	pojmenování	OK	OK
Landscape	Na šířku (k)	OLE (object linking &	OLE (vkládání a propojování
left aligned	zarovnaný vlevo (l)	embedding)	objektů)
LEFT ARROW	klávesa ŠIPKA VLEVO	OLE application	aplikace OLE
left scroll arrow	šipka přetáčení doleva	**Open**	**Otevři (o)**
left window border	levý okraj okna	option button	tlačítko přepínače, přepínací
Line (Ln)	ř.		tlačítko
link	propojení	Options	Volitelné
linked object	propojený objekt	**Options menu**	**Volitelné (v)**
linked text and list box	sloučené ediční pole	Orientation	Orientace (o)
	se seznamem	Overtype on (OVR)	PŘES
list box	pole se seznamem, seznam	package	balíček
List Files of Type	Typ zobrazených souborů (t)	Page (Pg)	str.
Macro menu	**Makro (m)**	Pages	Počet stran (s)
Macro Recorder on (REC)	MAKRO	**Page Setup**	**Nastavení vzhledu stránky (h)**
Main	Hlavní skupina	palette	paleta
main application	hlavní aplikace	pane	podokno
main document	hlavní dokument	**Paragraph...**	**Odstavec... (o)**
manual link	ruční propojení	Paper Size	Formát papíru (f)
Match Case	Rozlišuj malá a velká písmena (r)	paste	přilepit
Match Whole Word Only	Pouze celá slova (p)	**Paste**	**Přilep (p)**
Maximize	**Maximalizuj (x)**	**Paste Link**	**Přilep propojení (i)**
Maximize button	maximalizační tlačítko,	**Paste Special**	**Rozšířené přilepení (l)**
	tlačítko pro maximalizaci	PAUSE	klávesa PAUSE
Media Player	Přehrávač záznamů	PG DN	klávesa PAGE DOWN (PG DN)
menu	nabídka	PG UP	klávesa PAGE UP (PG UP)
menu bar	nabídkový pruh	PIF Editor	Editor PIF
menu command	nabídkový povel	point	ukázat na
menu name	jméno nabídky	pointer	ukazovátko
message	zpráva	Portrait	Na výšku (v)
message box	okno se zprávou	**Preferences**	**Preference (r)**
message line	řádek pro zobrazení zprávy,	press and hold down	držet (stisknuto)
	řádek se zprávou	**Print**	**Vytiskni (t)**
MIDI Sequencer...	**Sekvencer MIDI... (m)**	Printer	Tiskárna (t)
Minimize	**Minimalizuj (n)**	**Printer Setup**	**Nastavení tiskárny (s)**
Minimize button	minimalizační tlačítko, tlačítko	Print Manager	Správce tisku
	pro minimalizaci	**Print Preview**	**Ukázka před tiskem (e)**
Mix with File...	**Smíchej se souborem... (s)**	Print Quality	Kvalita tisku (v)
More	Více	Print Range	Vytisknout stránky (s)
Mouse	**Myš (m)**	PRINT SCREEN	klávesa PRINT SCREEN

ENGLISH	CZECH	ENGLISH	CZECH
Print Setup...	**Nastavení způsobu tisku... (z)**	**Search for Help on Section...**	**Vyhledej nápovědu (v) Oddíl... (l)**
Print to File	Tisk do souboru (s)	Section (Sec)	odd.
Print Topic	**Vytiskni heslo (v)**	select	vybrat (si), zvolit (si)
program group	seskupení programů	select (check box, option button)	zaškrtnout (políčko k zaškrtnutí),
program item	programová položka		vybrat si jedno z tlačítek
program-item icon	ikona programové položky	select (data)	vybrat (si), zvolit (si)
progress indicator	indikace průběhu, indikátor průběhu	select (drop-down menu)	vybrat (si), zvolit (si)
		selected command	vysvícený povel
Program Manager	Správce programů	Selection	Výběr (v)
push button	tlačítko	selection cursor	kurzor pro provádění výběru
Quit	Konec	select (list box)	vybrat (si), zvolit (si)
radio button	knoflík	Set	Nastavit
Read Only	Pouze čtení (p)	Setup	Nastavení
Record...	**Záznam... (z)**	SHIFT	klávesa SHIFT
Recorder	Makrokamera	shortcut key	zkratková klávesa
Redo	Znovu	**Short Menus**	**Zkrácená nabídka (z)**
reduce selection	(z)redukovat výběr, zúžit výběr	size	změnit velikost
		Size	**Změň velikost (v)**
Remove Split	**Zruš rozdělení (r)**	Size (font size)	Velikost (v)
Repeat	**Opakuj (a)**	sizing handle	úchopný bod pro nastavení velikosti
Replace...	**Zaměň... (z)**		
Replace All	Zaměnit všude (d)	slider	běžec
Replace With	Zaměnit za (z)	slider indicator	indikátor polohy běžce
Reset	Vynulovat	small capitals	kapitálky (a)
resize	změnit velikost	**Sound...**	**Zvuky... (z)**
restore	obnovit (velikost)	Sound Recorder	Záznam zvuku
Restore	**Obnov (o)**	Source (paper)	Zdroj (z)
Restore button	obnovovací tlačítko, tlačítko (pro) obnovení	source application	zdrojová aplikace
		source document	zdrojový dokument
Resume	Obnovit	SPACEBAR	MEZERNÍK
Retry	Zkusit znovu	spin box	protáčející se políčko
Reverse	**Reverzuj (r)**	Split	Rozděl (r)
Revert...	**Obnov... (b)**	split	rozdělit
right aligned	zarovnaný vpravo (p)	**Split**	**Změň rozdělení (r)**
RIGHT ARROW	klávesa ŠIPKA VPRAVO	split bar	dělící pruh
right scroll arrow	šipka přetáčení doprava	split box	dělící políčko, políčko pro změnu (roz)dělení
right window border	pravý okraj okna		
ruler	pravítko	StartUp	Spustit při startu
Run...	**Spusť... (u)**	status bar	stavový pruh
Run...	**Spusť... (s)**	status-bar indicator	indikátor na stavovém pruhu
Sample	Vzorek (z)	submenu	vnořená nabídka
Save	**Ulož (u)**	switch	přepnout
Save All	**Ulož vše (l)**	Switch to	Přepnout
Save As...	**Ulož pod jménem... (p)**	**Switch To...**	**Přepni do jiné úlohy... (p)**
Save File as Type	Tvar uložení souboru (t)	SYS RQ	klávesa SYS RQ
scale	změnit měřítko	TAB	klávesa TAB
Scale menu	**Měřítko (m)**	Terminal	Terminál
Scaling	Měřítko (m)	text box	textové pole
scroll	přetáčet	text frame	textový rámec
scroll arrow	přetáčecí šipka	**Tile**	**Dlaždice (d)**
scroll bar	přetáčecí pruh	tiled windows	dlaždicové uspořádání oken
scroll box	přetáčecí běžec	**Time**	**Čas (a)**
SCROLL LOCK	klávesa SCROLL LOCK	title bar	titulkový pruh
Scroll Lock on (SCRL)	SCRL	To	Kam (k)
Search	Hledání (h)	tool	nástroj
Search	Hledat	toolbar	nástrojový pruh
Search...	**Vyhledej... (v)**	toolbox	nástroje

ENGLISH	CZECH	ENGLISH	CZECH
Tools menu	**Nástroje (t)**	view	zobrazit
top window border	horní okraj okna	**View menu**	**Zobrazení (z)**
Tracks	**Stopy (s)**	wallpaper	tapeta
Tutorial	**Kurs (k)**	warning message	výstražná zpráva
type	zadat, napsat	wildcard	znak obecné náhrady
unavailable command	nedostupný povel	window	okno
underline	podtržení (o)	window background	pozadí okna
Undo	**Zpět (z)**	window border	okraj okna
unfreeze	zrušit zmrazení	window corner	roh okna
Unfreeze Panes	**Zruš zmrazení podoken (z)**	window frame	rám okna
Unhide...	**Zruš skrytí... (s)**	**Window menu**	**Okno (o)**
Up	Nahoru (n)	window size	velikost okna
UP ARROW	klávesa ŠIPKA NAHORU	window title	titulek okna
up scroll arrow	šipka přetáčení vzhůru	Windows Setup	Instalační program Windows Setup
update	aktualizace		
Update	**Aktualizuj (a)**	workspace	pracovní prostor
Utilities menu	**Pomůcky (p)**	Yes	Ano
value set	nastavení hodnoty	zoom in	+ lupa
vertical scroll bar	svislý přetáčecí pruh	zoom out	- lupa
vertical split bar	svislý dělící pruh	**Zoom...**	**Lupa... (l)**

CHAPTER 9

Danish

This chapter lists the Danish translations of all terms formatted in *italic* in Part 1. Terminology is listed in two ways: by category and in alphabetical order. The first section includes translations in the following categories: Window Elements, Menus, Dialog Boxes, Message Boxes, Other GUI Screen Elements, Keys, User Actions, and Applications For Microsoft Windows.

Terminology by Category

ENGLISH	DANISH	ENGLISH	DANISH
WINDOW ELEMENTS			
Main window elements		window frame	vinduesramme
active window	aktivt vindue	window size	vinduesstørrelse
application window	programvindue	window title	vinduestitel
border	ramme	workspace	arbejdsområde
bottom window border	nedre vinduesramme		
cascading windows	overlappende vinduer	**Window controls**	
desktop	desktop	Control-menu box	kontrolmenuboks
document window	dokumentvindue	down scroll arrow	rullepil ned
group window	gruppevindue	horizontal scroll bar	vandret rullepanel
Help window	Hjælp-vindue	horizontal split bar	vandret delelinje
inactive window	ikke-aktivt vindue	left scroll arrow	venstre rullepil
left window border	venstre vinduesramme	Maximize button	maksimeringsknap
menu bar	menulinje	Minimize button	minimeringsknap
pane	rude	Restore button	gendannelsesknap
right window border	højre vinduesramme	right scroll arrow	højre rullepil
ruler	lineal	scroll arrow	rullepil
status bar	statuslinje	scroll bar	rullepanel
tiled windows	vinduer side om side	scroll box	rulleboks
title bar	titellinje	split bar	delelinje
toolbar	værktøjslinje	split box	deleboks
top window border	øvre vinduesramme	up scroll arrow	rullepil op
wallpaper	tapet	vertical scroll bar	lodret rullepanel
window	vindue	vertical split bar	lodret delelinje
window background	vinduesbaggrund		
window border	vinduesramme		
window corner	vindueshjørne		

ENGLISH	DANISH	ENGLISH	DANISH
Pointers		Move	Flyt (f)
arrow	pil	Size	Tilpas størrelse (t)
arrow pointer	pilmarkør	Minimize	Minimer (i)
cross-hair pointer	krydsmarkør	Maximize	Maksimer (m)
hourglass pointer	timeglas	Next	Næste (n)
I-beam pointer	tekstmarkør	Close	Luk (l)
insertion point	indsætningspunkt	Run...	Kør... (k)
mouse pointer	musmarkør	Switch To...	Skift til... (s)
pointer	markør	Split	Opdel (o)
selection cursor	markør		
		File menu	Filer (f)
Icons		New...	Ny(t)... (n)
application icon	programikon	Open	Åbn (b)
directory icon	biblioteksikon	Close	Luk (l)
disk icon	disketteikon	Close All	Luk alt (l)
document file icon	dokumentfilikon	Save	Gem (g)
document icon	dokumentikon	Save As...	Gem som... (m)
drive icon	drevikon	Save All	Gem alt (e)
group icon	gruppeikon	Delete	Slet (s)
icon	ikon	Page Setup	Sideopsætning (i)
program-item icon	programobjektikon	Print	Udskriv (u)
		Print Preview	Vis udskrift (v)
General terms		Printer Setup	Indstil printer (i)
access key	hurtigtast	Exit	Afslut (a)
check mark	afkrydsning	Exit and Return to	Afslut og returner til (a)
ellipsis	ellipse	Update	Opdater (o)
font	skrifttype		
object	objekt	Edit menu	Rediger (r)
program group	programgruppe	Undo	Fortryd (r)
program item	programobjekt	Repeat	Gentag (g)
shortcut key	genvejstast	Cut	Klip (k)
sizing handle	størrelseshåndtag	Copy	Kopier (o)
status-bar indicator	statuslinjeindikator	Copy Special	Kopier speciel (c)
tool	værktøj	Paste	Sæt ind (n)
unavailable command	ikke-tilgængelig kommando	Paste Link	Indsæt kæde (e)
		Paste Special	Indsæt speciel (p)
MENUS		Clear	Ryd (d)
Menu elements		Clear All	Ryd alt (d)
cascading menu	undermenu	Find...	Søg... (s)
checked command	afkrydset kommando	Search...	Søg... (s)
command	kommando	Replace...	Erstat... (e)
command separator	kommandoseparator	Go To...	Gå til... (l)
drop-down menu	rullemenu	Delete...	Slet... (s)
menu	menu	Insert...	Indsæt... (i)
menu command	menukommando	Object...	Objekt... (b)
menu name	menunavn	Insert Object...	Indsæt objekt... (t)
selected command	markeret kommando		
submenu	undermenu	Options menu	Indstillinger (i)
		Preferences	Indstillinger (i)
Menus and commands		Full Menus	Lange menuer (m)
View menu	Vis (v)	Short Menus	Korte menuer (m)
Insert menu	Indsæt (i)		
		Format menu	Formater (t)
Control menu	Kontrolmenu	Character...	Tegn... (t)
Restore	Gendan (g)	Paragraph...	Afsnit... (a)

ENGLISH	DANISH	ENGLISH	DANISH
Section...	Sektion... (s)	Decrease Volume	Reducer lydstyrken (c)
Document...	Dokument... (d)	Increase Speed (by 100%)	Forøg hastigheden
Number...	Tal... (l)		(med 100 %) (f)
Alignment...	Justering... (j)	Decrease Speed	Reducer hastigheden (r)
		Add Echo	Tilføj ekko (t)
Utilities menu	Funktioner (k)	Reverse	Baglæns (b)
Tools menu	Funktioner (k)		
Customize	Tilpas (t)	**Help application**	
		File menu	Filer (f)
Macro menu	Makro (m)	Open	Åbn (b)
Record...	Indspil... (i)	Print Topic	Udskriv emne (u)
Run...	Afspil... (a)	Print Setup...	Indstil printer... (i)
Edit	Rediger (r)	Exit	Afslut (a)
Assign to Key	Tildel tast (t)		
Assign to Menu	Tildel menu (m)	Edit menu	Rediger (r)
		Copy...	Kopier... (o)
Window menu	Vindue (u)	Annotate...	Anmærk... (a)
New Window	Nyt vindue (n)		
Cascade	Overlappet (o)	Bookmark menu	Bogmærke (m)
Tile	Side om side (s)	Define...	Definer... (d)
Next Window	Næste vindue (v)		
Arrange All	Arranger alle (a)	Help menu	Hjælp (h)
Hide	Skjul (s)	How to use Help	Brug af Hjælp (b)
Unhide...	Vis... (v)	Always on Top	Altid øverst (ø)
Split	Opdel (o)	About Help...	Om Hjælp... (o)
Freeze Panes	Frys ruder (f)		
Remove Split	Fjern opdeling (o)	**Buttons**	
Unfreeze Panes	Frigør ruder (f)	Contents	Indhold (i)
Zoom...	Zoom... (z)	Search	Søg (s)
		Back	Tilbage (t)
Help menu	Hjælp (h)	History	Oversigt (o)
Contents	Indhold (i)	Glossary	Leksikon (l)
How to use Help	Brug af Hjælp (b)		
Search for Help on	Søg efter hjælp om (s)	**DIALOG BOXES**	
Active Window	Aktivt vindue (a)	dialog box	dialogboks
Keyboard	Tastatur (t)	wildcard	jokertegn
Mouse	Mus (m)		
Tutorial	Selvstudium (e)	**Dialog box elements**	
About	Om (o)	button	knap
		check box	afkrydsningsfelt
Device menu	Enhed (e)	chevrons	«-tegn
Scale menu	Skala (s)	combo box	kombinationsboks
MIDI Sequencer...	MIDI-sequencer...	command button	kommandoknap
Sound...	Lyd... (l)	dialog box title	dialogbokstitel
Time	Tid (t)	drop-down combo box	kombinationsboks
Tracks	Spor (s)	drop-down list box	rulleliste
		Goto/Gosub button	hopknap
Effects menu	Effekter (e)	group box	gruppeboks
Revert...	Genindlæs... (g)	label	navn
Insert File...	Indsæt fil... (f)	linked text and list box	kombineret tekstboks/liste
Mix with File...	Mix med fil... (m)	list box	liste
Delete Before Current Position	Slet op til nuværende	option button	alternativknap
	position (t)	progress indicator	statusindikator
Delete After Current Position	Slet fra nuværende position (s)	push button	trykknap
Increase Volume (by 25%)	Forøg lydstyrken	radio button	alternativknap
	(med 25 %) (ø)		

ENGLISH	DANISH	ENGLISH	DANISH
slider	skala	Print Quality	Kvalitet (v)
slider indicator	skalaindikator	Print Range	Udskriftsområde
spin box	rotationsboks	Print to File	Skriv til fil (l)
text box	tekstboks	Read Only	Skrivebeskyttet (s)
value set	værdisæt	Replace All	Erstat alle
		Replace With	Erstat med (e)
Dialog box buttons		Sample	Eksempel
Add	Tilføj	Save File as Type	Filtype (t)
Apply	Anvend	Scaling	Skalering (r)
Cancel	Annuller	Selection	Det markerede (m)
Change	Skift	Size (font size)	Størrelse (ø)
Create	Opret	Source (paper)	Kilde (k)
Default	Standard	To	Til (t)
Define	Definer	Up	Tilbage (t)
Done	Udført/Luk		
Go To	Gå til		
Help	Hjælp	**MESSAGE BOXES**	
More	Mere	critical message	alvorlig meddelelse
No	Nej	message	meddelelse
OK	OK	message box	meddelelsesboks
Options	Indstillinger	message line	meddelelseslinje
Quit	Afslut	warning message	advarsel
Redo	Gør om		
Reset	Nulstil	**OTHER GUI SCREEN**	
Resume	Fortsæt	**ELEMENTS**	
Retry	Forsøg igen	**Graphical options**	
Search	Søg	gallery	galleri
Set	Angiv/Vælg/Indstil	palette	palet
Setup	Indstil	text frame	tekstrude
Switch to	Skift til	toolbox	værktøjskasse
Yes	Ja		
		Status bar abbreviations	
Dialog box labels		Caps Lock on (CAPS)	CAPS
All	Alt (a)	Column (Col)	Kol
Collate copies	Sorter kopier (o)	Extend selection on (EXT)	UDV
Copies	Kopier (k)	Line (Ln)	Li
Direction	Retning	Macro Recorder on (REC)	INDS
Directories	Biblioteker (b)	Num Lock on (NUM)	NUM
Down	Fremad (f)	Overtype on (OVR)	OVR
Drives	Drev (d)	Page (Pg)	Si
File Name	Filnavn (n)	Scroll Lock on (SCRL)	SCRL
Find Next	Find næste (n)	Section (Sec)	Sek
Find What	Søg efter (s)		
Font	Skrifttype (s)	**Character formats**	
Font Style	Typografi (t)	bold	fed (f)
From	Fra (f)	double underline	dobbelt understreget (d)
Landscape	Liggende (l)	italic	kursiv (k)
List Files of Type	Filtype (t)	small capitals	kapitæler (a)
Match Case	Forskel på store/små bogstaver (b)	underline	understreget (u)
Match Whole Word Only	Kun hele ord (k)	**Paragraph formats**	
Orientation	Papirretning	centered	centreret (c)
Pages	Sider (s)	justified	lige margener (l)
Paper Size	Størrelse (ø)	left aligned	venstrejusteret (v)
Portrait	Stående (s)	right aligned	højrejusteret (h)
Printer	Printer		

ENGLISH	DANISH
KEYS	
Shortcut keys	
CTRL+B (Bold)	CTRL+F
CTRL+C (Copy)	CTRL+C
CTRL+D (Double underline)	CTRL+D
CTRL+E (Center)	CTRL+E
CTRL+I (Italics)	CTRL+K
CTRL+J (Justify)	CTRL+J
CTRL+L (Left align)	CTRL+L
CTRL+R (Right align)	CTRL+R
CTRL+U (Underline)	CTRL+U
CTRL+V (Paste)	CTRL+V
CTRL+W (Word underline)	CTRL+W
CTRL+X (Cut)	CTRL+X
CTRL+Z (Undo)	CTRL+Z
DEL (Clear)	DEL
Keynames	
(keypad) *	NUM *
(keypad) +	NUM +
(keypad) -	NUM -
(keypad) /	NUM /
ALT	ALT
ALT GR	ALT GR
BACKSPACE	TILBAGE
BREAK	BREAK
CAPS LOCK	CAPS LOCK
CTRL	CTRL
DEL	DEL
DOWN ARROW	PIL NED
END	END
ENTER	ENTER
ENTER (keypad)	NUM ENTER
ESC	ESC
HOME	HOME
INS	INS
LEFT ARROW	VENSTRE PIL
NUM LOCK	NUM LOCK
PAUSE	PAUSE
PG DN	PGDN
PG UP	PGUP
PRINT SCREEN	PRINTSCRN
RIGHT ARROW	HØJRE PIL
SCROLL LOCK	SCROLL LOCK
SHIFT	SKIFT
SPACEBAR	MELLEMRUM
SYS RQ	SYS RQ
TAB	TAB
UP ARROW	PIL OP
USER ACTIONS	
Keyboard actions	
enter	skrive
press and hold down	trykke på og holde nede
type	skrive

ENGLISH	DANISH
Mouse actions	
click	klikke på
double-click	dobbeltklikke på
drag	trække
drag-and-drop	trække og slippe
drop	slippe
point	pege på
Manipulating window appearance	
arrange	arrangere
close	lukke
freeze	fryse
hide	skjule
move	flytte
resize	tilpasse størrelse
restore	gendanne
select	markere/vælge
size	tilpasse størrelse
split	opdele
switch	skifte
unfreeze	frigøre
Selecting options or content	
cancel	annullere
check	afkrydse
choose	vælge
clear (undo Select)	fjerne afkrydsning
extend selection	udvide markering
reduce selection	formindske markering
select	markere/vælge
select (check box, option button)	markere (afkrydsningsfelt, alternativ)
select (data)	markere (data)
select (drop-down menu)	vælge (menu, kommando)
select (list box)	vælge (liste)
Viewing content	
autoscroll	automatisk rulning
browse	gennemse
collapse	skjule
expand	udvide
scroll	rulle
view	vise
zoom in	zoome ind
zoom out	zoome ud
Removing content	
clear	rydde
copy	kopiere
cut	klippe ud
delete	slette
paste	sætte ind

ENGLISH	DANISH
Manipulating objects	
arrange	arrangere
automatic link	automatisk kæde
Clipboard	Udklipsholder
container application	klientprogram
container document	klientdokument
copy	kopiere
crop	beskære
destination application	destinationsprogram
destination document	destinationsdokument
drag-and-drop	trække og slippe
embed	integrere
embedded object	integreret objekt
group	gruppere
link	kæde sammen
linked object	sammenkædet objekt
main application	hovedprogram
main document	hoveddokument
manual link	manuel kæde
object	objekt
object linking & embedding (OLE)	objektsammenkædning og integrering (OLE)
OLE (object linking & embedding)	OLE (Object Linking & Embedding)
OLE application	OLE-program
package	objektpakke
paste	sætte ind
scale	skalere
size	tilpasse størrelse
source application	kildeprogram

ENGLISH	DANISH
source document	kildedokument
update	opdatere
APPLICATIONS FOR MICROSOFT WINDOWS	
Accessories	Tilbehør
Applications	Programmer
Calculator	Lommeregner
Calendar	Kalender
Cardfile	Kartotek
Character Map	Tegnoversigt
Clipboard Viewer	Udklipsholder
Clock	Ur
Control Panel	Kontrolpanel
File Manager	Filhåndtering
Games	Underholdning
Main	Systemgruppe
Media Player	Medieafspiller
MS-DOS Prompt	MS-DOS-prompt
Notepad	Notesblok
Object Packager	Objektpakning
PIF Editor	PIF-editor
Print Manager	Udskriftsstyring
Program Manager	Programstyring
Recorder	Makrooptager
Sound Recorder	Audiosampler
StartUp	Start
Terminal	Terminal
Windows Setup	Windows Installation

Terminology by Alphabet

Notes:
1. All terms formatted in **bold** refer to menu names or command names.
2. All characters between parentheses are preferred access keys.

ENGLISH	DANISH	ENGLISH	DANISH
(keypad) *	NUM *	Cardfile	Kartotek
(keypad) +	NUM +	**Cascade**	**Overlappet (o)**
(keypad) -	NUM -	cascading menu	undermenu
(keypad) /	NUM /	cascading windows	overlappende vinduer
About	**Om (o)**	centered	centreret (c)
About Help...	**Om Hjælp... (o)**	Change	Skift
access key	hurtigtast	**Character...**	**Tegn... (t)**
Accessories	Tilbehør	Character Map	Tegnoversigt
active window	aktivt vindue	check	afkrydse
Active Window	**Aktivt vindue (a)**	check box	afkrydsningsfelt
Add	Tilføj	checked command	afkrydset kommando
Add Echo	**Tilføj ekko (t)**	check mark	afkrydsning
Alignment...	**Justering... (j)**	chevrons	«-tegn
All	Alt (a)	choose	vælge
ALT	ALT	**Clear**	**Ryd (d)**
ALT GR	ALT GR	clear	rydde
Always on Top	**Altid øverst (ø)**	clear (undo Select)	fjerne afkrydsning
Annotate...	**Anmærk... (a)**	**Clear All**	**Ryd alt (d)**
application icon	programikon	click	klikke på
application window	programvindue	Clipboard	Udklipsholder
Applications	Programmer	Clipboard Viewer	Udklipsholder
Apply	Anvend	Clock	Ur
arrange	arrangere	**Close**	**Luk (l)**
Arrange All	**Arranger alle (a)**	close	lukke
arrow	pil	**Close All**	**Luk alt (l)**
arrow pointer	pilmarkør	collapse	skjule
Assign to Key	**Tildel tast (t)**	Collate copies	Sorter kopier (o)
Assign to Menu	**Tildel menu (m)**	Column (Col)	Kol
automatic link	automatisk kæde	combo box	kombinationsboks
autoscroll	automatisk rulning	command	kommando
Back	Tilbage (t)	command button	kommandoknap
BACKSPACE	TILBAGE	command separator	kommandoseparator
bold	fed (f)	container application	klientprogram
Bookmark menu	**Bogmærke (m)**	container document	klientdokument
border	ramme	**Contents**	**Indhold (i)**
bottom window border	nedre vinduesramme	Contents	Indhold (i)
BREAK	BREAK	**Control menu**	**Kontrolmenu**
browse	gennemse	Control-menu box	kontrolmenuboks
button	knap	Control Panel	Kontrolpanel
Calculator	Lommeregner	Copies	Kopier (k)
Calendar	Kalender	**Copy**	**Kopier (o)**
Cancel	Annuller	copy	kopiere
cancel	annullere	**Copy...**	**Kopier... (o)**
CAPS LOCK	CAPS LOCK	**Copy Special**	**Kopier speciel (c)**
Caps Lock on (CAPS)	CAPS	Create	Opret

ENGLISH	DANISH	ENGLISH	DANISH
critical message	alvorlig meddelelse	Drives	Drev (d)
crop	beskære	drop	slippe
cross-hair pointer	krydsmarkør	drop-down combo box	kombinationsboks
CTRL	CTRL	drop-down list box	rulleliste
CTRL+B (Bold)	CTRL+F	drop-down menu	rullemenu
CTRL+C (Copy)	CTRL+C	**Edit**	**Rediger (r)**
CTRL+D (Double underline)	CTRL+D	**Edit menu**	**Rediger (r)**
CTRL+E (Center)	CTRL+E	**Effects menu**	**Effekter (e)**
CTRL+I (Italics)	CTRL+K	ellipsis	ellipse
CTRL+J (Justify)	CTRL+J	embed	integrere
CTRL+L (Left align)	CTRL+L	embedded object	integreret objekt
CTRL+R (Right align)	CTRL+R	END	END
CTRL+U (Underline)	CTRL+U	enter	skrive
CTRL+V (Paste)	CTRL+V	ENTER	ENTER
CTRL+W (Word underline)	CTRL+W	ENTER (keypad)	NUM ENTER
CTRL+X (Cut)	CTRL+X	ESC	ESC
CTRL+Z (Undo)	CTRL+Z	**Exit**	**Afslut (a)**
Customize	**Tilpas (t)**	**Exit and Return to**	**Afslut og returner til (a)**
Cut	**Klip (k)**	expand	udvide
cut	klippe ud	extend selection	udvide markering
Decrease Speed	**Reducer hastigheden (r)**	Extend selection on (EXT)	UDV
Decrease Volume	**Reducer lydstyrken (c)**	File Manager	Filhåndtering
Default	Standard	**File menu**	**Filer (f)**
Define	Definer	File Name	Filnavn (n)
Define...	**Definer... (d)**	**Find...**	**Søg... (s)**
DEL	DEL	Find Next	Find næste (n)
DEL (Clear)	DEL	Find What	Søg efter (s)
delete	slette	font	skrifttype
Delete	**Slet (s)**	Font	Skrifttype (s)
Delete...	**Slet... (s)**	Font Style	Typografi (t)
Delete After Current Position	**Slet fra nuværende position (s)**	**Format menu**	**Formater (t)**
Delete Before Current Position	**Slet op til nuværende position (t)**	freeze	fryse
		Freeze Panes	**Frys ruder (f)**
desktop	desktop	From	Fra (f)
destination application	destinationsprogram	**Full Menus**	**Lange menuer (m)**
destination document	destinationsdokument	gallery	galleri
Device menu	**Enhed (e)**	Games	Underholdning
dialog box	dialogboks	Glossary	Leksikon (l)
dialog box title	dialogbokstitel	Go To	Gå til
Direction	Retning	**Go To...**	**Gå til... (l)**
Directories	Biblioteker (b)	Goto/Gosub button	hopknap
directory icon	biblioteksikon	group	gruppere
disk icon	disketteikon	group box	gruppeboks
Document...	**Dokument... (d)**	group icon	gruppeikon
document file icon	dokumentfilikon	group window	gruppevindue
document icon	dokumentikon	Help	Hjælp
document window	dokumentvindue	**Help menu**	**Hjælp (h)**
Done	Udført/Luk	Help window	Hjælp-vindue
double-click	dobbeltklikke på	**Hide**	**Skjul (s)**
double underline	dobbelt understreget (d)	hide	skjule
Down	Fremad (f)	History	Oversigt (o)
DOWN ARROW	PIL NED	HOME	HOME
down scroll arrow	rullepil ned	horizontal scroll bar	vandret rullepanel
drag	trække	horizontal split bar	vandret delelinje
drag-and-drop	trække og slippe	hourglass pointer	timeglas
drive icon	drevikon	**How to use Help**	**Brug af Hjælp (b)**

ENGLISH	DANISH	ENGLISH	DANISH
I-beam pointer	tekstmarkør	MS-DOS Prompt	MS-DOS-prompt
icon	ikon	**New...**	**Ny(t)... (n)**
inactive window	ikke-aktivt vindue	**New Window**	**Nyt vindue (n)**
Increase Speed (by 100%)	**Forøg hastigheden (med 100 %) (f)**	Next	Næste (n)
		Next Window	**Næste vindue (v)**
Increase Volume (by 25%)	**Forøg lydstyrken (med 25 %) (ø)**	No	Nej
		Notepad	Notesblok
INS	INS	**Number...**	**Tal... (l)**
Insert...	**Indsæt... (i)**	NUM LOCK	NUM LOCK
Insert File...	**Indsæt fil... (f)**	Num Lock on (NUM)	NUM
insertion point	indsætningspunkt	object	objekt
Insert menu	**Indsæt (i)**	**Object...**	**Objekt... (b)**
Insert Object...	**Indsæt objekt... (t)**	object linking & embedding (OLE)	objektsammenkædning og integrering (OLE)
italic	kursiv (k)		
justified	lige margener (l)	Object Packager	Objektpakning
Keyboard	**Tastatur (t)**	OK	OK
label	navn	OLE application	OLE-program
Landscape	Liggende (l)	OLE (object linking & embedding)	OLE (Object Linking & Embedding)
left aligned	venstrejusteret (v)		
LEFT ARROW	VENSTRE PIL	**Open**	**Åbn (b)**
left scroll arrow	venstre rullepil	option button	alternativknap
left window border	venstre vinduesramme	Options	Indstillinger
Line (Ln)	Li	**Options menu**	**Indstillinger (i)**
link	kæde sammen	Orientation	Papirretning
linked object	sammenkædet objekt	Overtype on (OVR)	OVR
linked text and list box	kombineret tekstboks/liste	package	objektpakke
list box	liste	Page (Pg)	Si
List Files of Type	Filtype (t)	Pages	Sider (s)
Macro menu	**Makro (m)**	**Page Setup**	**Sideopsætning (i)**
Macro Recorder on (REC)	INDS	palette	palet
Main	Systemgruppe	pane	rude
main application	hovedprogram	Paper Size	Størrelse (ø)
main document	hoveddokument	**Paragraph...**	**Afsnit... (a)**
manual link	manuel kæde	**Paste**	**Sæt ind (n)**
Match Case	Forskel på store/små bogstaver (b)	paste	sætte ind
		Paste Link	**Indsæt kæde (e)**
Match Whole Word Only	Kun hele ord (k)	**Paste Special**	**Indsæt speciel (p)**
Maximize	**Maksimer (m)**	PAUSE	PAUSE
Maximize button	maksimeringsknap	PG DN	PGDN
Media Player	Medieafspiller	PG UP	PGUP
menu	menu	PIF Editor	PIF-editor
menu bar	menulinje	point	pege på
menu command	menukommando	pointer	markør
menu name	menunavn	Portrait	Stående (s)
message	meddelelse	**Preferences**	**Indstillinger (i)**
message box	meddelelsesboks	press and hold down	trykke på og holde nede
message line	meddelelseslinje	**Print**	**Udskriv (u)**
MIDI Sequencer...	**MIDI-sequencer...**	Printer	Printer
Minimize	**Minimer (i)**	**Printer Setup**	**Indstil printer (i)**
Minimize button	minimeringsknap	Print Manager	Udskriftsstyring
Mix with File...	**Mix med fil... (m)**	**Print Preview**	**Vis udskrift (v)**
More	Mere	Print Quality	Kvalitet (v)
Mouse	**Mus (m)**	Print Range	Udskriftsområde
mouse pointer	musmarkør	PRINT SCREEN	PRINTSCRN
Move	**Flyt (f)**	**Print Setup...**	**Indstil printer... (i)**
move	flytte	Print to File	Skriv til fil (l)

ENGLISH	DANISH	ENGLISH	DANISH
Print Topic	**Udskriv emne (u)**	select (check box, option button)	markere (afkrydsningsfelt, alternativ)
program group	programgruppe		
program item	programobjekt	select (data)	markere (data)
program-item icon	programobjektikon	select (drop-down menu)	vælge (menu, kommando)
Program Manager	Programstyring	selected command	markeret kommando
progress indicator	statusindikator	Selection	Det markerede (m)
push button	trykknap	selection cursor	markør
Quit	Afslut	select (list box)	vælge (liste)
radio button	alternativknap	Set	Angiv/Vælg/Indstil
Read Only	Skrivebeskyttet (s)	Setup	Indstil
Record...	**Indspil... (i)**	SHIFT	SKIFT
Recorder	Makrooptager	shortcut key	genvejstast
Redo	Gør om	**Short Menus**	**Korte menuer (m)**
reduce selection	formindske markering	**Size**	**Tilpas størrelse (t)**
Remove Split	**Fjern opdeling (o)**	size	tilpasse størrelse
Repeat	**Gentag (g)**	Size (font size)	Størrelse (ø)
Replace...	**Erstat... (e)**	sizing handle	størrelseshåndtag
Replace All	Erstat alle	slider	skala
Replace With	Erstat med (e)	slider indicator	skalaindikator
Reset	Nulstil	small capitals	kapitæler (a)
resize	tilpasse størrelse	**Sound...**	**Lyd... (l)**
Restore	**Gendan (g)**	Sound Recorder	Audiosampler
restore	gendanne	source application	kildeprogram
Restore button	gendannelsesknap	Source (paper)	Kilde (k)
Resume	Fortsæt	source document	kildedokument
Retry	Forsøg igen	SPACEBAR	MELLEMRUM
Reverse	**Baglæns (b)**	spin box	rotationsboks
Revert...	**Genindlæs... (g)**	**Split**	**Opdel (o)**
right aligned	højrejusteret (h)	split	opdele
RIGHT ARROW	HØJRE PIL	split bar	delelinje
right scroll arrow	højre rullepil	split box	deleboks
right window border	højre vinduesramme	StartUp	Start
ruler	lineal	status bar	statuslinje
Run...	**Kør... (k)**	status-bar indicator	statuslinjeindikator
Run...	**Afspil... (a)**	submenu	undermenu
Sample	Eksempel	switch	skifte
Save	**Gem (g)**	Switch to	Skift til
Save All	**Gem alt (e)**	**Switch To...**	**Skift til... (s)**
Save As...	**Gem som... (m)**	SYS RQ	SYS RQ
Save File as Type	Filtype (t)	TAB	TAB
scale	skalere	Terminal	Terminal
Scale menu	**Skala (s)**	text box	tekstboks
Scaling	Skalering (r)	text frame	tekstrude
scroll	rulle	**Tile**	**Side om side (s)**
scroll arrow	rullepil	tiled windows	vinduer side om side
scroll bar	rullepanel	**Time**	**Tid (t)**
scroll box	rulleboks	title bar	titellinje
SCROLL LOCK	SCROLL LOCK	To	Til (t)
Scroll Lock on (SCRL)	SCRL	tool	værktøj
Search	Søg (s)	toolbar	værktøjslinje
Search	Søg	toolbox	værktøjskasse
Search...	**Søg... (s)**	**Tools menu**	**Funktioner (k)**
Search for Help on	**Søg efter hjælp om (s)**	top window border	øvre vinduesramme
Section...	**Sektion... (s)**	**Tracks**	**Spor (s)**
Section (Sec)	Sek	**Tutorial**	**Selvstudium (e)**
select	markere/vælge	type	skrive

ENGLISH	DANISH
unavailable command	ikke-tilgængelig kommando
underline	understreget (u)
Undo	**Fortryd (r)**
unfreeze	frigøre
Unfreeze Panes	**Frigør ruder (f)**
Unhide...	**Vis... (v)**
Up	Tilbage (t)
UP ARROW	PIL OP
up scroll arrow	rullepil op
Update	**Opdater (o)**
update	opdatere
Utilities	**Funktioner (k)**
value set	værdisæt
vertical scroll bar	lodret rullepanel
vertical split bar	lodret delelinje
view	vise
View menu	**Vis (v)**

ENGLISH	DANISH
wallpaper	tapet
warning message	advarsel
wildcard	jokertegn
window	vindue
window background	vinduesbaggrund
window border	vinduesramme
window corner	vindueshjørne
window frame	vinduesramme
Window menu	**Vindue (u)**
window size	vinduesstørrelse
window title	vinduestitel
Windows Setup	Windows Installation
workspace	arbejdsområde
Yes	Ja
Zoom...	**Zoom... (z)**
zoom in	zoome ind
zoom out	zoome ud

CHAPTER 10

Dutch

This chapter lists the Dutch translations of all terms formatted in *italic* in Part 1. Terminology is listed in two ways: by category and in alphabetical order. The first section includes translations in the following categories: Window Elements, Menus, Dialog Boxes, Message Boxes, Other GUI Screen Elements, Keys, User Actions, and Applications For Microsoft Windows.

Terminology by Category

ENGLISH	DUTCH	ENGLISH	DUTCH
WINDOW ELEMENTS		window border	vensterkader
Main window elements		window corner	vensterhoek
active window	werkvenster	window frame	vensterkader
application window	toepassingsvenster	window size	vensterformaat
border	kader; rand	window title	venstertitel
bottom window border	onderrand van venster	workspace	werkruimte
cascading windows	trapsgewijs gerangschikte vensters		
desktop	bureaublad	**Window controls**	
document window	documentvenster	Control-menu box	symbool Systeemmenu
group window	groepsvenster	down scroll arrow	schuifpijl-omlaag
Help window	Help-venster	horizontal scroll bar	horizontale schuifbalk
inactive window	achtergrondvenster	horizontal split bar	horizontale splitsbalk
left window border	linkerrand van venster	left scroll arrow	schuifpijl-links
menu bar	menubalk	Maximize button	knop Maximumvenster
pane	deelvenster	Minimize button	knop Pictogram
right window border	rechterrand van venster	Restore button	knop Vorig formaat
ruler	liniaal	right scroll arrow	schuifpijl-rechts
status bar	statusbalk	scroll arrow	schuifpijl
tiled windows	naast elkaar gerangschikte vensters	scroll bar	schuifbalk
		scroll box	schuifblokje
title bar	titelbalk	split bar	splitsbalk
toolbar	werkbalk	split box	splitsblokje
top window border	bovenrand van venster	up scroll arrow	schuifpijl-omhoog
wallpaper	achtergrond	vertical scroll bar	verticale schuifbalk
window	venster	vertical split bar	verticale splitsbalk
window background	vensterachtergrond		

ENGLISH	DUTCH
Pointers	
arrow	pijl
arrow pointer	aanwijzer
cross-hair pointer	kruiscursor
hourglass pointer	zandloper
I-beam pointer	invoegsymbool
insertion point	invoegpositie
mouse pointer	muisaanwijzer
pointer	aanwijzer
selection cursor	selectiecursor
Icons	
application icon	toepassingspictogram
directory icon	directorypictogram
disk icon	schijfpictogram
document file icon	bestandspictogram
document icon	documentpictogram
drive icon	stationspictogram
group icon	groepspictogram
icon	pictogram
program-item icon	programmapictogram
General terms	
access key	toegangstoets
check mark	vinkje
ellipsis	puntjes (...)
font	lettertype
object	object
program group	programmagroep
program item	programma
shortcut key	sneltoets
sizing handle	formaatgreep
status-bar indicator	statusbalkindicatie
tool	knop
unavailable command	niet-beschikbare opdracht
MENUS	
Menu elements	
cascading menu	vervolgmenu
checked command	ingeschakelde opdracht
command	opdracht
command separator	opdrachtenscheidingslijn
drop-down menu	menu
menu	menu
menu command	(menu-)opdracht
menu name	menunaam
selected command	geselecteerde opdracht
submenu	vervolgmenu
Menus and commands	
View menu	Beeld (d)
Insert menu	Invoegen (i)
Control menu	Systeemmenu
Restore	Vorig formaat (v)

ENGLISH	DUTCH
Move	Verplaatsen (e)
Size	Formaat wijzigen (f)
Minimize	Pictogram (p)
Maximize	Maximumvenster (m)
Next	Volgende (d)
Close	Sluiten (s)
Run...	Starten... (t)
Switch To...	Taakoverzicht... (o)
Split	Splitsen (i)
File menu	Bestand (b)
New...	Nieuw... (n)
Open	Openen (o)
Close	Sluiten (s)
Close All	Alles sluiten (u)
Save	Opslaan (p)
Save As...	Opslaan als... (l)
Save All	Alles opslaan (e)
Delete	Verwijderen (v)
Page Setup	Pagina-instelling (g)
Print	Afdrukken (d)
Print Preview	Afdrukvoorbeeld (f)
Printer Setup	Printerinstelling (i)
Exit	Afsluiten (a)
Exit and Return to	Afsluiten en terug naar (a)
Update	Bijwerken (w)
Edit menu	Bewerken (w)
Undo	Ongedaan maken (o)
Repeat	Herhalen (h)
Cut	Knippen (n)
Copy	Kopiëren (k)
Copy Special	Kopiëren speciaal (c)
Paste	Plakken (p)
Paste Link	Koppeling plakken (e)
Paste Special	Plakken speciaal (s)
Clear	Wissen (w)
Clear All	Alles wissen (a)
Find...	Zoeken... (z)
Search...	Zoeken... (z)
Replace...	Vervangen... (v)
Go To...	Ga naar... (g)
Delete...	Verwijderen... (v)
Insert...	Invoegen... (i)
Object...	Object... (b)
Insert Object...	Object invoegen... (c)
Options menu	Opties (o)
Preferences	Voorkeuren (v)
Full Menus	Volledige menu's (m)
Short Menus	Beknopte menu's (m)
Format menu	Opmaak (k)
Character...	Teken... (e)
Paragraph...	Alinea... (a)

ENGLISH	DUTCH	ENGLISH	DUTCH
Section...	Sectie... (s)	Increase Volume (by 25%)	Volume verhogen (met 25%) (v)
Document...	Document... (d)		
Number...	Getal... (g)	Decrease Volume	Volume verlagen (o)
Alignment...	Uitlijning... (u)	Increase Speed (by 100%)	Snelheid vermeerderen (met 100%) (s)
Utilities menu	Extra (x)	Decrease Speed	Snelheid verminderen (n)
Tools menu	Extra (x)	Add Echo	Echo toevoegen (c)
Customize	Aanpassen (a)	Reverse	Achteruit spelen (a)
Macro menu	Macro (m)	**Help application**	
Record...	Opnemen... (o)	File menu	Bestand (b)
Run...	Starten... (s)	Open	Openen (o)
Edit	Bewerken (w)	Print Topic	Onderwerp afdrukken (n)
Assign to Key	Toewijzen aan toets (t)	Print Setup...	Printerinstelling... (i)
Assign to Menu	Toewijzen aan menu (m)	Exit	Afsluiten (a)
Window menu	Venster (v)	Edit menu	Bewerken (w)
New Window	Nieuw venster (w)	Copy...	Kopiëren... (k)
Cascade	Trapsgewijs (t)	Annotate...	Aantekening... (a)
Tile	Naast elkaar (n)		
Next Window	Volgend venster (v)	Bookmark menu	Bladwijzer (a)
Arrange All	Alle vensters (a)	Define...	Bepalen... (b)
Hide	Verbergen (b)		
Unhide...	Zichtbaar maken... (z)	Help menu	?
Split	Splitsen (i)	How to use Help	Help gebruiken (e)
Freeze Panes	Titels blokkeren (t)	Always on Top	Altijd op voorgrond (a)
Remove Split	Splitsing ongedaan maken (i)	About Help...	Info... (i)
Unfreeze Panes	Titelblokkering opheffen (t)	**Buttons**	
Zoom...	In-/uitzoomen... (u)	Contents	Inhoud (i)
		Search	Zoeken (z)
Help menu	?	Back	Terug (t)
Contents	Inhoudsopgave (o)	History	Vorige (v)
How to use Help	Help gebruiken (e)	Glossary	Definities (d)
Search for Help on	Zoeken (z)		
Active Window	Werkvenster (w)	**DIALOG BOXES**	
Keyboard	Toetsenbord (t)		
Mouse	Muis (m)	dialog box	dialoogvenster
Tutorial	Zelfstudie (s)	wildcard	jokerteken
About	Info (i)	**Dialog box elements**	
Device menu	Apparaat (a)	button	knop
Scale menu	Schaal (s)	check box	aankruisvakje
MIDI Sequencer...	MIDI Sequencer...	chevrons	dubbele punthaken
Sound...	Geluid... (g)	combo box	keuzelijst met invoervak
Time	Tijd (t)	command button	opdrachtknop
Tracks	Sporen (s)	dialog box title	dialoogvensternaam
		drop-down combo box	vervolgkeuzelijst met invoervak
Effects menu	Effecten (e)		
Revert...	Terug... (t)	drop-down list box	vervolgkeuzelijst
Insert File...	Bestand invoegen... (b)	Goto/Gosub button	vervolgknop
Mix with File...	Met bestand mengen... (m)	group box	groepsvak
Delete Before Current Position	Voor huidige positie verwijderen (v)	label	label
Delete After Current Position	Na huidige positie verwijderen (n)	linked text and list box	invoervak/keuzelijst-combinatie

ENGLISH	DUTCH	ENGLISH	DUTCH
list box	keuzelijst	Orientation	Afdrukstand
option button	keuzerondje	Pages	Pagina's (p)
progress indicator	voortgangsindicatie	Paper Size	Papierformaat (f)
push button	opdrachtknop	Portrait	Staand (t)
radio button	keuzerondje	Printer	Printer
slider	schuifregelaar	Print Quality	Afdrukkwaliteit (f)
slider indicator	regelknop	Print Range	Bereik
spin box	ringveld	Print to File	Naar bestand (b)
text box	tekstvak	Read Only	Alleen-lezen (a)
value set	mogelijke keuzen	Replace All	Alles vervangen
		Replace With	Vervangen door (d)
Dialog box buttons		Sample	Voorbeeld
Add	Toevoegen	Save File as Type	Bestand opslaan als (b)
Apply	Toepassen	Scaling	Aanpassen (s)
Cancel	Annuleren	Selection	Selectie (s)
Change	Wijzigen	Size (font size)	Punten/Pt (p)
Create	Maken	Source (paper)	Invoer (i)
Default	Standaard	To	T/m (t)
Define	Bepalen	Up	Omhoog (o)
Done	Gereed		
Go To	Ga naar	**MESSAGE BOXES**	
Help	Help	critical message	foutbericht
More	Overige	message	statusbericht
No	Nee	message box	berichtvenster
OK	OK	message line	berichtregel
Options	Opties	warning message	waarschuwing(sbericht)
Quit	Afsluiten		
Redo	Opnieuw	**OTHER GUI SCREEN**	
Reset	Beginwaarde(n)	**ELEMENTS**	
Resume	Doorgaan	**Graphical options**	
Retry	Nogmaals	gallery	galerie
Search	Zoeken	palette	palet
Set	Instellen	text frame	tekstkader
Setup	Instellen	toolbox	werkset
Switch to	Activeren		
Yes	Ja	**Status bar abbreviations**	
		Caps Lock on (CAPS)	CAPS
Dialog box labels		Column (Col)	Ko
All	Alles (l)	Extend selection on (EXT)	UIT
Collate copies	Sorteren (r)	Line (Ln)	Rg
Copies	Aantal (a)	Macro Recorder on (REC)	OPN
Direction	Richting	Num Lock on (NUM)	NUM
Directories	Directory's (d)	Overtype on (OVR)	OVR
Down	Stations (s)	Page (Pg)	Pg
Drives	Omlaag (l)	Scroll Lock on (SCRL)	SCRL
File Name	Bestandsnaam (n)	Section (Sec)	Se
Find Next	Volgende zoeken (v)		
Find What	Zoeken naar (z)	**Character formats**	
Font	Lettertype (l)	bold	vet (b)
Font Style	Lettertype-opmaak (e)	double underline	dubbel onderstrepen (d)
From	Van (v)	italic	cursief (i)
Landscape	Liggend (l)	small capitals	klein kapitaal (k)
List Files of Type	Bestandstypen (t)	underline	onderstrepen (u)
Match Case	Identieke hoofdletters/kleine letters (i)		
Match Whole Word Only	Heel woord (h)		

ENGLISH	DUTCH
Paragraph formats	
centered	centreren (e)
justified	uitvullen (j)
left aligned	links uitlijnen (l)
right aligned	rechts uitlijnen (r)
KEYS	
Shortcut keys	
CTRL+B (Bold)	CTRL+B
CTRL+C (Copy)	CTRL+C
CTRL+D (Double underline)	CTRL+D
CTRL+E (Center)	CTRL+E
CTRL+I (Italics)	CTRL+I
CTRL+J (Justify)	CTRL+J
CTRL+L (Left align)	CTRL+L
CTRL+R (Right align)	CTRL+R
CTRL+U (Underline)	CTRL+U
CTRL+V (Paste)	CTRL+V
CTRL+W (Word underline)	CTRL+W
CTRL+X (Cut)	CTRL+X
CTRL+Z (Undo)	CTRL+Z
DEL (Clear)	DEL
Keynames	
(keypad) *	NUM-STERRETJE
(keypad) +	NUM-PLUSTEKEN
keypad) -	NUM-MINTEKEN
(keypad) /	NUM-SLASH
ALT	ALT
ALT GR	ALT-GR
BACKSPACE	BACKSPACE
BREAK	BREAK
CAPS LOCK	CAPS-LOCK
CTRL	CTRL
DEL	DEL
DOWN ARROW	PIJL-OMLAAG
END	END
ENTER	ENTER
ENTER (keypad)	ENTER (NUM-BLOK)
ESC	ESC
HOME	HOME
INS	INS
LEFT ARROW	PIJL-LINKS
NUM LOCK	NUM-LOCK
PAUSE	PAUSE
PG DN	PGDN
PG UP	PGUP
PRINT SCREEN	PRINT-SCRN
RIGHT ARROW	PIJL-RECHTS
SCROLL LOCK	SCROLL-LOCK
SHIFT	SHIFT
SPACEBAR	SPATIEBALK
SYS RQ	SYS-RQ
TAB	TAB
UP ARROW	PIJL-OMHOOG

ENGLISH	DUTCH
USER ACTIONS	
Keyboard actions	
enter	invoeren (typen en op ENTER drukken)
press and hold down	ingedrukt houden
type	typen
Mouse actions	
click	klikken
double-click	dubbelklikken
drag	slepen
drag-and-drop	slepen en neerzetten
drop	neerzetten
point	aanwijzen
Manipulating window appearance	
arrange	schikken
close	sluiten
freeze	blokkeren
hide	verbergen
move	verplaatsen
resize	formaat wijzigen
restore	vorig formaat herstellen
select	selecteren
size	formaat wijzigen
split	splitsen
switch	overschakelen
unfreeze	blokkering opheffen
Selecting options or content	
cancel	annuleren
check	inschakelen
choose	kiezen
clear (undo Select)	uitschakelen
extend selection	selectie uitbreiden
reduce selection	selectie verkleinen
select	selecteren
select (check box, option button)	inschakelen (aankruisvakje); selecteren (keuzerondje)
select (data)	selecteren
select (drop-down menu)	kiezen
select (list box)	openen
Viewing content	
autoscroll	automatisch schuiven
browse	bladeren
collapse	samenvouwen
expand	uitvouwen
scroll	schuiven
view	bekijken
zoom in	inzoomen
zoom out	uitzoomen

ENGLISH	DUTCH	ENGLISH	DUTCH
Removing content		paste	plakken
clear	wissen	scale	formaat; formaat wijzigen
copy	kopiëren	size	formaat wijzigen
cut	knippen	source application	brontoepassing
delete	verwijderen	source document	brondocument
paste	plakken	update	bijwerken
Manipulating objects		**APPLICATIONS FOR**	
arrange	schikken	**MICROSOFT WINDOWS**	
automatic link	automatische koppeling		
Clipboard	Klembord	Accessories	Bureau-accessoires
container application	hoofdtoepassing	Applications	Toepassingen
container document	hoofddocument	Calculator	Rekenmachine
copy	kopiëren	Calendar	Agenda
crop	bijsnijden	Cardfile	Kaartenbak
destination application	doeltoepassing	Character Map	Speciale tekens
destination document	doeldocument	Clipboard Viewer	Klembord
drag-and-drop	slepen en neerzetten	Clock	Klok
embed	insluiten	Control Panel	Configuratiescherm
embedded object	ingesloten object	File Manager	Bestandsbeheer
group	groeperen	Games	Ontspanning
link	koppelen	Main	Hoofdgroep
linked object	gekoppeld object	Media Player	Media-speler
main application	hoofdtoepassing	MS-DOS Prompt	MS-DOS-aanwijzing
main document	hoofddocument	Notepad	Kladblok
manual link	handmatige koppeling	Object Packager	Objectenbeheer
object	object	PIF Editor	PIF-editor
object linking & embedding (OLE)	Object Linking & Embedding (OLE, objecten koppelen en insluiten)	Print Manager	Afdrukbeheer
		Program Manager	Programmabeheer
OLE (object linking & embedding)	OLE (Object Linking & Embedding, objecten koppelen en insluiten)	Recorder	Macrorecorder
		Sound Recorder	Geluidsrecorder
		StartUp	Opstarten
OLE application	OLE-toepassing	Terminal	Terminal
package	OLE-object	Windows Setup	Windows Setup

Terminology by Alphabet

Notes:
1. All terms formatted in **bold** refer to menu names or command names.
2. All characters between parentheses are preferred access keys.

ENGLISH	DUTCH	ENGLISH	DUTCH
(keypad) *	NUM-STERRETJE	Cardfile	Kaartenbak
(keypad) +	NUM-PLUSTEKEN	**Cascade**	**Trapsgewijs (t)**
(keypad) -	NUM-MINTEKEN	cascading menu	vervolgmenu
(keypad) /	NUM-SLASH	cascading windows	trapsgewijs gerangschikte
About	**Info (i)**		vensters
About Help...	**Info... (i)**	centered	centreren (e)
access key	toegangstoets	Change	Wijzigen
Accessories	Bureau-accessoires	**Character...**	**Teken... (e)**
active window	werkvenster	Character Map	Speciale tekens
Active Window	**Werkvenster (w)**	check	inschakelen
Add	Toevoegen	check box	aankruisvakje
Add Echo	**Echo toevoegen (c)**	checked command	ingeschakelde opdracht
Alignment...	**Uitlijning... (u)**	check mark	vinkje
All	Alles (l)	chevrons	dubbele punthaken
ALT	ALT	choose	kiezen
ALT GR	ALT-GR	**Clear**	**Wissen (w)**
Always on Top	**Altijd op voorgrond (a)**	clear	wissen
Annotate...	**Aantekening... (a)**	**Clear All**	**Alles wissen (a)**
application icon	toepassingspictogram	clear (undo Select)	uitschakelen
application window	toepassingsvenster	click	klikken
Applications	Toepassingen	Clipboard	Klembord
Apply	Toepassen	Clipboard Viewer	Klembord
arrange	schikken	Clock	Klok
Arrange All	**Alle vensters (a)**	**Close**	**Sluiten (s)**
arrow	pijl	close	sluiten
arrow pointer	aanwijzer	**Close All**	**Alles sluiten (u)**
Assign to Key	**Toewijzen aan toets (t)**	collapse	samenvouwen
Assign to Menu	**Toewijzen aan menu (m)**	Collate copies	Sorteren (r)
automatic link	automatische koppeling	Column (Col)	Ko
autoscroll	automatisch schuiven	combo box	keuzelijst met invoervak
Back	Terug (t)	command	opdracht
BACKSPACE	BACKSPACE	command button	opdrachtknop
bold	vet (b)	command separator	opdrachtenscheidingslijn
Bookmark menu	**Bladwijzer (a)**	container application	hoofdtoepassing
border	kader; rand	container document	hoofddocument
bottom window border	onderrand van venster	**Contents**	**Inhoudsopgave (o)**
BREAK	BREAK	Contents	Inhoud (i)
browse	bladeren	**Control menu**	**Systeemmenu**
button	knop	Control-menu box	symbool Systeemmenu
Calculator	Rekenmachine	Control Panel	Configuratiescherm
Calendar	Agenda	Copies	Aantal (a)
Cancel	Annuleren	copy	kopiëren
cancel	annuleren	**Copy**	**Kopiëren (k)**
CAPS LOCK	CAPS-LOCK	**Copy Special**	**Kopiëren speciaal (c)**
Caps Lock on (CAPS)	CAPS	Create	Maken

ENGLISH	DUTCH	ENGLISH	DUTCH
critical message	foutbericht	drop	neerzetten
crop	bijsnijden	drop-down combo box	vervolgkeuzelijst met
cross-hair pointer	kruiscursor		invoervak
CTRL	CTRL	drop-down list box	vervolgkeuzelijst
CTRL+B (Bold)	CTRL+B	drop-down menu	menu
CTRL+C (Copy)	CTRL+C	**Edit**	**Bewerken (w)**
CTRL+D (Double underline)	CTRL+D	**Edit menu**	**Bewerken (w)**
CTRL+E (Center)	CTRL+E	**Effects menu**	**Effecten (e)**
CTRL+I (Italics)	CTRL+I	ellipsis	puntjes (...)
CTRL+J (Justify)	CTRL+J	embed	insluiten
CTRL+L (Left align)	CTRL+L	embedded object	ingesloten object
CTRL+R (Right align)	CTRL+R	END	END
CTRL+U (Underline)	CTRL+U	enter	invoeren (typen en op
CTRL+V (Paste)	CTRL+V		ENTER drukken)
CTRL+W (Word underline)	CTRL+W	ENTER	ENTER
CTRL+X (Cut)	CTRL+X	ENTER (keypad)	ENTER (NUM-BLOK)
CTRL+Z (Undo)	CTRL+Z	ESC	ESC
Customize	**Aanpassen (a)**	**Exit**	**Afsluiten (a)**
Cut	**Knippen (n)**	**Exit and Return to**	**Afsluiten en terug naar (a)**
cut	knippen	expand	uitvouwen
Decrease Speed	**Snelheid verminderen (n)**	extend selection	selectie uitbreiden
Decrease Volume	**Volume verlagen (o)**	Extend selection on (EXT)	UIT
Default	Standaard	File Manager	Bestandsbeheer
Define	Bepalen	**File menu**	**Bestand (b)**
Define...	**Bepalen... (b)**	File Name	Bestandsnaam (n)
DEL	DEL	**Find...**	**Zoeken... (z)**
DEL (Clear)	DEL	Find Next	Volgende zoeken (v)
Delete	**Verwijderen (v)**	Find What	Zoeken naar (z)
delete	verwijderen	font	lettertype
Delete After Current Position	**Na huidige positie verwijderen (n)**	Font	Lettertype (l)
		Font Style	Lettertype-opmaak (e)
Delete Before Current Position	**Voor huidige positie verwijderen (v)**	**Format menu**	**Opmaak (k)**
		freeze	blokkeren
desktop	bureaublad	**Freeze Panes**	**Titels blokkeren (t)**
destination application	doeltoepassing	From	Van (v)
destination document	doeldocument	**Full Menus**	**Volledige menu's (m)**
Device menu	**Apparaat (a)**	gallery	galerie
dialog box	dialoogvenster	Games	Ontspanning
dialog box title	dialoogvensternaam	Glossary	Definities (d)
Direction	Richting	Go To	Ga naar
Directories	Directory's (d)	**Go To...**	**Ga naar... (g)**
directory icon	directorypictogram	Goto/Gosub button	vervolgknop
disk icon	schijfpictogram	group	groeperen
Document...	**Document... (d)**	group box	groepsvak
document file icon	bestandspictogram	group icon	groepspictogram
document icon	documentpictogram	group window	groepsvenster
document window	documentvenster	Help	Help
Done	Gereed	**Help menu**	**?**
double-click	dubbelklikken	Help window	Help-venster
double underline	dubbel onderstrepen (d)	**Hide**	**Verbergen (b)**
Down	Stations (s)	hide	verbergen
DOWN ARROW	PIJL-OMLAAG	History	Vorige (v)
down scroll arrow	schuifpijl-omlaag	HOME	HOME
drag	slepen	horizontal scroll bar	horizontale schuifbalk
drag-and-drop	slepen en neerzetten	horizontal split bar	horizontale splitsbalk
drive icon	stationspictogram	hourglass pointer	zandloper
Drives	Omlaag (l)		

ENGLISH	DUTCH
How to use Help	Help gebruiken (e)
I-beam pointer	invoegsymbool
icon	pictogram
inactive window	achtergrondvenster
Increase Speed (by 100%)	Snelheid vermeerderen
	(met 100%) (s)
Increase Volume (by 25%)	Volume verhogen
	(met 25%) (v)
INS	INS
Insert...	Invoegen... (i)
Insert File...	Bestand invoegen... (b)
insertion point	invoegpositie
Insert menu	Invoegen (i)
Insert Object...	Object invoegen... (c)
italic	cursief (i)
justified	uitvullen (j)
Keyboard	Toetsenbord (t)
label	label
Landscape	Liggend (l)
left aligned	links uitlijnen (l)
LEFT ARROW	PIJL-LINKS
left scroll arrow	schuifpijl-links
left window border	linkerrand van venster
Line (Ln)	Rg
link	koppelen
linked object	gekoppeld object
linked text and list box	invoervak/keuzelijst-
	combinatie
list box	keuzelijst
List Files of Type	Bestandstypen (t)
Macro menu	Macro (m)
Macro Recorder on (REC)	OPN
Main	Hoofdgroep
main application	hoofdtoepassing
main document	hoofddocument
manual link	handmatige koppeling
Match Case	Identieke hoofdletters/kleine
	letters (i)
Match Whole Word Only	Heel woord (h)
Maximize	Maximumvenster (m)
Maximize button	knop Maximumvenster
Media Player	Media-speler
menu	menu
menu bar	menubalk
menu command	(menu-)opdracht
menu name	menunaam
message	statusbericht
message box	berichtvenster
message line	berichtregel
MIDI Sequencer...	MIDI Sequencer...
Minimize	Pictogram (p)
Minimize button	knop Pictogram
Mix with File...	Met bestand mengen... (m)
More	Overige
Mouse	Muis (m)
mouse pointer	muisaanwijzer
Move	Verplaatsen (e)

ENGLISH	DUTCH
move	verplaatsen
MS-DOS Prompt	MS-DOS-aanwijzing
New...	Nieuw... (n)
New Window	Nieuw venster (w)
Next	Volgende (d)
Next Window	Volgend venster (v)
No	Nee
Notepad	Kladblok
Number...	Getal... (g)
NUM LOCK	NUM-LOCK
Num Lock on (NUM)	NUM
object	object
Object...	Object... (h)
object linking & embedding	Object Linking & Embedding
(OLE)	(OLE, objecten koppelen en
	insluiten)
Object Packager	Objectenbeheer
OK	OK
OLE application	OLE-toepassing
OLE (object linking &	OLE (Object Linking &
embedding)	Embedding, objecten koppelen
	en insluiten)
Open	Openen (o)
option button	keuzerondje
Options	Opties
Options menu	Opties (o)
Orientation	Afdrukstand
Overtype on (OVR)	OVR
package	OLE-object
Page (Pg)	Pg
Page Setup	Pagina-instelling (g)
Pages	Pagina's (p)
palette	palet
pane	deelvenster
Paper Size	Papierformaat (f)
Paragraph...	Alinea... (a)
Paste	Plakken (p)
paste	plakken
Paste Link	Koppeling plakken (c)
Paste Special	Plakken speciaal (s)
PAUSE	PAUSE
PG DN	PGDN
PG UP	PGUP
PIF Editor	PIF-editor
point	aanwijzen
pointer	aanwijzer
Portrait	Staand (t)
Preferences	Voorkeuren (v)
press and hold down	ingedrukt houden
Print	Afdrukken (d)
Printer	Printer
Printer Setup	Printerinstelling (i)
Print Manager	Afdrukbeheer
Print Preview	Afdrukvoorbeeld (f)
Print Quality	Afdrukkwaliteit (f)
Print Range	Bereik

ENGLISH	DUTCH	ENGLISH	DUTCH
PRINT SCREEN	PRINT-SCRN	Section...	Sectie... (s)
Print Setup...	**Printerinstelling... (i)**	Section (Sec)	Se
Print to File	Naar bestand (b)	select	selecteren
Print Topic	**Onderwerp afdrukken (n)**	select (check box, option button)	inschakelen (aankruisvakje);
program group	programmagroep		selecteren (keuzerondje)
program item	programma	select (data)	selecteren
program-item icon	programmapictogram	select (drop-down menu)	kiezen
Program Manager	Programmabeheer	selected command	geselecteerde opdracht
progress indicator	voortgangsindicatie	Selection	Selectie (s)
push button	opdrachtknop	selection cursor	selectiecursor
Quit	Afsluiten	select (list box)	openen
radio button	keuzerondje	Set	Instellen
Read Only	Alleen-lezen (a)	Setup	Instellen
Record...	**Opnemen... (o)**	SHIFT	SHIFT
Recorder	Macrorecorder	shortcut key	sneltoets
Redo	Opnieuw	**Short Menus**	**Beknopte menu's (m)**
reduce selection	selectie verkleinen	**Size**	**Formaat wijzigen (f)**
Remove Split	**Splitsing ongedaan maken (i)**	size	formaat wijzigen
Repeat	**Herhalen (h)**	Size (font size)	Punten/Pt (p)
Replace...	**Vervangen... (v)**	sizing handle	formaatgreep
Replace All	Alles vervangen	slider	schuifregelaar
Replace With	Vervangen door (d)	slider indicator	regelknop
Reset	Beginwaarde(n)	small capitals	klein kapitaal (k)
resize	formaat wijzigen	**Sound...**	**Geluid... (g)**
Restore	**Vorig formaat (v)**	Sound Recorder	Geluidsrecorder
restore	vorig formaat herstellen	source application	brontoepassing
Restore button	knop Vorig formaat	source document	brondocument
Resume	Doorgaan	Source (paper)	Invoer (i)
Retry	Nogmaals	SPACEBAR	SPATIEBALK
Reverse	**Achteruit spelen (a)**	spin box	ringveld
Revert...	**Terug... (t)**	**Split**	**Splitsen (i)**
right aligned	rechts uitlijnen (r)	split	splitsen
RIGHT ARROW	PIJL-RECHTS	split bar	splitsbalk
right scroll arrow	schuifpijl-rechts	split box	splitsblokje
right window border	rechterrand van venster	StartUp	Opstarten
ruler	liniaal	status bar	statusbalk
Run...	**Starten... (t)**	status-bar indicator	statusbalkindicatie
Run...	**Starten... (s)**	submenu	vervolgmenu
Sample	Voorbeeld	switch	overschakelen
Save	**Opslaan (p)**	Switch to	Activeren
Save All	**Alles opslaan (e)**	**Switch To...**	**Taakoverzicht... (o)**
Save As...	**Opslaan als... (l)**	SYS RQ	SYS-RQ
Save File as Type	Bestand opslaan als (b)	TAB	TAB
scale	formaat; formaat wijzigen	Terminal	Terminal
Scale menu	**Schaal (s)**	text box	tekstvak
Scaling	Aanpassen (s)	text frame	tekstkader
scroll	schuiven	**Tile**	**Naast elkaar (n)**
scroll arrow	schuifpijl	tiled windows	naast elkaar gerangschikte
scroll bar	schuifbalk		vensters
scroll box	schuifblokje	**Time**	**Tijd (t)**
SCROLL LOCK	SCROLL-LOCK	title bar	titelbalk
Scroll Lock on (SCRL)	SCRL	To	T/m (t)
Search	Zoeken (z)	tool	knop
Search	Zoeken	toolbar	werkbalk
Search...	**Zoeken... (z)**	toolbox	werkset
Search for Help on	**Zoeken (z)**	**Tools menu**	**Extra (x)**

ENGLISH	DUTCH	ENGLISH	DUTCH
top window border	bovenrand van venster	view	bekijken
Tracks	**Sporen (s)**	**View menu**	**Beeld (d)**
Tutorial	**Zelfstudie (s)**	wallpaper	achtergrond
type	typen	warning message	waarschuwing(sbericht)
unavailable command	niet-beschikbare opdracht	wildcard	jokerteken
underline	onderstrepen (u)	window	venster
Undo	**Ongedaan maken (o)**	window background	vensterachtergrond
unfreeze	blokkering opheffen	window border	vensterkader
Unfreeze Panes	**Titelblokkering**	window corner	vensterhoek
	opheffen (t)	window frame	vensterkader
Unhide...	**Zichtbaar maken... (z)**	**Window menu**	**Venster (v)**
Up	Omhoog (o)	window size	vensterformaat
UP ARROW	PIJL-OMHOOG	window title	venstertitel
up scroll arrow	schuifpijl-omhoog	Windows Setup	Windows Setup
Update	**Bijwerken (w)**	workspace	werkruimte
update	bijwerken	Yes	Ja
Utilities menu	**Extra (x)**	**Zoom...**	**In-/uitzoomen... (u)**
value set	mogelijke keuzen	zoom in	inzoomen
vertical scroll bar	verticale schuifbalk	zoom out	uitzoomen
vertical split bar	verticale splitsbalk		

CHAPTER 11

Finnish

This chapter lists the Finnish translations of all terms formatted in *italic* in Part 1. Terminology is listed in two ways: by category and in alphabetical order. The first section includes translations in the following categories: Window Elements, Menus, Dialog Boxes, Message Boxes, Other GUI Screen Elements, Keys, User Actions, and Applications For Microsoft Windows.

Terminology by Category

ENGLISH	FINNISH	ENGLISH	FINNISH
WINDOW ELEMENTS		window frame	ikkunan kehys
Main window elements		window size	ikkunan koko
active window	aktiivinen ikkuna	window title	ikkunan otsikko
application window	sovellusikkuna	workspace	työtila
border	reunaviiva		
bottom window border	ikkunan alareuna	**Window controls**	
cascading windows	limittäiset ikkunat	Control-menu box	ohjausvalikkoruutu
desktop	työpöytä	down scroll arrow	alavieritysnuoli
document window	asiakirjaikkuna	horizontal scroll bar	vaakasuora vierityspalkki
group window	ryhmäikkuna	horizontal split bar	vaakasuora jakopalkki
Help window	Ohje-ikkuna	left scroll arrow	vasen vieritysnuoli
inactive window	passiivinen ikkuna	Maximize button	suurennuspainike
left window border	ikkunan vasen reuna	Minimize button	pienennyspainike
menu bar	valikkorivi	Restore button	palautuspainike
pane	ruutu	right scroll arrow	oikea vieritysnuoli
right window border	ikkunan oikea reuna	scroll arrow	vieritysnuoli
ruler	viivain	scroll bar	vierityspalkki
status bar	tilarivi	scroll box	vieritysruutu
tiled windows	vierekkäiset ikkunat	split bar	jakopalkki
title bar	otsikkorivi	split box	jakoruutu
toolbar	työkalurivi	up scroll arrow	ylävieritysnuoli
top window border	ikkunan yläreuna	vertical scroll bar	pystysuora vierityspalkki
wallpaper	taustakuva	vertical split bar	pystysuora jakopalkki
window	ikkuna		
window background	ikkunan tausta		
window border	ikkunan reuna		
window corner	ikkunan kulma		

ENGLISH	FINNISH	ENGLISH	FINNISH
Pointers		Control menu	ohjausvalikko
arrow	nuoli	Restore	Palauta (p)
arrow pointer	nuoliosoitin	Move	Siirrä (r)
cross-hair pointer	ristiosoitin	Size	Muuta kokoa (m)
hourglass pointer	tiimalasiosoitin	Minimize	Pienennä (i)
I-beam pointer	I-osoitin	Maximize	Suurenna (u)
		Next	Seuraava (e)
insertion point	lisäyskohta	Close	Sulje (s)
mouse pointer	hiiriosoitin	Run...	Suorita... (t)
pointer	osoitin	Switch To...	Vaihda... (v)
selection cursor	valintakohdistin	Split	Jaa (j)
Icons		File menu	Tiedosto (t)
application icon	sovelluskuvake	New...	Uusi... (u)
directory icon	hakemistokuvake	Open	Avaa (a)
disk icon	levykuvake	Close	Sulje (s)
document file icon	asiakirjatiedostokuvake	Close All	Sulje kaikki (s)
document icon	asiakirjakuvake	Save	Tallenna (t)
drive icon	asemakuvake	Save As...	Tallenna nimellä... (n)
group icon	ryhmäkuvake	Save All	Tallenna kaikki (i)
icon	kuvake	Delete	Poista (p)
program-item icon	ohjelmakuvake	Page Setup	Sivun asetukset (v)
		Print	Tulosta (o)
General terms		Print Preview	Esikatsele (e)
access key	valintanäppäin	Printer Setup	Kirjoittimen asetukset (k)
check mark	valintamerkki	Exit	Lopeta (l)
ellipsis	kolme pistettä	Exit and Return to	Lopeta ja palaa tiedostoon (l)
font	fontti	Update	Päivitä (p)
object	objekti		
program group	ohjelmaryhmä	Edit menu	Muokkaa (m)
program item	ohjelma	Undo	Kumoa (k)
shortcut key	pikanäppäin	Repeat	Toista (t)
sizing handle	koonmuuttokahva	Cut	Leikkaa (l)
status-bar indicator	tilarivi-ilmaisin	Copy	Kopioi (o)
tool	työkalu	Copy Special	Kopioi määräten (m)
unavailable command	komento, joka ei ole	Paste	Liitä (i)
	käytettävissä	Paste Link	Liitä linkki (i)
		Paste Special	Liitä määräten (n)
		Clear	Tyhjennä (y)
MENUS		Clear All	Tyhjennä kaikki (y)
Menu elements		Find...	Etsi... (e)
cascading menu	alivalikko	Search...	Etsi... (e)
checked command	valittu komento	Replace...	Korvaa... (r)
command	komento	Go To...	Siirry... (s)
command separator	komentojen erotinviiva	Delete...	Poista... (p)
drop-down menu	avattava valikko	Insert...	Lisää... (ä)
menu	valikko	Object...	Objekti... (b)
menu command	valikon komento	Insert Object...	Lisää objekti... (b)
menu name	valikon nimi		
selected command	valittu komento	Options menu	Asetukset (a)
submenu	alivalikko	Preferences	Oletukset (o)
		Full Menus	Pitkät valikot (v)
Menus and commands		Short Menus	Lyhyet valikot (v)
View menu	Näytä (n)		
Insert menu	Lisää (l)		

ENGLISH	FINNISH	ENGLISH	FINNISH
Format menu	Muotoile (e)	Delete After Current Position	Poista nykyisen kohdan
Character...	Merkki... (m)		jälkeen (p)
Paragraph...	Kappale... (k)	Increase Volume (by 25%)	Lisää äänenvoimakkuutta
Section...	Osa... (o)		(25%) (k)
Document...	Asiakirja... (a)	Decrease Volume	Vähennä äänenvoimakkuutta
Number...	Luku... (l)		(v)
Alignment...	Tasaus... (s)	Increase Speed (by 100%)	Lisää nopeutta (100%) (n)
		Decrease Speed	Vähennä nopeutta (o)
Utilities menu	Muut (u)	Add Echo	Lisää kaiku (l)
Tools menu	Työkalut (y)	Reverse	Käännä suunta (s)
Customize	Mukauta (m)		
		Help application	
Macro menu	Makro (r)	File menu	Tiedosto (t)
Record...	Nauhoita... (a)	Open	Avaa (a)
Run...	Suorita...(s)	Print Topic	Tulosta aihe (t)
Edit	Muokkaa (m)	Print Setup...	Kirjoittimen asetukset... (k)
Assign to Key	Liitä näppäimeen (n)	Exit	Lopeta (l)
Assign to Menu	Liitä valikkoon (v)		
		Edit menu	Muokkaa (m)
Window menu	Ikkuna (i)	Copy...	Kopioi... (o)
New Window	Uusi ikkuna (u)	Annotate...	Huomautus... (h)
Cascade	Limittäin (l)		
Tile	Vierekkäin (v)	Bookmark menu	Kirjanmerkki (k)
Next Window	Seuraava ikkuna (s)	Define	Määritä... (m)
Arrange All	Järjestä kaikki (j)		
Hide	Piilota (p)	Help menu	Ohje (o)
Unhide...	Tuo esiin... (e)	How to use Help	Ohjeen käyttö (k)
Split	Jaa (a)	Always on Top	Aina päällimmäisenä (a)
Freeze Panes	Kiinnitä ruudut (r)	About Help...	Tietoja... (t)
Remove Split	Poista jako (a)		
Unfreeze Panes	Vapauta ruudut (r)	**Buttons**	
Zoom...	Zoomaa... (z)	Contents	Sisällys (s)
		Search	Etsi (e)
Help menu	Ohje (o)	Back	Takaisin (a)
Contents	Sisällys (s)	History	Luetut (l)
How to use Help	Ohjeen käyttö (k)	Glossary	Sanasto (n)
Search for Help on	Etsi ohje aiheesta (e)		
Active Window	Aktiivinen ikkuna (a)	**DIALOG BOXES**	
Keyboard	Näppäimistö (n)	dialog box	valintaikkuna
Mouse	Hiiri (h)	wildcard	yleismerkki
Tutorial	Opetusohjelma (o)		
About	Tietoja (t)	**Dialog box elements**	
		button	painike, nappi
Device menu	Laite (l)	check box	valintaruutu
Scale menu	Skaala (s)	chevrons	kulmasulkeet
MIDI Sequencer...	MIDI-sekvensseri...	combo box	yhdistelmäruutu
Sound...	Ääni... (ä)	command button	komentopainike
Time	Aika (a)	dialog box title	valintaikkunan nimi
Tracks	Raidat (r)	drop-down combo box	avattava yhdistelmäruutu
		drop-down list box	avattava luetteloruutu
Effects menu	Säädöt (ä)	Goto/Gosub button	valintaikkunan avaava painike
Revert...	Muunna takaisin... (m)	group box	ryhmän kehys
Insert File...	Lisää tiedosto... (l)	label	nimi, otsikko
Mix with File...	Miksaa toiseen tiedostoon... (s)		
Delete Before Current Position	Poista ennen nykyistä kohtaa (e)		

ENGLISH	FINNISH	ENGLISH	FINNISH
linked text and list box	yhdistetty muokkaus- ja luetteloruutu	Match Case	Kirjainkoko (o)
		Match Whole Word Only	Koko sana (k)
list box	luetteloruutu	Orientation	Suunta
option button	valintanappi	Pages	Sivuja (s)
progress indicator	tilanneilmaisin	Paper Size	Koko (k)
push button	komentopainike	Portrait	Pysty (p)
radio button	valintanappi	Printer	Kirjoitin
slider	liukusäädin	Print Quality	Tulostustarkkuus (t)
slider indicator	liukuruutu	Print Range	Tulostusalue
spin box	askellusruutu	Print to File	Tulosta tiedostoon (i)
text box	muokkausruutu	Read Only	Vain luku (v)
value set	valintajoukko	Replace All	Korvaa kaikki
		Replace With	Korvaava (r)
Dialog box buttons		Sample	Malli
Add	Lisää	Save File as Type	Tallenna tiedosto muodossa (m)
Apply	Käytä		
Cancel	Peruuta	Scaling	Skaalaus (s)
Change	Muuta	Selection	Valinta (v)
Create	Luo	Size (font size)	Koko (k)
Default	Oletukset	Source (paper)	Lähde (h)
Define	Määritä	To	Mihin (h)
Done	Valmis	Up	Ylös (y)
Go To	Siirry		
Help	Ohje		
More	Lisää	**MESSAGE BOXES**	
No	Ei	critical message	ilmoitus vakavasta virheestä
OK	OK	message	sanoma
Options	Asetukset	message box	sanomaruutu
Quit	Lopeta	message line	sanomarivi
Redo	Tee uudelleen	warning message	varoitus
Reset	Palauta		
Resume	Jatka	**OTHER GUI SCREEN ELEMENTS**	
Retry	Yritä uudelleen		
Search	Etsi	**Graphical options**	
Set	Aseta	gallery	galleria
Setup	Aseta	palette	värivalikoima
Switch to	Vaihda	text frame	tekstikehys
Yes	Kyllä	toolbox	työkaluryhmä
Dialog box labels		**Status bar abbreviations**	
All	Kaikki (k)	Caps Lock on (CAPS)	ISOT
Collate copies	Lajittele kopiot (l)	Column (Col)	SAR
Copies	Kopioita (o)	Extend selection on (EXT)	LAAJ
Direction	Suunta	Line (Ln)	RI
Directories	Hakemistot (h)	Macro Recorder on (REC)	NAUH
Down	Alas (a)	Num Lock on (NUM)	NUM
Drives	Asemat (a)	Overtype on (OVR)	KORV
File Name	Tiedostonimi (n)	Page (Pg)	SI
Find Next	Etsi seuraava (e)	Scroll Lock on (SCRL)	VIER
Find What	Etsittävä (e)	Section (Sec)	OSA
Font	Fontti (f)		
Font Style	Tyyli (t)	**Character formats**	
From	Mistä (m)	bold	Lihavoitu (l)
Landscape	Vaaka (v)	double underline	Kaksoisalleviivattu (t)
List Files of Type	Luettele tiedostot tyypeittäin (l)	italic	Kursivoitu (k)

ENGLISH	FINNISH
small capitals	Kapiteelit (i)
underline	Alleviivattu (a)

Paragraph formats

centered	Keskitetty (e)
justified	Molemmat reunat (m)
left aligned	Vasen (v)
right aligned	Oikea (o)

KEYS

Shortcut keys

CTRL+B (Bold)	CTRL+B
CTRL+C (Copy)	CTRL+C
CTRL+D (Double underline)	CTRL+D
CTRL+E (Center)	CTRL+E
CTRL+I (Italics)	CTRL+I
CTRL+J (Justify)	CTRL+J
CTRL+L (Left align)	CTRL+L
CTRL+R (Right align)	CTRL+R
CTRL+U (Underline)	CTRL+U
CTRL+V (Paste)	CTRL+V
CTRL+W (Word underline)	CTRL+W
CTRL+X (Cut)	CTRL+X
CTRL+Z (Undo)	CTRL+Z
DEL (Clear)	DEL

Keynames

(keypad) *	NUM *
(keypad) +	NUM +
(keypad) -	NUM -
(keypad) /	NUM /
ALT	ALT
ALT GR	ALT GR
BACKSPACE	ASKELPALAUTIN
BREAK	BREAK
CAPS LOCK	CAPS LOCK
CTRL	CTRL
DEL	DEL
DOWN ARROW	ALANUOLI
END	END
ENTER	ENTER
ENTER (keypad)	NUM ENTER
ESC	ESC
HOME	HOME
INS	INS
LEFT ARROW	VASEN NUOLI
NUM LOCK	NUM LOCK
PAUSE	PAUSE
PG DN	PAGE DOWN
PG UP	PAGE UP
PRINT SCREEN	PRINT SCREEN
RIGHT ARROW	OIKEA NUOLI
SCROLL LOCK	SCROLL LOCK
SHIFT	VAIHTONÄPPÄIN
SPACEBAR	VÄLINÄPPÄIN

ENGLISH	FINNISH
SYS RQ	SYS RQ
TAB	SARKAIN
UP ARROW	YLÄNUOLI

USER ACTIONS

Keyboard actions

enter	kirjoittaa
press and hold down	painaa ja pitää alhaalla
type	kirjoittaa

Mouse actions

click	napsauttaa
double-click	kaksoisnapsauttaa
drag	vetää
drag-and-drop	vetää ja pudottaa
drop	pudottaa
point	osoittaa

Manipulating window appearance

arrange	järjestää
close	sulkea
freeze	kiinnittää
hide	piilottaa
move	siirtää
resize	muuttaa kokoa
restore	palauttaa
select	valita
size	muuttaa kokoa
split	jakaa
switch	vaihtaa
unfreeze	vapauttaa

Selecting options or content

cancel	peruuttaa
check	valita
choose	valita
clear (undo Select)	poistaa valintamerkki
extend selection	laajentaa valintaa
reduce selection	pienentää valintaa
select	valita
select (check box, option button)	valita (valintaruutu, valintanappi)
select (data)	valita (tietoa, dataa)
select (drop-down menu)	valita (avattavasta valikosta)
select (list box)	valita (luetteloruudusta)

Viewing content

autoscroll	automaattinen vieritys
browse	selata
collapse	tiivistää, kutistaa (hakemistopuun haara)
expand	laajentaa

ENGLISH	FINNISH
scroll	vierittää
view	näyttää
zoom in	pienentää
zoom out	suurentaa

Removing content

clear	tyhjentää, poistaa
copy	kopioida
cut	leikata
delete	poistaa
paste	liittää

Manipulating objects

arrange	järjestää
automatic link	automaattinen linkki
Clipboard	Leikepöytä
container application	säilösovellus
container document	säilöasiakirja
copy	kopioida
crop	rajata
destination application	kohdesovellus
destination document	kohdeasiakirja
drag-and-drop	vetää ja pudottaa
embed	upottaa
embedded object	upotettu objekti
group	ryhmittää
link	linkittää
linked object	linkitetty objekti
main application	pääsovellus
main document	pääasiakirja
manual link	manuaalinen linkki
object	objekti
object linking & embedding (OLE)	objektin linkittäminen ja upottaminen (OLE)
OLE (object linking & embedding)	OLE (Object Linking & Embedding)

ENGLISH	FINNISH
package	pakkaus
paste	liittää
scale	skaalata
OLE application	OLE-sovellus
size	muuttaa kokoa
source application	lähdesovellus
source document	lähdeasiakirja
update	päivittää

APPLICATIONS FOR MICROSOFT WINDOWS

Accessories	Apuohjelmat
Applications	Sovellukset
Calculator	Laskin
Calendar	Kalenteri
Cardfile	Kortisto
Character Map	Merkistö
Clipboard Viewer	Leikepöydän tarkastelu
Clock	Kello
Control Panel	Ohjauspaneeli
File Manager	Tiedostonhallinta
Games	Pelit
Main	Varusohjelmat
Media Player	Mediasoitin
MS-DOS Prompt	MS-DOS-kehote
Notepad	Muistio
Object Packager	Objektin pakkaus
PIF Editor	PIF-editori
Print Manager	Tulostuksenhallinta
Program Manager	Järjestelmänhallinta
Recorder	Nauhuri
Sound Recorder	Ääninauhuri
StartUp	Käynnistys
Terminal	Pääte
Windows Setup	Windows Asennus

Terminology by Alphabet

Notes:
1. All terms formatted in **bold** refer to menu names or command names.
2. All characters between parentheses are preferred access keys.

ENGLISH	FINNISH	ENGLISH	FINNISH
\		Cardfile	Kortisto
(keypad) *	NUM *	**Cascade**	**Limittäin (l)**
(keypad) +	NUM +	cascading menu	alivalikko
(keypad) -	NUM -	cascading windows	limittäiset ikkunat
(keypad) /	NUM /	centered	Keskitetty (e)
About	**Tietoja (t)**	Change	Muuta
About Help...	**Tietoja... (t)**	**Character...**	**Merkki... (m)**
access key	valintanäppäin	Character Map	Merkistö
Accessories	Apuohjelmat	check	valita
active window	aktiivinen ikkuna	check box	valintaruutu
Active Window	**Aktiivinen ikkuna (a)**	checked command	valittu komento
Add	Lisää	check mark	valintamerkki
Add Echo	**Lisää kaiku (l)**	chevrons	kulmasulkeet
Alignment...	**Tasaus... (s)**	choose	valita
All	Kaikki (k)	**Clear**	**Tyhjennä (y)**
ALT	ALT	clear	tyhjentää, poistaa
ALT GR	ALT GR	**Clear All**	**Tyhjennä kaikki (y)**
Always on Top	**Aina päällimmäisenä (a)**	clear (undo Select)	poistaa valintamerkki
Annotate...	**Huomautus... (h)**	click	napsauttaa
application icon	sovelluskuvake	Clipboard	Leikepöytä
Applications	Sovellukset	Clipboard Viewer	Leikepöydän tarkastelu
application window	sovellusikkuna	Clock	Kello
Apply	Käytä	**Close**	**Sulje (s)**
arrange	järjestää	close	sulkea
Arrange All	**Järjestä kaikki (j)**	**Close All**	**Sulje kaikki (s)**
arrow	nuoli	collapse	tiivistää, kutistaa
arrow pointer	nuoliosoitin		(hakemistopuun haara)
Assign to Key	**Liitä näppäimeen (n)**	Collate copies	Lajittele kopiot (l)
Assign to Menu	**Liitä valikkoon (v)**	Column (Col)	SAR
automatic link	automaattinen linkki	combo box	yhdistelmäruutu
autoscroll	automaattinen vieritys	command	komento
Back	Takaisin (a)	command button	komentopainike
BACKSPACE	ASKELPALAUTIN	command separator	komentojen erotinviiva
bold	Lihavoitu (l)	container application	säilösovellus
Bookmark menu	**Kirjanmerkki (k)**	container document	säilöasiakirja
border	reunaviiva	**Contents**	**Sisällys (s)**
bottom window border	ikkunan alareuna	**Control menu**	**ohjausvalikko**
BREAK	BREAK	Control-menu box	ohjausvalikkoruutu
browse	selata	Control Panel	Ohjauspaneeli
button	painike, nappi	Copies	Kopioita (o)
Calculator	Laskin	copy	kopioida
Calendar	Kalenteri	**Copy**	**Kopioi (o)**
Cancel	Peruuta	**Copy...**	**Kopioi... (o)**
cancel	peruuttaa	**Copy Special**	**Kopioi määräten (m)**
CAPS LOCK	CAPS LOCK	Create	Luo
Caps Lock on (CAPS)	ISOT		

ENGLISH	FINNISH	ENGLISH	FINNISH
critical message	ilmoitus vakavasta virheestä	drag-and-drop	vetää ja pudottaa
crop	rajata	drive icon	asemakuvake
cross-hair pointer	ristiosoitin	Drives	Asemat (a)
CTRL	CTRL	drop	pudottaa
CTRL+B (Bold)	CTRL+B	drop-down combo box	avattava yhdistelmäruutu
CTRL+C (Copy)	CTRL+C	drop-down list box	avattava luetteloruutu
CTRL+D (Double underline)	CTRL+D	drop-down menu	avattava valikko
CTRL+E (Center)	CTRL+E	**Edit**	**Muokkaa (m)**
CTRL+I (Italics)	CTRL+I	**Edit menu**	**Muokkaa (m)**
CTRL+J (Justify)	CTRL+J	**Effects menu**	**Säädöt (ä)**
CTRL+L (Left align)	CTRL+L	ellipsis	kolme pistettä
CTRL+R (Right align)	CTRL+R	embed	upottaa
CTRL+U (Underline)	CTRL+U	embedded object	upotettu objekti
CTRL+V (Paste)	CTRL+V	END	END
CTRL+W (Word underline)	CTRL+W	ENTER	ENTER
CTRL+X (Cut)	CTRL+X	enter	kirjoittaa
CTRL+Z (Undo)	CTRL+Z	ENTER (keypad)	NUM ENTER
Customize	**Mukauta (m)**	ESC	ESC
Cut	**Leikkaa (l)**	**Exit**	**Lopeta (l)**
cut	leikata	**Exit and Return to**	**Lopeta ja palaa**
Decrease Speed	**Vähennä nopeutta (o)**		**tiedostoon (l)**
Decrease Volume	**Vähennä äänenvoimakkuutta**	expand	laajentaa
	(v)	extend selection	laajentaa valintaa
Default	Oletukset	Extend selection on (EXT)	LAAJ
Define	Määritä	File Manager	Tiedostonhallinta
Define...	**Määritä... (m)**	**File menu**	**Tiedosto (t)**
DEL	DEL	File Name	Tiedostonimi (n)
DEL (Clear)	DEL	**Find...**	**Etsi... (e)**
delete	poistaa	Find Next	Etsi seuraava (e)
Delete	**Poista (p)**	Find What	Etsittävä (e)
Delete...	**Poista... (p)**	font	fontti
Delete After Current Position	**Poista nykyisen kohdan**	Font	Fontti (f)
	jälkeen (p)	Font Style	Tyyli (t)
Delete Before Current Position	**Poista ennen nykyistä**	**Format menu**	**Muotoile (e)**
	kohtaa (e)	freeze	kiinnittää
desktop	työpöytä	**Freeze Panes**	**Kiinnitä ruudut (r)**
destination application	kohdesovellus	From	Mistä (m)
destination document	kohdeasiakirja	**Full Menus**	**Pitkät valikot (v)**
Device menu	**Laite (l)**	gallery	galleria
dialog box	valintaikkuna	Games	Pelit
dialog box title	valintaikkunan nimi	Glossary	Sanasto (n)
Direction	Suunta	Go To	Siirry
Directories	Hakemistot (h)	**Go To...**	**Siirry... (s)**
directory icon	hakemistokuvake	Goto/Gosub button	valintaikkunan avaava painike
disk icon	levykuvake	group	ryhmittää
Document...	**Asiakirja... (a)**	group box	ryhmän kehys
document file icon	asiakirjatiedostokuvake	group icon	ryhmäkuvake
document icon	asiakirjakuvake	group window	ryhmäikkuna
document window	asiakirjaikkuna	Help	Ohje
Done	Valmis	**Help menu**	**Ohje (o)**
double-click	kaksoisnapsauttaa	Help window	Ohje-ikkuna
double underline	Kaksoisalleviivattu (t)	**Hide**	**Piilota (p)**
Down	Alas (a)	hide	piilottaa
DOWN ARROW	ALANUOLI	History	Luetut (l)
down scroll arrow	alavieritysnuoli	HOME	HOME
drag	vetää	horizontal scroll bar	vaakasuora vierityspalkki

ENGLISH	FINNISH	ENGLISH	FINNISH
horizontal split bar	vaakasuora jakopalkki	**Mouse**	**Hiiri (h)**
hourglass pointer	tiimalasiosoitin	mouse pointer	hiiriosoitin
How to use Help	**Ohjeen käyttö (k)**	**Move**	**Siirrä (r)**
I-beam pointer	I-osoitin	move	siirtää
icon	kuvake	MS-DOS Prompt	MS-DOS-kehote
inactive window	passiivinen ikkuna	**New...**	**Uusi... (u)**
Increase Speed (by 100%)	**Lisää nopeutta (100%) (n)**	**New Window**	**Uusi ikkuna (u)**
Increase Volume (by 25%)	**Lisää äänenvoimakkuutta**	**Next**	**Seuraava (e)**
	(25%) (k)	**Next Window**	**Seuraava ikkuna (s)**
INS	INS	No	Ei
Insert...	**Lisää... (ä)**	Notepad	Muistio
Insert File...	**Lisää tiedosto... (l)**	**Number...**	**Luku... (l)**
insertion point	lisäyskohta	NUM LOCK	NUM LOCK
Insert menu	**Lisää (l)**	Num Lock on (NUM)	NUM
Insert Object...	**Lisää objekti... (b)**	object	objekti
italic	Kursivoitu (k)	**Object...**	**Objekti... (b)**
justified	Molemmat reunat (m)	object linking & embedding	objektin linkittäminen ja
Keyboard	**Näppäimistö (n)**	(OLE)	upottaminen (OLE)
label	nimi, otsikko	Object Packager	Objektin pakkaus
Landscape	Vaaka (v)	OK	OK
left aligned	Vasen (v)	OLE application	OLE-sovellus
LEFT ARROW	VASEN NUOLI	OLE (object linking &	OLE (Object Linking &
left scroll arrow	vasen vieritysnuoli	embedding)	Embedding)
left window border	ikkunan vasen reuna	**Open**	**Avaa (a)**
Line (Ln)	RI	option button	valintanappi
link	linkittää	Options	Asetukset
linked object	linkitetty objekti	**Options menu**	**Asetukset (a)**
linked text and list box	yhdistetty muokkaus- ja	Orientation	Suunta
	luetteloruutu	Overtype on (OVR)	KORV
list box	luetteloruutu	package	pakkaus
List Files of Type	Luettele tiedostot	Page (Pg)	SI
	tyypeittäin (l)	Pages	Sivuja (s)
Macro menu	**Makro (r)**	**Page Setup**	**Sivun asetukset (v)**
Macro Recorder on (REC)	NAUH	palette	värivalikoima
Main	Varusohjelmat	pane	ruutu
main application	pääsovellus	Paper Size	Koko (k)
main document	pääasiakirja	**Paragraph...**	**Kappale... (k)**
manual link	manuaalinen linkki	**Paste**	**Liitä (i)**
Match Case	Kirjainkoko (o)	paste	liittää
Match Whole Word Only	Koko sana (k)	**Paste Link**	**Liitä linkki (i)**
Maximize	**Suurenna (u)**	**Paste Special**	**Liitä määräten (n)**
Maximize button	suurennuspainike	PAUSE	PAUSE
Media Player	Mediasoitin	PG DN	PAGE DOWN
menu	valikko	PG UP	PAGE UP
menu bar	valikkorivi	PIF Editor	PIF-editori
menu command	valikon komento	point	osoittaa
menu name	valikon nimi	pointer	osoitin
message	sanoma	Portrait	Pysty (p)
message box	sanomaruutu	**Preferences**	**Oletukset (o)**
message line	sanomarivi	press and hold down	painaa ja pitää alhaalla
MIDI Sequencer...	**MIDI-sekvensseri...**	**Print**	**Tulosta (o)**
Minimize	**Pienennä (i)**	Printer	Kirjoitin
Minimize button	pienennyspainike	**Printer Setup**	**Kirjoittimen asetukset (k)**
Mix with File...	**Miksaa toiseen**	Print Manager	Tulostuksenhallinta
	tiedostoon... (s)	**Print Preview**	**Esikatsele (e)**
More	Lisää	Print Quality	Tulostustarkkuus (t)

ENGLISH	FINNISH
Print Range	Tulostusalue
PRINT SCREEN	PRINT SCREEN
Print Setup...	**Kirjoittimen**
	asetukset... (k)
Print to File	Tulosta tiedostoon (i)
Print Topic	**Tulosta aihe (t)**
program group	ohjelmaryhmä
program item	ohjelma
program-item icon	ohjelmakuvake
Program Manager	Järjestelmänhallinta
progress indicator	tilanneilmaisin
push button	komentopainike
Quit	Lopeta
radio button	valintanappi
Read Only	Vain luku (v)
Record...	**Nauhoita... (a)**
Recorder	Nauhuri
Redo	Tee uudelleen
reduce selection	pienentää valintaa
Remove Split	**Poista jako (a)**
Repeat	**Toista (t)**
Replace...	**Korvaa... (r)**
Replace All	Korvaa kaikki
Replace With	Korvaava (r)
Reset	Palauta
resize	muuttaa kokoa
Restore	**Palauta (p)**
restore	palauttaa
Restore button	palautuspainike
Resume	Jatka
Retry	Yritä uudelleen
Reverse	**Käännä suunta (s)**
Revert...	**Muunna takaisin... (m)**
right aligned	Oikea (o)
RIGHT ARROW	OIKEA NUOLI
right scroll arrow	oikea vieritysnuoli
right window border	ikkunan oikea reuna
ruler	viivain
Run...	**Suorita...(s)**
Sample	Malli
Save	**Tallenna (t)**
Save All	**Tallenna kaikki (i)**
Save As...	**Tallenna nimellä... (n)**
Save File as Type	Tallenna tiedosto
	muodossa (m)
scale	skaalata
Scale menu	**Skaala (s)**
Scaling	Skaalaus (s)
scroll	vierittää
scroll arrow	vieritysnuoli
scroll bar	vierityspalkki
scroll box	vieritysruutu
SCROLL LOCK	SCROLL LOCK
Scroll Lock on (SCRL)	VIER
Search	**Etsi (e)**
Search	Etsi

ENGLISH	FINNISH
Search...	**Etsi... (e)**
Search for Help on	**Etsi ohje aiheesta (e)**
Section...	**Osa... (o)**
Section (Sec)	OSA
select	valita
select (check box, option button)	valita (valintaruutu, valintanappi)
select (data)	valita (tietoa, dataa)
select (drop-down menu)	valita (avattavasta valikosta)
selected command	valittu komento
Selection	Valinta (v)
selection cursor	valintakohdistin
select (list box)	valita (luetteloruudusta)
Set	Aseta
Setup	Aseta
SHIFT	VAIHTONÄPPÄIN
shortcut key	pikanäppäin
Short Menus	**Lyhyet valikot (v)**
Size	**Muuta kokoa (m)**
size	muuttaa kokoa
Size (font size)	Koko (k)
sizing handle	koonmuuttokahva
slider	liukusäädin
slider indicator	liukuruutu
small capitals	Kapiteelit (i)
Sound...	**Ääni... (ä)**
Sound Recorder	Ääninauhuri
source application	lähdesovellus
source document	lähdeasiakirja
Source (paper)	Lähde (h)
SPACEBAR	VÄLINÄPPÄIN
spin box	askellusruutu
Split	**Jaa (a)**
Split	**Jaa (j)**
split	jakaa
split bar	jakopalkki
split box	jakoruutu
StartUp	Käynnistys
status bar	tilarivi
status-bar indicator	tilarivi-ilmaisin
submenu	alivalikko
switch	vaihtaa
Switch to	Vaihda
Switch To...	**Vaihda... (v)**
SYS RQ	SYS RQ
TAB	SARKAIN
Terminal	Pääte
text box	muokkausruutu
text frame	tekstikehys
Tile	**Vierekkäin (v)**
tiled windows	vierekkäiset ikkunat
Time	**Aika (a)**
title bar	otsikkorivi
To	Mihin (h)
tool	työkalu
toolbar	työkalurivi

ENGLISH	FINNISH	ENGLISH	FINNISH
toolbox	työkaluryhmä	vertical split bar	pystysuora jakopalkki
Tools menu	**Työkalut (y)**	view	näyttää
top window border	ikkunan yläreuna	**View menu**	**Näytä (n)**
Tracks	**Raidat (r)**	wallpaper	taustakuva
Tutorial	**Opetusohjelma (o)**	warning message	varoitus
type	kirjoittaa	wildcard	yleismerkki
unavailable command	komento, joka ei ole	window	ikkuna
	käytettävissä	window background	ikkunan tausta
underline	Alleviivattu (a)	window border	ikkunan reuna
Undo	**Kumoa (k)**	window corner	ikkunan kulma
unfreeze	vapauttaa	window frame	ikkunan kehys
Unfreeze Panes	**Vapauta ruudut (r)**	**Window menu**	**Ikkuna (i)**
Unhide...	**Tuo esiin... (e)**	window size	ikkunan koko
Up	Ylös (y)	Windows Setup	Windows Asennus
UP ARROW	YLÄNUOLI	window title	ikkunan otsikko
up scroll arrow	ylävieritysnuoli	workspace	työtila
Update	**Päivitä (p)**	Yes	Kyllä
update	päivittää	**Zoom...**	**Zoomaa... (z)**
Utilities menu	**Muut (u)**	zoom in	pienentää
value set	valintajoukko	zoom out	suurentaa
vertical scroll bar	pystysuora vierityspalkki		

CHAPTER 12

French

This chapter lists the French translations of all terms formatted in *italic* in Part 1. Terminology is listed in two ways: by category and in alphabetical order. The first section includes translations in the following categories: Window Elements, Menus, Dialog Boxes, Message Boxes, Other GUI Screen Elements, Keys, User Actions, and Applications For Microsoft Windows.

Terminology by Category

ENGLISH	FRENCH	ENGLISH	FRENCH
WINDOW ELEMENTS		window corner	coin de la fenêtre
Main window elements		window frame	filet de bordure
active window	fenêtre active	window size	taille de la fenêtre
application window	fenêtre d'application	window title	titre de la fenêtre
border	bordure	workspace	espace de travail
bottom window border	bordure inférieure de la fenêtre		
cascading windows	fenêtres en cascade	**Window controls**	
desktop	bureau (électronique)	Control-menu box	case du menu Système
document window	fenêtre de document	down scroll arrow	flèche de défilement vers
group window	fenêtre de groupe		le bas
Help window	fenêtre d'aide	horizontal scroll bar	barre de défilement horizontale
inactive window	fenêtre inactive	horizontal split bar	barre de fractionnement
left window border	bordure gauche de la fenêtre		horizontale
menu bar	barre de menus	left scroll arrow	flèche de défilement vers la
pane	volet		gauche
right window border	bordure droite de la fenêtre	Maximize button	bouton Agrandissement
ruler	règle	Minimize button	bouton Réduction
status bar	barre d'état	Restore button	bouton Restauration
tiled windows	fenêtres en mosaïque	right scroll arrow	flèche de défilement vers la
title bar	barre de titre		droite
toolbar	barre d'outils	scroll arrow	flèche de défilement
top window border	bordure supérieure de la fenêtre	scroll bar	barre de défilement
wallpaper	papier peint	scroll box	curseur de défilement
window	fenêtre	split bar	barre de fractionnement
window background	fond de la fenêtre	split box	curseur de fractionnement
window border	bordure de la fenêtre		

ENGLISH	FRENCH	ENGLISH	FRENCH
up scroll arrow	flèche de défilement vers le haut	**Menus and commands**	
		View menu	Affichage (a)
vertical scroll bar	barre de défilement verticale	Insert menu	Insère (i)
vertical split bar	barre de fractionnement verticale		
		Control menu	menu Système
		Restore	Restauration (r)
Pointers		Move	Déplacement (d)
arrow	flèche	Size	Dimension (m)
arrow pointer	pointeur flèche	Minimize	Réduction (i)
cross-hair pointer	pointeur en croix	Maximize	Agrandissement (a)
hourglass pointer	sablier	Next	Suivant (s)
I-beam pointer	pointeur en I	Close	Fermeture (f)
insertion point	point d'insertion	Run...	Exécuter... (x)
mouse pointer	pointeur de la souris	Switch To...	Basculer vers... (b)
pointer	pointeur	Split	Fractionner/Fractionnement (c)
selection cursor	curseur de sélection	File menu	Fichier (f)
		New...	Nouveau... (n)
Icons		Open	Ouvrir (o)
application icon	icône d'application	Close	Fermer (f)
directory icon	icône de répertoire	Close All	Fermer tout (f)
disk icon	icône disque/disquette	Save	Enregistrer (e)
document file icon	icône de fichier de données	Save As...	Enregistrer sous... (r)
document icon	icône de document	Save All	Enregistrer tout (t)
drive icon	icône de lecteur de disques	Delete	Supprimer (s)
group icon	icône de groupe	Page Setup	Mise en page (m)
icon	icône (une)	Print	Imprimer (i)
program-item icon	icône de programme	Print Preview	Aperçu avant impression (a)
		Printer Setup	Configuration de l'imprimante (c)
General terms			
access key	touche d'accès rapide	Exit	Quitter (q)
check mark	coche	Exit and Return to	Quitter et retourner dans (q)
ellipsis	points de suspension	Update	Mise à jour (u)
font	police		
object	objet	Edit menu	Edition (e)
program group	groupe de programmes	Undo	Annuler (a)
program item	programme	Repeat	Répéter (r)
shortcut key	touche de raccourci	Cut	Couper (c)
sizing handle	poignée de redimensionnement	Copy	Copier (p)
status-bar indicator	indicateur de la barre d'état	Copy Special	Copie spéciale (s)
tool	outil	Paste	Coller (o)
unavailable command	commande non disponible	Paste Link	Coller avec liaison (n)
		Paste Special	Collage spécial (l)
		Clear	Effacer (e)
MENUS		Clear All	Effacer tout (t)
Menu elements		Find...	Rechercher... (h)
cascading menu	menu en cascade	Search...	Rechercher... (h)
checked command	commande cochée	Replace...	Remplacer... (e)
command	commande	Go To...	Atteindre... (t)
command separator	séparateur de commande	Delete...	Supprimer... (s)
drop-down menu	menu déroulant	Insert...	Insérer... (i)
menu	menu	Object...	Objet... (b)
menu command	commande	Insert Object...	Insérer un objet... (t)
menu name	nom de menu		
selected command	commande en surbrillance	Options menu	Options (o)
submenu	menu secondaire	Preferences	Préférences (f)

ENGLISH	FRENCH
Full Menus	Menus longs (m)
Short Menus	Menus courts (m)
Format menu	Format (t)
Character...	Caractère... (c)
Paragraph...	Paragraphe... (p)
Section...	Section... (s)
Document...	Document... (d)
Number...	Nombre... (n)
Alignment...	Position... (p)
Utilities menu	Outils (o)
Tools menu	Outils (o)
Customize	Personnaliser (p)
Macro menu	Macro (m)
Record...	Enregistrer... (e)
Run...	Exécuter... (x)
Edit	Modifier (m)
Assign to Key	Affecter à une touche (f)
Assign to Menu	Affecter à un menu (a)
Window menu	Ecran (c)
New Window	Nouvelle fenêtre (n)
Cascade	Cascade (c)
Tile	Mosaïque (m)
Next Window	Fenêtre suivante (s)
Arrange All	Réorganiser (r)
Hide	Masquer (m)
Unhide...	Afficher... (f)
Split	Fractionner (t)
Freeze Panes	Figer les volets (v)
Remove Split	Supprimer Partager (p)
Unfreeze Panes	Libérer les volets (v)
Zoom...	Zoom... (z)
Help menu	?
Contents	Index (i)
How to use Help	Utiliser l'Aide (u)
Search for Help on	Rechercher l'Aide sur (r)
Active Window	Fenêtre active (f)
Keyboard	Clavier (c)
Mouse	Souris (s)
Tutorial	Didacticiel (d)
About	A propos (a)
Device menu	Périphérique (r)
Scale menu	Echelle (E)
MIDI Sequencer...	Séquenceur MIDI...
Sound...	Son... (n)
Time	Temps (T)
Tracks	Plages (P)
Effects menu	Effets (s)
Revert...	Récupérer... (c)
Insert File...	Insérer un fichier... (i)

ENGLISH	FRENCH
Mix with File...	Mixer avec un fichier... (m)
Delete Before Current Position	Effacer avant la position actuelle (a)
Delete After Current Position	Effacer après la position actuelle (r)
Increase Volume (by 25%)	Augmenter le volume (de 25%) (A)
Decrease Volume	Réduire le volume (R)
Increase Speed (by 100%)	Augmenter la vitesse (de 100%) (m)
Decrease Speed	Réduire la vitesse (d)
Add Echo	Ajouter de l'écho (u)
Reverse	Inverser (e)
Help application	
File menu	Fichier (f)
Open	Ouvrir (o)
Print Topic	Imprimer la rubrique (i)
Print Setup...	Configuration de l'imprimante... (c)
Exit	Quitter (q)
Edit menu	Edition (e)
Copy...	Copier... (p)
Annotate...	Annotation... (a)
Bookmark menu	Signet (s)
Define...	Définir... (d)
Help menu	?
How to use Help	Utiliser l'Aide (u)
Always on Top	Toujours visible (t)
About Help...	A propos... (a)
Buttons	
Contents	Index (i)
Search	Rechercher (r)
Back	Précédent (p)
History	Historique (h)
Glossary	Glossaire (g)
DIALOG BOXES	
dialog box	boîte de dialogue
wildcard	caractère générique
Dialog box elements	
button	bouton
check box	case à cocher
chevrons	chevrons
combo box	zone de liste déroulante
command button	bouton de commande
dialog box title	titre de la boîte de dialogue
drop-down combo box	zone de liste déroulante fixe
drop-down list box	zone de liste déroulante modifiable

ENGLISH	FRENCH	ENGLISH	FRENCH
Goto/Gosub button	bouton Aller à	List Files of Type	Liste des fichiers de type (t)
group box	zone de groupe	Match Case	Majuscule/Minuscule (u)
label	nom de volume / étiquette	Match Whole Word Only	Mot entier (m)
linked text and list box	zone de liste déroulante	Orientation	Orientation
list box	zone de liste	Pages	Pages (p)
option button	case d'option	Paper Size	Taille (t)
progress indicator	indicateur d'état	Portrait	Portrait (r)
push button	bouton de commande	Printer	Imprimante (i)
radio button	case d'option	Print Quality	Qualité d'impression (q)
slider	barre de défilement	Print Range	Etendue
slider indicator	curseur de défilement	Print to File	Fichier d'impression (f)
spin box	pointeur Toupie	Read Only	Lecture seule (l)
text box	zone de texte	Replace All	Remplacer tout (t)
value set	jeu de valeurs	Replace With	Remplacer par (m)
		Sample	Exemple
Dialog box buttons		Save File as Type	Enregistrer sous le format (f)
Add	Ajouter	Scaling	Echelle (h)
Apply	Appliquer	Selection	Sélection (e)
Cancel	Annuler	Size (font size)	Taille (t)
Change	Modifier / Remplacer	Source (paper)	Alimentation (a)
Create	Créer	To	A (a)
Default	Par défaut	Up	Haut (h)
Define	Définir		
Done	Terminer	**MESSAGE BOXES**	
Go To	Aller à	critical message	message d'alerte
Help	Aide / Info / ?	message	message d'information
More	Suite	message box	boîte de message
No	Non	message line	ligne de message
OK	OK	warning message	message d'avertissement
Options	Options		
Quit	Quitter	**OTHER GUI SCREEN**	
Redo	Annuler Annuler	**ELEMENTS**	
Reset	Restaurer	**Graphical options**	
Resume	Reprendre	gallery	présentation
Retry	Répéter	palette	palette
Search	Rechercher	text frame	cadre
Set	Paramétrer / Etablir	toolbox	boîte à outils
Setup	Install		
Switch to	Basculer vers	**Status bar abbreviations**	
Yes	Oui	Caps Lock on (CAPS)	MAJ
		Column (Col)	Co
Dialog box labels		Extend selection on (EXT)	EXT
All	Tout (t)	Line (Ln)	Li
Collate copies	Copies triées (s)	Macro Recorder on (REC)	REC
Copies	Copies (c)	Num Lock on (NUM)	NUM
Direction	Direction	Overtype on (OVR)	REF
Directories	Répertoires (r)	Page (Pg)	Pg
Down	Bas (b)	Scroll Lock on (SCRL)	DEF
Drives	Lecteurs (e)	Section (Sec)	Sec
File Name	Nom de fichier (n)		
Find Next	Suivant (s)	**Character formats**	
Find What	Rechercher (h)	bold	gras (a)
Font	Police (p)	double underline	souligné double (d)
Font Style	Style de police (l)	italic	italique (i)
From	De/Du (d)		
Landscape	Paysage (e)		

ENGLISH	FRENCH	ENGLISH	FRENCH
small capitals	petites majuscules (k)	PRINT SCREEN	IMPRESSION ECRAN
underline	souligné (continu) (s)		(IMPR.ECRAN)
		RIGHT ARROW	DROITE
Paragraph formats		SCROLL LOCK	DEFILEMENT (DEFIL)
centered	centré (c)	SHIFT	MAJUSCULE (MAJ)
justified	justifié (j)	SPACEBAR	ESPACE
left aligned	aligné à gauche (g)	SYS RQ	SYST
right aligned	aligné à droite (r)	TAB	TABULATION (TAB)
		UP ARROW	HAUT
KEYS			
Shortcut keys		**USER ACTIONS**	
CTRL+B (Bold)	CTRL+G	**Keyboard actions**	
CTRL+C (Copy)	CTRL+C	enter	entrer
CTRL+D (Double underline)	CTRL+D	press and hold down	maintenir la touche enfoncée
CTRL+E (Center)	CTRL+MAJ+C	type	taper
CTRL+I (Italics)	CTRL+I		
CTRL+J (Justify)	CTRL+J	**Mouse actions**	
CTRL+L (Left align)	CTRL+MAJ+G	click	cliquer sur (à l'écran) /
CTRL+R (Right align)	CTRL+MAJ+D		cliquer le (bouton souris)
CTRL+U (Underline)	CTRL+S	double-click	cliquer deux fois
CTRL+V (Paste)	CTRL+V	drag	faire glisser
CTRL+W (Word underline)	CTRL+U	drag-and-drop	glisser-déplacer
CTRL+X (Cut)	CTRL+X	drop	déplacer
CTRL+Z (Undo)	CTRL+Z	point	amener le pointeur sur
DEL (Clear)	DEL		
		Manipulating window	
Keynames		**appearance**	
(keypad) *	* (pavé num.)	arrange	réorganiser
(keypad) +	+ (pavé num.)	close	fermer
(keypad) -	- (pavé num.)	freeze	figer
(keypad) /	/ (pavé num.)	hide	masquer
ALT	ALT	move	déplacer
ALT GR	ALT GR	resize	redimensionner
BACKSPACE	RETOUR ARRIERE	restore	restauration/rendre à xxx sa
	(RET.ARR)		taille précédente
BREAK	ATTN	select	sélectionner
CAPS LOCK	VERROUILLAGE	size	dimensionner
	MAJUSCULE (VERR.MAJ)	split	fractionner
CTRL	CONTROLE (CTRL)	switch	basculer
DEL	SUPPRESSION (SUPPR)	unfreeze	libérer
DOWN ARROW	BAS		
END	FIN	**Selecting options or content**	
ENTER	ENTREE	cancel	annuler
ENTER (keypad)	ENTREE (pavé num.)	check	cocher
ESC	ECHAPPEMENT (ECHAP)	choose	choisir
HOME	ORIGINE	clear (undo Select)	supprimer la coche (case à
INS	INSERTION (INS)		cocher)
LEFT ARROW	GAUCHE	extend selection	étendre la sélection
NUM LOCK	VERROUILLAGE	reduce selection	réduire la sélection
	NUMERIQUE	select	sélectionner
	(VERR.NUM)	select (check box, option button)	choisir (case à cocher/d'option)
PAUSE	PAUSE	select (data)	sélectionner (des données)
PG DN	PAGE SUIVANTE (PG.SUIV)	select (drop-down menu)	choisir (une commande)
PG UP	PAGE PRECEDENTE	select (list box)	sélectionner (dans une liste)
	(PG.PREC)		

ENGLISH	FRENCH
Viewing content	
autoscroll	sélection par défilement
browse	parcourir
collapse	réduire
expand	développer
scroll	faire défiler
view	afficher
zoom in	(faire un) zoom Avant
zoom out	(faire un) zoom Arrière
Removing content	
clear	effacer
copy	copier
cut	couper
delete	supprimer
paste	coller
Manipulating objects	
arrange	réorganiser
automatic link	liaison automatique
Clipboard	Presse-papiers
container application	application incorporante
container document	document incorporant
copy	copier/copie
crop	découper
destination application	application destinataire
destination document	document destinataire
drag-and-drop	glisser-déplacer
embed	incorporer
embedded object	objet incorporé
group	groupe
link	lier/liaison
linked object	objet lié
main application	application principale
main document	document principal
manual link	liaison manuelle
object	objet
object linking & embedding (OLE)	liaison et incorporation d'objet

ENGLISH	FRENCH
OLE (object linking & embedding)	OLE (object linking & embedding; liaison et incorporation d'objet)
OLE application	application OLE
package	ensemble
paste	coller
scale	échelle/mettre à l'échelle
size	taille/dimensionner
source application	application source
source document	document source
update	mettre à jour

APPLICATIONS FOR MICROSOFT WINDOWS

Accessories	Accessoires
Applications	Applications
Calculator	Calculatrice
Calendar	Agenda
Cardfile	Répertoire
Character Map	Table des caractères
Clipboard Viewer	Presse-papiers
Clock	Horloge
Control Panel	Panneau de configuration
File Manager	Gestionnaire de fichiers
Games	Jeux
Main	Groupe principal
Media Player	Diffuseur de médias
MS-DOS Prompt	Message d'attente de MS-DOS
Notepad	Bloc-notes
Object Packager	Gestionnaire de liaisons
PIF Editor	Pifedit
Print Manager	Gestionnaire d'impression
Program Manager	Gestionnaire de programmes
Recorder	Enregistreur
Sound Recorder	Enregistreur de sons
StartUp	Démarrage
Terminal	Terminal
Windows Setup	Windows Installation

Terminology by Alphabet

Notes:
1.   All terms formatted in **bold** refer to menu names or command names.
2.   All characters between parentheses are preferred access keys.

ENGLISH	FRENCH	ENGLISH	FRENCH
(keypad) *	* (pavé num.)	CAPS LOCK	VERROUILLAGE MAJUSCULE (VERR.MAJ)
(keypad) +	+ (pavé num.)		
(keypad) -	- (pavé num.)	Caps Lock on (CAPS)	MAJ
(keypad) /	/ (pavé num.)	Cardfile	Répertoire
About	**A propos (a)**	**Cascade**	**Cascade (c)**
About Help...	**A propos... (a)**	cascading menu	menu en cascade
access key	touche d'accès rapide	cascading windows	fenêtres en cascade
Accessories	Accessoires	centered	centré (c)
active window	fenêtre active	Change	Modifier / Remplacer
Active Window	**Fenêtre active (f)**	**Character...**	**Caractère... (c)**
Add	Ajouter	Character Map	Table des caractères
Add Echo	**Ajouter de l'écho (u)**	check	cocher
Alignment...	**Position... (p)**	check box	case à cocher
All	Tout (t)	checked command	commande cochée
ALT	ALT	check mark	coche
ALT GR	ALT GR	chevrons	chevrons
Always on Top	**Toujours visible (t)**	choose	choisir
Annotate...	**Annotation... (a)**	**Clear**	**Effacer (e)**
application icon	icône d'application	clear	effacer
Applications	Applications	**Clear All**	**Effacer tout (t)**
application window	fenêtre d'application	clear (undo Select)	supprimer la coche (case à cocher)
Apply	Appliquer		
arrange	réorganiser	click	cliquer sur (à l'écran) / cliquer le (bouton souris)
Arrange All	**Réorganiser (r)**		
arrow	flèche	Clipboard	Presse-papiers
arrow pointer	pointeur flèche	Clipboard Viewer	Presse-papiers
Assign to Key	**Affecter à une touche (f)**	Clock	Horloge
Assign to Menu	**Affecter à un menu (a)**	**Close**	**Fermeture (f)**
automatic link	liaison automatique	Close	Fermer (f)
autoscroll	sélection par défilement	close	fermer
Back	Précédent (p)	**Close All**	**Fermer tout (f)**
BACKSPACE	RETOUR ARRIERE (RET.ARR)	collapse	réduire
		Collate copies	Copies triées (s)
bold	gras (a)	Column (Col)	Co
Bookmark menu	**Signet (s)**	combo box	zone de liste déroulante
border	bordure	command	commande
bottom window border	bordure inférieure de la fenêtre	command button	bouton de commande
BREAK	ATTN	command separator	séparateur de commande
browse	parcourir	container application	application incorporante
button	bouton	container document	document incorporant
Calculator	Calculatrice	**Contents**	**Index (i)**
Calendar	Agenda	Contents	Index (i)
Cancel	Annuler	**Control menu**	**menu Système**
cancel	annuler	Control-menu box	case du menu Système

ENGLISH	FRENCH	ENGLISH	FRENCH
Control Panel	Panneau de configuration	double underline	souligné double (d)
Copies	Copies (c)	Down	Bas (b)
Copy	**Copier (p)**	DOWN ARROW	BAS
copy	copier	down scroll arrow	flèche de défilement vers
copy	copier/copie		le bas
Copy Special	**Copie spéciale (s)**	drag	faire glisser
Create	Créer	drag-and-drop	glisser-déplacer
critical message	message d'alerte	drive icon	icône de lecteur de disques
crop	découper	Drives	Lecteurs (e)
cross-hair pointer	pointeur en croix	drop	déplacer
CTRL	CONTROLE (CTRL)	drop-down combo box	zone de liste déroulante fixe
CTRL+B (Bold)	CTRL+G	drop-down list box	zone de liste déroulante
CTRL+C (Copy)	CTRL+C		modifiable
CTRL+D (Double underline)	CTRL+D	drop-down menu	menu déroulant
CTRL+E (Center)	CTRL+MAJ+C	**Edit**	**Modifier (m)**
CTRL+I (Italics)	CTRL+I	**Edit menu**	**Edition (e)**
CTRL+J (Justify)	CTRL+J	**Effects menu**	**Effets (s)**
CTRL+L (Left align)	CTRL+MAJ+G	ellipsis	points de suspension
CTRL+R (Right align)	CTRL+MAJ+D	embed	incorporer
CTRL+U (Underline)	CTRL+S	embedded object	objet incorporé
CTRL+V (Paste)	CTRL+V	END	FIN
CTRL+W (Word underline)	CTRL+U	ENTER	ENTREE
CTRL+X (Cut)	CTRL+X	enter	entrer
CTRL+Z (Undo)	CTRL+Z	ENTER (keypad)	ENTREE (pavé num.)
Customize	**Personnaliser (p)**	ESC	ECHAPPEMENT (ECHAP)
Cut	**Couper (c)**	**Exit**	**Quitter (q)**
cut	couper	**Exit and Return to**	**Quitter et retourner**
Decrease Speed	**Réduire la vitesse (d)**		**dans (q)**
Decrease Volume	**Réduire le volume (R)**	expand	développer
Default	Par défaut	extend selection	étendre la sélection
Define	Définir	Extend selection on (EXT)	EXT
Define...	**Définir... (d)**	File Manager	Gestionnaire de fichiers
DEL	SUPPRESSION (SUPPR)	**File menu**	**Fichier (f)**
DEL (Clear)	DEL	File Name	Nom de fichier (n)
Delete	**Supprimer (s)**	**Find...**	**Rechercher... (h)**
delete	supprimer	Find Next	Suivant (s)
Delete After Current Position	**Effacer après la position**	Find What	Rechercher (h)
	actuelle (r)	font	police
Delete Before Current Position	**Effacer avant la position**	Font	Police (p)
	actuelle (a)	Font Style	Style de police (l)
desktop	bureau (électronique)	**Format menu**	**Format (t)**
destination application	application destinataire	freeze	figer
destination document	document destinataire	**Freeze Panes**	**Figer les volets (v)**
Device menu	**Périphérique (r)**	From	De/Du (d)
dialog box	boîte de dialogue	**Full Menus**	**Menus longs (m)**
dialog box title	titre de la boîte de dialogue	gallery	présentation
Direction	Direction	Games	Jeux
Directories	Répertoires (r)	Glossary	Glossaire (g)
directory icon	icône de répertoire	Go To	Aller à
disk icon	icône disque/disquette	**Go To...**	**Atteindre... (t)**
Document...	**Document... (d)**	Goto/Gosub button	bouton Aller à
document file icon	icône de fichier de données	group	groupe
document icon	icône de document	group box	zone de groupe
document window	fenêtre de document	group icon	icône de groupe
Done	Terminer	group window	fenêtre de groupe
double-click	cliquer deux fois	Help	Aide / Info / ?

ENGLISH	FRENCH	ENGLISH	FRENCH
Help menu	**?**	message	message d'information
Help window	fenêtre d'aide	message box	boîte de message
Hide	**Masquer (m)**	message line	ligne de message
hide	masquer	**MIDI Sequencer...**	**Séquenceur MIDI...**
History	Historique (h)	**Minimize**	**Réduction (i)**
HOME	ORIGINE	Minimize button	bouton Réduction
horizontal scroll bar	barre de défilement	**Mix with File...**	**Mixer avec un fichier... (m)**
	horizontale	More	Suite
horizontal split bar	barre de fractionnement	**Mouse**	**Souris (s)**
	horizontale	mouse pointer	pointeur de la souris
hourglass pointer	sablier	**Move**	**Déplacement (d)**
How to use Help	**Utiliser l'Aide (u)**	move	déplacer
I-beam pointer	pointeur en I	MS-DOS Prompt	Message d'attente de MS-DOS
icon	icône (une)	**New...**	**Nouveau... (n)**
inactive window	fenêtre inactive	**New Window**	**Nouvelle fenêtre (n)**
Increase Speed (by 100%)	**Augmenter la vitesse**	Next	**Suivant (s)**
	(de 100%) (m)	**Next Window**	**Fenêtre suivante (s)**
Increase Volume (by 25%)	**Augmenter le volume**	No	Non
	(de 25%) (A)	Notepad	Bloc-notes
INS	INSERTION (INS)	**Number...**	**Nombre... (n)**
Insert...	**Insérer... (i)**	NUM LOCK	VERROUILLAGE
Insert File...	**Insérer un fichier... (i)**		NUMERIQUE
insertion point	point d'insertion		(VERR.NUM)
Insert menu	**Insère (i)**	Num Lock on (NUM)	NUM
Insert Object...	**Insérer un objet... (t)**	object	objet
italic	italique (i)	**Object...**	**Objet... (b)**
justified	justifié (j)	object linking & embedding	liaison et incorporation
Keyboard	**Clavier (c)**	(OLE)	d'objet
label	nom de volume / étiquette	Object Packager	Gestionnaire de liaisons
Landscape	Paysage (e)	OK	OK
left aligned	aligné à gauche (g)	OLE application	application OLE
LEFT ARROW	GAUCHE	OLE (object linking &	OLE (object linking &
left scroll arrow	flèche de défilement vers la	embedding)	embedding; liaison et
	gauche		incorporation d'objet)
left window border	bordure gauche de la fenêtre	**Open**	**Ouvrir (o)**
Line (Ln)	Li	option button	case d'option
link	lier/liaison	Options	Options
linked object	objet lié	**Options menu**	**Options (o)**
linked text and list box	zone de liste déroulante	Orientation	Orientation
list box	zone de liste	Overtype on (OVR)	REF
List Files of Type	Liste des fichiers de type (t)	package	ensemble
Macro menu	**Macro (m)**	Page (Pg)	Pg
Macro Recorder on (REC)	REC	Pages	Pages (p)
Main	Groupe principal	**Page Setup**	**Mise en page (m)**
main application	application principale	palette	palette
main document	document principal	pane	volet
manual link	liaison manuelle	Paper Size	Taille (t)
Match Case	Majuscule/Minuscule (u)	**Paragraph...**	**Paragraphe... (p)**
Match Whole Word Only	Mot entier (m)	**Paste**	**Coller (o)**
Maximize	**Agrandissement (a)**	paste	coller
Maximize button	bouton Agrandissement	**Paste Link**	**Coller avec liaison (n)**
Media Player	Diffuseur de médias	**Paste Special**	**Collage spécial (l)**
menu	menu	PAUSE	PAUSE
menu bar	barre de menus	PG DN	PAGE SUIVANTE (PG.SUIV)
menu command	commande	PG UP	PAGE PRECEDENTE
menu name	nom de menu		(PG.PREC)

ENGLISH	FRENCH	ENGLISH	FRENCH
PIF Editor	Pifedit	Sample	Exemple
point	amener le pointeur sur	**Save**	**Enregistrer (e)**
pointer	pointeur	**Save All**	**Enregistrer tout (t)**
Portrait	Portrait (r)	**Save As...**	**Enregistrer sous... (r)**
Preferences	**Préférences (f)**	Save File as Type	Enregistrer sous le format (f)
press and hold down	maintenir la touche enfoncée	scale	échelle/mettre à l'échelle
Print	**Imprimer (i)**	**Scale menu**	**Echelle (E)**
Printer	Imprimante (i)	Scaling	Echelle (h)
Printer Setup	**Configuration de**	scroll	faire défiler
	l'imprimante (c)	scroll arrow	flèche de défilement
Print Manager	Gestionnaire d'impression	scroll bar	barre de défilement
Print Preview	**Aperçu avant**	scroll box	curseur de défilement
	impression (a)	SCROLL LOCK	DEFILEMENT (DEFIL)
Print Quality	Qualité d'impression (q)	Scroll Lock on (SCRL)	DEF
Print Range	Etendue	Search	Rechercher (r)
PRINT SCREEN	IMPRESSION ECRAN	Search	Rechercher
	(IMPR.ECRAN)	**Search...**	**Rechercher... (h)**
Print Setup...	**Configuration de**	**Search for Help on**	**Rechercher l'Aide sur (r)**
	l'imprimante... (c)	**Section...**	**Section... (s)**
Print to File	Fichier d'impression (f)	Section (Sec)	Sec
Print Topic	**Imprimer la rubrique (i)**	select	sélectionner
program group	groupe de programmes	select (check box, option	choisir (case à cocher/
program item	programme	button)	d'option)
program-item icon	icône de programme	select (data)	sélectionner (des données)
Program Manager	Gestionnaire de programmes	select (drop-down menu)	choisir (une commande)
progress indicator	indicateur d'état	selected command	commande en surbrillance
push button	bouton de commande	Selection	Sélection (e)
Quit	Quitter	selection cursor	curseur de sélection
radio button	case d'option	select (list box)	sélectionner (dans une liste)
Read Only	Lecture seule (l)	Set	Paramétrer / Etablir
Record...	**Enregistrer... (e)**	Setup	Install
Recorder	Enregistreur	SHIFT	MAJUSCULE (MAJ)
Redo	Annuler Annuler	shortcut key	touche de raccourci
reduce selection	réduire la sélection	**Short Menus**	**Menus courts (m)**
Remove Split	**Supprimer Partager (p)**	**Size**	**Dimension (m)**
Repeat	**Répéter (r)**	size	dimensionner
Replace...	**Remplacer... (e)**	size	taille/dimensionner
Replace All	Remplacer tout (t)	Size (font size)	Taille (t)
Replace With	Remplacer par (m)	sizing handle	poignée de redimensionnement
Reset	Restaurer	slider	barre de défilement
resize	redimensionner	slider indicator	curseur de défilement
Restore	**Restauration (r)**	small capitals	petites majuscules (k)
restore	restauration/rendre à xxx sa	**Sound...**	**Son... (n)**
	taille précédente	Sound Recorder	Enregistreur de sons
Restore button	bouton Restauration	source application	application source
Resume	Reprendre	Source (paper)	Alimentation (a)
Retry	Répéter	source document	document source
Reverse	**Inverser (e)**	SPACEBAR	ESPACE
Revert...	**Récupérer... (c)**	spin box	pointeur Toupie
right aligned	aligné à droite (r)	**Split**	**Fractionner/**
RIGHT ARROW	DROITE		**Fractionnement (c)**
right scroll arrow	flèche de défilement vers la	**Split**	**Fractionner (t)**
	droite	split	fractionner
right window border	bordure droite de la fenêtre	split bar	barre de fractionnement
ruler	règle	split box	curseur de fractionnement
Run...	**Exécuter... (x)**	StartUp	Démarrage

ENGLISH	FRENCH	ENGLISH	FRENCH
status bar	barre d'état	Up	Haut (h)
status-bar indicator	indicateur de la barre d'état	UP ARROW	HAUT
submenu	menu secondaire	up scroll arrow	flèche de défilement vers le haut
switch	basculer	**Update**	**Mise à jour (u)**
Switch to	Basculer vers	update	mettre à jour
Switch To...	**Basculer vers... (b)**	**Utilities menu**	**Outils (o)**
SYS RQ	SYST	value set	jeu de valeurs
TAB	TABULATION (TAB)	vertical scroll bar	barre de défilement verticale
Terminal	Terminal	vertical split bar	barre de fractionnement
text box	zone de texte		verticale
text frame	cadre	view	afficher
Tile	**Mosaïque (m)**	**View menu**	**Affichage (a)**
tiled windows	fenêtres en mosaïque	wallpaper	papier peint
Time	**Temps (T)**	warning message	message d'avertissement
title bar	barre de titre	wildcard	caractère générique
To	A (a)	window	fenêtre
tool	outil	window background	fond de la fenêtre
toolbar	barre d'outils	window border	bordure de la fenêtre
toolbox	boîte à outils	window corner	coin de la fenêtre
Tools menu	**Outils (o)**	window frame	filet de bordure
top window border	bordure supérieure de la fenêtre	**Window menu**	**Ecran (c)**
Tracks	**Plages (P)**	window size	taille de la fenêtre
Tutorial	**Didacticiel (d)**	window title	titre de la fenêtre
type	taper	Windows Setup	Windows Installation
unavailable command	commande non disponible	workspace	espace de travail
underline	souligné (continu) (s)	Yes	Oui
Undo	**Annuler (a)**	**Zoom...**	**Zoom... (z)**
unfreeze	libérer	zoom in	(faire un) zoom Avant
Unfreeze Panes	**Libérer les volets (v)**	zoom out	(faire un) zoom Arrière
Unhide...	**Afficher... (f)**		

CHAPTER 13

German

This chapter lists the German translations of all terms formatted in *italic* in Part 1. Terminology is listed in two ways: by category and in alphabetical order. The first section includes translations in the following categories: Window Elements, Menus, Dialog Boxes, Message Boxes, Other GUI Screen Elements, Keys, User Actions, and Applications For Microsoft Windows.

Terminology by Category

ENGLISH	GERMAN	ENGLISH	GERMAN
WINDOW ELEMENTS		window corner	Fensterecke
Main window elements		window frame	Fensterrahmen
active window	Aktives Fenster	window size	Fenstergröße
application window	Anwendungsfenster	window title	Fenstertitel
border	Rand, Rahmen	workspace	Arbeitsbereich
bottom window border	Unterer Fensterrand		
cascading windows	Überlappende Fenster	**Window controls**	
desktop	Desktop	Control-menu box	Systemmenüfeld
document window	Dokumentfenster	down scroll arrow	Bildlaufpfeil abwärts
group window	Gruppenfenster	horizontal scroll bar	Horizontale Bildlaufleiste
Help window	Hilfefenster	horizontal split bar	Horizontaler Fensterteiler
inactive window	Inaktives Fenster	left scroll arrow	Bildlaufpfeil links
left window border	Linker Fensterrand	Maximize button	Schaltfläche für Maximieren
menu bar	Menüleiste	Minimize button	Schaltfläche für Minimieren
pane	Ausschnitt	Restore button	Schaltfläche für Wiederherstellen
right window border	Rechter Fensterrand		
ruler	Lineal; Absatzlineal	right scroll arrow	Bildlaufpfeil rechts
status bar	Statusleiste	scroll arrow	Bildlaufpfeil
tiled windows	Nebeneinander angeordnete Fenster	scroll bar	Bildlaufleiste
		scroll box	Bildlauffeld
title bar	Titelleiste	split bar	Fensterteiler
toolbar	Symbolleiste	split box	Teilungsfeld
top window border	Oberer Fensterrand	up scroll arrow	Bildlaufpfeil aufwärts
wallpaper	Hintergrundbild	vertical scroll bar	Vertikale Bildlaufleiste
window	Fenster	vertical split bar	Vertikaler Fensterteiler
window background	Fensterhintergrund		
window border	Fensterrand		

ENGLISH	GERMAN
Pointers	
arrow	Pfeil
arrow pointer	Vierfachpfeil
cross-hair pointer	Fadenkreuz
hourglass pointer	Sanduhr
I-beam pointer	I-förmiger Mauszeiger
insertion point	Einfügemarke
mouse pointer	Mauszeiger
pointer	Zeiger
selection cursor	Auswahl-Cursor
Icons	
application icon	Anwendungssymbol
directory icon	Verzeichnissymbol
disk icon	Datenträgersymbol
document file icon	Dateisymbol
document icon	Dokumentsymbol
drive icon	Laufwerksymbol
group icon	Gruppensymbol
icon	Symbol
program-item icon	Anwendungssymbol
General terms	
access key	Zugriffstaste
check mark	Häkchen
ellipsis	Auslassungspunkte
font	Schriftart
object	Objekt
program group	Programmgruppe
program item	Programm
shortcut key	Tastaturbefehl
sizing handle	Ziehpunkt
status-bar indicator	Statusanzeige
tool	Symbol
unavailable command	Nicht verfügbarer Befehl
MENUS	
Menu elements	
cascading menu	Überlappende Menüs
checked command	Aktivierter/gewählter Befehl
command	Befehl
command separator	Befehlstrennlinie
drop-down menu	Dropdown-Menü
menu	Menü
menu command	Menübefehl
menu name	Menüname
selected command	Hervorgehobener Befehl
submenu	Untermenü
Menus and commands	
View menu	Ansicht (A)
Insert menu	Einfügen (E)
Control menu	Systemmenü
Restore	Wiederherstellen (W)

ENGLISH	GERMAN
Move	Verschieben (V)
Size	Größe ändern (G)
Minimize	Symbol (S)
Maximize	Vollbild (B)
Next	Nächstes (N)
Close	Schließen (L)
Run...	Ausführen...(A)
Switch To...	Wechseln zu... (Z)
Split	Teilen (T)
File menu	Datei (D)
New...	Neu... (N)
Open	Öffnen (F)
Close	Schließen (S)
Close All	Alles schließen (A)
Save	Speichern (P)
Save As...	Speichern unter... (U)
Save All	Alles speichern (A)
Delete	Löschen (L)
Page Setup	Seite einrichten (E)
Print	Drucken (D)
Print Preview	Seitenansicht (T)
Printer Setup	Druckereinrichtung (E)
Exit	Beenden (B)
Exit and Return to	Beenden & Zurück zu (B)
Update	Aktualisieren (A)
Edit menu	Bearbeiten (B)
Undo	Rückgängig (R)
Repeat	Wiederholen (W)
Cut	Ausschneiden (A)
Copy	Kopieren (K)
Copy Special	Inhalte kopieren (I)
Paste	Einfügen (I)
Paste Link	Verknüpfung einfügen (V)
Paste Special	Inhalte einfügen (I)
Clear	Löschen (L)
Clear All	Alles Löschen (A)
Find...	Suchen... (S)
Search...	Suchen... (S)
Replace...	Ersetzen... (E)
Go To...	Gehe zu... (G)
Delete...	Löschen... (L)
Insert...	Einfügen... (I)
Object...	Objekt... (O)
Insert Object...	Objekt einfügen... (O)
Options menu	Optionen (O)
Preferences	Bildschirmeinstellungen (B)
Full Menus	Ganze Menüs (M)
Short Menus	Kurze Menüs (M)
Format menu	Format (T)
Character...	Zeichen... (Z)
Paragraph...	Absatz... (A)

ENGLISH	GERMAN
Section...	Abschnitt...(I)
Document...	Dokument... (K)
Number...	Zahlenformat... (Z)
Alignment...	Ausrichtung... (A)
Utilities menu	Extras (X)
Tools menu	Extras (X)
Customize	Einstellungen (E)
Macro menu	Makro (M)
Record...	Aufzeichnen... (A)
Run...	Ausführen... (U)
Edit	Bearbeiten (B)
Assign to Key	Tastenzuordnung (T)
Assign to Menu	Menüzuordnung (M)
Window menu	Fenster (F)
New Window	Neues Fenster (N)
Cascade	Überlappend (L)
Tile	Nebeneinander (N)
Next Window	Nächstes Fenster (N)
Arrange All	Alles anordnen (A)
Hide	Ausblenden (A)
Unhide...	Einblenden... (E)
Split	Teilen (R)
Freeze Panes	Fenster fixieren (F)
Remove Split	Teilung aufheben (T)
Unfreeze Panes	Fensterfixierung aufheben (F)
Zoom...	Zoom... (Z)
Help menu	?
Contents	Inhalt (I)
How to use Help	Hilfe benutzen (H)
Search for Help on	Suchen (S)
Active Window	Aktives Fenster
Keyboard	Tastatur (T)
Mouse	Maus (M)
Tutorial	Lernprogramm (P)
About	Info (O)
Device menu	Gerät (g)
Scale menu	Skala (s)
MIDI Sequencer...	MIDI-Sequenzer...
Sound...	Klang... (k)
Time	Zeit (z)
Tracks	Titel (t)
Effects menu	Effekte (e)
Revert...	Wiederherstellen... (w)
Insert File...	Datei einfügen... (d)
Mix with File...	Datei einmischen... (a)
Delete Before Current Position	Löschen vor aktueller Position (n)
Delete After Current Position	Löschen nach aktueller Position (v)

ENGLISH	GERMAN
Increase Volume (by 25%)	Lautstärke erhöhen (um 25%) (e)
Decrease Volume	Lautstärke verringern (v)
Increase Speed (by 100%)	Geschwindigkeit erhöhen (um 100%) (h)
Decrease Speed	Geschwindigkeit verringern (r)
Add Echo	Echo hinzufügen (c)
Reverse	Umkehren (u)
Help application	
File menu	Datei (D)
Open	Öffnen (F)
Print Topic	Thema drucken (D)
Print Setup...	Druckereinrichtung... (E)
Exit	Beenden (B)
Edit menu	Bearbeiten (B)
Copy...	Kopieren... (K)
Annotate...	Anmerken... (A)
Bookmark menu	Lesezeichen
Define...	Definieren... (D)
Help menu	?
How to use Help	Hilfe benutzen (H)
Always on Top	Immer im Vordergrund (V)
About Help...	Info... (I)
Buttons	
Contents	Inhalt (I)
Search	Suchen (S)
Back	Zurück (Z)
History	Bisher (R)
Glossary	Glossar (G)
DIALOG BOXES	
dialog box	Dialogfeld
wildcard	Stellvertreterzeichen
Dialog box elements	
button	Schaltfläche
check box	Kontrollkästchen
chevrons	Steuerzeichen
combo box	Kombinationsfeld
command button	Befehlsschaltfläche
dialog box title	Dialogfeldtitel
drop-down combo box	Dropdown-Kombinationsfeld
drop-down list box	Dropdown-Listenfeld
Goto/Gosub button	Schaltfläche "Gehe zu"
group box	Gruppenfeld
label	Beschriftung, Etikett, Marke
linked text and list box	Verknüpftes Textfeld/ Listenfeld
list box	Listenfeld

ENGLISH	GERMAN
option button	(Rundes) Optionsfeld
progress indicator	Statusanzeiger
push button	Schaltfläche
radio button	Rundes Optionsfeld
slider	Bildlauffeld
slider indicator	Bildlaufanzeige
spin box	Drehfeld
text box	Textfeld
value set	Festgelegter Wert

Dialog box buttons

Add	Hinzufügen
Apply	Anwenden
Cancel	Abbrechen
Change	Ändern
Create	Erstellen
Default	Standard
Define	Definieren
Done	Fertig
Go To	Gehe zu
Help	Hilfe
More	Weitere Optionen
No	Nein
OK	OK
Options	Optionen
Quit	Beenden
Redo	Wiederherstellen, Wiederholen
Reset	Zurücksetzen
Resume	Fortsetzen
Retry	Wiederholen
Search	Suchen
Set	Festlegen
Setup	Einrichten, Setup
Switch to	Wechseln zu
Yes	Ja

Dialog box labels

All	Alles (A)
Collate copies	Kopien sortieren (t)
Copies	Kopien (K)
Direction	Suchrichtung
Directories	Verzeichnisse (V)
Down	Abwärts (b)
Drives	Laufwerke (L)
File Name	Dateiname (n)
Find Next	Weitersuchen (W)
Find What	Suchen nach (n)
Font	Schriftart (a)
Font Style	Schriftstil (S)
From	Von (V)
Landscape	Querformat (Q)
List Files of Type	Dateiformat (f)
Match Case	Groß-/Kleinschreibung (G)
Match Whole Word Only	Als Wort (A)
Orientation	Format

ENGLISH	GERMAN
Pages	Seiten (S)
Paper Size	Papiergröße (P)
Portrait	Hochformat (f)
Printer	Drucker
Print Quality	Druckqualität (u)
Print Range	Druckbereich
Print to File	Druckausgabe in Datei umleiten (r)
Read Only	Schreibgeschützt (S)
Replace All	Alles ersetzen (s)
Replace With	Ersetzen durch (d)
Sample	Muster
Save File as Type	Dateiformat (f)
Scaling	Skalierung (r)
Selection	Markierung (M)
Size (font size)	Schriftgröße (g)
Source (paper)	Zufuhr (Z)
To	Bis (B)
Up	Aufwärts (u)

MESSAGE BOXES

critical message	Wichtige Meldung, Systemfehlermeldung
message	Information, Meldung
message box	Meldungsfeld
message line	Meldungszeile
warning message	Warnmeldung

OTHER GUI SCREEN ELEMENTS

Graphical options

gallery	Muster
palette	Palette
text frame	Textrahmen
toolbox	Toolbox

Status bar abbreviations

Caps Lock on (CAPS)	UF
Column (Col)	Sp
Extend selection on (EXT)	ER
Line (Ln)	Ze
Macro Recorder on (REC)	MA
Num Lock on (NUM)	NF
Overtype on (OVR)	ÜB
Page (Pg)	S
Scroll Lock on (SCRL)	RF
Section (Sec)	Ab

Character formats

bold	Fett (F)
double underline	Doppelt unterstrichen (D)
italic	Kursiv (K)
small capitals	Kapitälchen
underline	Unterstrichen (U)

ENGLISH	GERMAN
Paragraph formats	
centered	Zentriert (Z)
justified	Blocksatz (B)
left aligned	Linksbündig (L)
right aligned	Rechtsbündig (R)
KEYS	
Shortcut keys	
CTRL+B (Bold)	Strg+F
CTRL+C (Copy)	Strg+C
CTRL+D (Double underline)	Strg+D
CTRL+E (Center)	Strg+E
CTRL+I (Italics)	Strg+K
CTRL+J (Justify)	Strg+B
CTRL+L (Left align)	Strg+L
CTRL+R (Right align)	Strg+R
CTRL+U (Underline)	Strg+U
CTRL+V (Paste)	Strg+V
CTRL+W (Word underline)	Strg+W
CTRL+X (Cut)	Strg+X
CTRL+Z (Undo)	Strg+Z
DEL (Clear)	ENTF
Keynames	
(keypad) *	* (Zehnertastatur)
(keypad) +	+ (Zehnertastatur)
(keypad) -	- (Zehnertastatur)
(keypad) /	/ (Zehnertastatur)
ALT	ALT
ALT GR	ALT GR
BACKSPACE	RÜCKTASTE (BKSP)
BREAK	UNTBR
CAPS LOCK	FESTSTELLTASTE
CTRL	STRG
DEL	ENTF
DOWN ARROW	NACH-UNTEN-TASTE
END	ENDE
ENTER	EINGABETASTE
ENTER (keypad)	EINGABETASTE (Zehnertastatur)
ESC	ESC
HOME	POS1
INS	EINFG
LEFT ARROW	NACH-LINKS-TASTE
NUM LOCK	NUM
PAUSE	PAUSE
PG DN	BILD-AB-TASTE
PG UP	BILD-AUF-TASTE
PRINT SCREEN	DRUCK
RIGHT ARROW	NACH-RECHTS-TASTE
SCROLL LOCK	ROLLEN
SHIFT	UMSCHALTTASTE
SPACEBAR	LEERTASTE
SYS RQ	S-ABF

ENGLISH	GERMAN
TAB	TAB
UP ARROW	NACH-OBEN-TASTE
USER ACTIONS	
Keyboard actions	
enter	EINGABETASTE drücken
press and hold down	Gedrückt halten
type	Eingeben
Mouse actions	
click	Klicken
double-click	Doppelklicken
drag	Ziehen
drag-and-drop	Ziehen und Ablegen
drop	Ablegen
point	Zeigen auf
Manipulating window appearance	
arrange	Anordnen
close	Schließen
freeze	Fixieren
hide	Ausblenden, Verbergen
move	Verschieben
resize	Größe ändern
restore	Wiederherstellen
select	Markieren, Auswählen
size	Größe (ändern)
split	Teilen
switch	Wechseln, Umschalten
unfreeze	Fixierung aufheben
Selecting options or content	
cancel	Abbrechen
check	Auswählen, Aktivieren
choose	Wählen, Auswählen
clear (undo Select)	Ausschalten, Deaktivieren
extend selection	Markierung erweitern
reduce selection	Markierung verkleinern
select	Markieren, Auswählen, Wählen
select (check box, option button)	Aktivieren (check box), Auswählen (Option button)
select (data)	Markieren
select (drop-down menu)	Wählen
select (list box)	Auswählen
Viewing content	
autoscroll	Automatisches Rollen
browse	Blättern
collapse	Ausblenden
expand	Erweitern

ENGLISH	GERMAN
scroll	Bildlauf durchführen
view	Anzeigen, Einsehen
zoom in	Vergrößern
zoom out	Verkleinern

Removing content

clear	Löschen
copy	Kopieren
cut	Ausschneiden
delete	Löschen
paste	Einfügen

Manipulating objects

arrange	Anordnen
automatic link	Automatische Verknüpfung
Clipboard	Zwischenablage
container application	Container-Anwendung
container document	Container-Dokument
copy	Kopieren
crop	Zuschneiden, Rahmenänderung
destination application	Zielanwendung
destination document	Zieldokument
drag-and-drop	Ziehen und Ablegen
embed	Einbetten
embedded object	Eingebettetes Objekt
group	Gruppieren
link	Verknüpfen
linked object	Verknüpftes Objekt
main application	Hauptanwendung
main document	Hauptdokument
manual link	Manuelle Verknüpfung
object	Objekt
object linking & embedding (OLE)	Objekte verknüpfen und einbetten (OLE)
OLE (object linking & embedding)	Objekte verknüpfen und einbetten (OLE)

ENGLISH	GERMAN
OLE application	OLE-Anwendung
package	Paket
paste	Einfügen
scale	Skalieren, Größe ändern
size	Vergrößern/Verkleinern
source application	Quellanwendung
source document	Quelldokument
update	Aktualisieren

APPLICATIONS FOR MICROSOFT WINDOWS

Accessories	Zubehör
Applications	Anwendungen
Calculator	Rechner
Calendar	Kalender
Cardfile	Kartei
Character Map	Zeichentabelle
Clipboard Viewer	Zwischenablage
Clock	Uhr
Control Panel	Systemsteuerung
File Manager	Datei-Manager
Games	Spiele
Main	Hauptgruppe
Media Player	Medien-Wiedergabe
MS-DOS Prompt	MS-DOS-Eingabeaufforderung
Notepad	Notizblock
Object Packager	Objekt-Manager
PIF Editor	PIF-Editor
Print Manager	Druck-Manager
Program Manager	Programm-Manager
Recorder	Rekorder
Sound Recorder	Klangrecorder
StartUp	Autostart
Terminal	Terminal
Windows Setup	Windows-Setup

Terminology by Alphabet

Notes:

1. All terms formatted in **bold** refer to menu names or command names.
2. All characters between parentheses are preferred access keys.

ENGLISH	GERMAN	ENGLISH	GERMAN
(keypad) *	* (Zehnertastatur)	Cardfile	Kartei
(keypad) +	+ (Zehnertastatur)	**Cascade**	**Überlappend (L)**
(keypad) -	- (Zehnertastatur)	cascading menu	Überlappende Menüs
(keypad) /	/ (Zehnertastatur)	cascading windows	Überlappende Fenster
About	**Info (O)**	centered	Zentriert (Z)
About Help...	**Info... (I)**	Change	Ändern
access key	Zugriffstaste	**Character...**	**Zeichen... (Z)**
Accessories	Zubehör	Character Map	Zeichentabelle
active window	Aktives Fenster	check	Auswählen, Aktivieren
Active Window	**Aktives Fenster**	check box	Kontrollkästchen
Add	Hinzufügen	checked command	Aktivierter/gewählter Befehl
Add Echo	**Echo hinzufügen (c)**	check mark	Häkchen
Alignment...	**Ausrichtung... (A)**	chevrons	Steuerzeichen
All	Alles (A)	choose	Wählen, Auswählen
ALT	ALT	**Clear**	**Löschen (L)**
ALT GR	ALT GR	clear	Löschen
Always on Top	**Immer im Vordergrund (V)**	**Clear All**	**Alles Löschen (A)**
Annotate...	**Anmerken... (A)**	clear (undo Select)	Ausschalten, Deaktivieren
application icon	Anwendungssymbol	click	Klicken
Applications	Anwendungen	Clipboard	Zwischenablage
application window	Anwendungsfenster	Clipboard Viewer	Zwischenablage
Apply	Anwenden	Clock	Uhr
arrange	Anordnen	**Close**	**Schließen (L)**
Arrange All	**Alles anordnen (A)**	Close	Schließen (S)
arrow	Pfeil	close	Schließen
arrow pointer	Vierfachpfeil	**Close All**	**Alles schließen (A)**
Assign to Key	**Tastenzuordnung (T)**	collapse	Ausblenden
Assign to Menu	**Menüzuordnung (M)**	Collate copies	Kopien sortieren (t)
automatic link	Automatische Verknüpfung	Column (Col)	Sp
autoscroll	Automatisches Rollen	combo box	Kombinationsfeld
Back	Zurück (Z)	command	Befehl
BACKSPACE	RÜCKTASTE (BKSP)	command button	Befehlsschaltfläche
bold	Fett (F)	command separator	Befehlstrennlinie
Bookmark menu	**Lesezeichen**	container application	Container-Anwendung
border	Rand, Rahmen	container document	Container-Dokument
bottom window border	Unterer Fensterrand	**Contents**	**Inhalt (I)**
BREAK	UNTBR	Contents	Inhalt (I)
browse	Blättern	**Control menu**	**Systemmenü**
button	Schaltfläche	Control-menu box	Systemmenüfeld
Calculator	Rechner	Control Panel	Systemsteuerung
Calendar	Kalender	Copies	Kopien (K)
Cancel	Abbrechen	**Copy**	**Kopieren (K)**
cancel	Abbrechen	**Copy...**	**Kopieren... (K)**
CAPS LOCK	FESTSTELLTASTE	copy	Kopieren
Caps Lock on (CAPS)	UF	**Copy Special**	**Inhalte kopieren (I)**

ENGLISH	GERMAN	ENGLISH	GERMAN
Create	Erstellen	down scroll arrow	Bildlaufpfeil abwärts
critical message	Wichtige Meldung,	drag	Ziehen
	Systemfehlermeldung	drag-and-drop	Ziehen und Ablegen
crop	Zuschneiden, Rahmenänderung	drive icon	Laufwerksymbol
cross-hair pointer	Fadenkreuz	Drives	Laufwerke (L)
CTRL	STRG	drop	Ablegen
CTRL+B (Bold)	Strg+F	drop-down combo box	Dropdown-Kombinationsfeld
CTRL+C (Copy)	Strg+C	drop-down list box	Dropdown-Listenfeld
CTRL+D (Double underline)	Strg+D	drop-down menu	Dropdown-Menü
CTRL+E (Center)	Strg+E	**Edit**	**Bearbeiten (B)**
CTRL+I (Italics)	Strg+K	**Edit menu**	**Bearbeiten (B)**
CTRL+J (Justify)	Strg+B	**Effects menu**	**Effekte (e)**
CTRL+L (Left align)	Strg+L	ellipsis	Auslassungspunkte
CTRL+R (Right align)	Strg+R	embed	Einbetten
CTRL+U (Underline)	Strg+U	embedded object	Eingebettetes Objekt
CTRL+V (Paste)	Strg+V	END	ENDE
CTRL+W (Word underline)	Strg+W	ENTER	EINGABETASTE
CTRL+X (Cut)	Strg+X	enter	EINGABETASTE drücken
CTRL+Z (Undo)	Strg+Z	ENTER (keypad)	EINGABETASTE
Customize	**Einstellungen (E)**		(Zehnertastatur)
Cut	**Ausschneiden (A)**	ESC	ESC
cut	Ausschneiden	**Exit**	**Beenden (B)**
Decrease Speed	**Geschwindigkeit**	**Exit and Return to**	**Beenden & Zurück zu (B)**
	verringern (r)	expand	Erweitern
Decrease Volume	**Lautstärke verringern (v)**	extend selection	Markierung erweitern
Default	Standard	Extend selection on (EXT)	ER
Define	Definieren	File Manager	Datei-Manager
Define...	**Definieren... (D)**	**File menu**	**Datei (D)**
DEL	ENTF	File Name	Dateiname (n)
DEL (Clear)	ENTF	**Find...**	**Suchen... (S)**
Delete	**Löschen (L)**	Find Next	Weitersuchen (W)
Delete...	**Löschen... (L)**	Find What	Suchen nach (n)
delete	Löschen	font	Schriftart
Delete After Current Position	**Löschen nach aktueller**	Font	Schriftart (a)
	Position (v)	Font Style	Schriftstil (S)
Delete Before Current Position	**Löschen vor aktueller**	**Format menu**	**Format (T)**
	Position (n)	freeze	Fixieren
desktop	Desktop	**Freeze Panes**	**Fenster fixieren (F)**
destination application	Zielanwendung	From	Von (V)
destination document	Zieldokument	**Full Menus**	**Ganze Menüs (M)**
Device menu	**Gerät (g)**	gallery	Muster
dialog box	Dialogfeld	Games	Spiele
dialog box title	Dialogfeldtitel	Glossary	Glossar (G)
Direction	Suchrichtung	Go To	Gehe zu
Directories	Verzeichnisse (V)	**Go To...**	**Gehe zu... (G)**
directory icon	Verzeichnissymbol	Goto/Gosub button	Schaltfläche "Gehe zu"
disk icon	Datenträgersymbol	group	Gruppieren
Document...	**Dokument... (K)**	group box	Gruppenfeld
document file icon	Dateisymbol	group icon	Gruppensymbol
document icon	Dokumentsymbol	group window	Gruppenfenster
document window	Dokumentfenster	Help	Hilfe
Done	Fertig	**Help menu**	**?**
double-click	Doppelklicken	Help window	Hilfefenster
double underline	Doppelt unterstrichen (D)	**Hide**	**Ausblenden (A)**
Down	Abwärts (b)	hide	Ausblenden, Verbergen
DOWN ARROW	NACH-UNTEN-TASTE	History	Bisher (R)

ENGLISH	GERMAN
HOME	POS1
horizontal scroll bar	Horizontale Bildlaufleiste
horizontal split bar	Horizontaler Fensterteiler
hourglass pointer	Sanduhr
How to use Help	**Hilfe benutzen (H)**
I-beam pointer	I-förmiger Mauszeiger
icon	Symbol
inactive window	Inaktives Fenster
Increase Speed (by 100%)	**Geschwindigkeit erhöhen (um 100%) (h)**
Increase Volume (by 25%)	**Lautstärke erhöhen (um 25%) (e)**
INS	EINFG
Insert...	**Einfügen... (I)**
insertion point	Einfügemarke
Insert File...	**Datei einfügen... (d)**
Insert menu	**Einfügen (E)**
Insert Object...	**Objekt einfügen... (O)**
italic	Kursiv (K)
justified	Blocksatz (B)
Keyboard	**Tastatur (T)**
label	Beschriftung, Etikett, Marke
Landscape	Querformat (Q)
left aligned	Linksbündig (L)
LEFT ARROW	NACH-LINKS-TASTE
left scroll arrow	Bildlaufpfeil links
left window border	Linker Fensterrand
Line (Ln)	Ze
link	Verknüpfen
linked object	Verknüpftes Objekt
linked text and list box	Verknüpftes Textfeld/ Listenfeld
list box	Listenfeld
List Files of Type	Dateiformat (f)
Macro menu	**Makro (M)**
Macro Recorder on (REC)	MA
Main	Hauptgruppe
main application	Hauptanwendung
main document	Hauptdokument
manual link	Manuelle Verknüpfung
Match Case	Groß-/Kleinschreibung (G)
Match Whole Word Only	Als Wort (A)
Maximize	**Vollbild (B)**
Maximize button	Schaltfläche für Maximieren
Media Player	Medien-Wiedergabe
menu	Menü
menu bar	Menüleiste
menu command	Menübefehl
menu name	Menüname
message	Information, Meldung
message box	Meldungsfeld
message line	Meldungszeile
MIDI Sequencer...	**MIDI-Sequenzer...**
Minimize	**Symbol (S)**
Minimize button	Schaltfläche für Minimieren
Mix with File...	**Datei einmischen... (a)**

ENGLISH	GERMAN
More	Weitere Optionen
Mouse	**Maus (M)**
mouse pointer	Mauszeiger
Move	**Verschieben (V)**
move	Verschieben
MS-DOS Prompt	MS-DOS-Eingabeaufforderung
New...	**Neu... (N)**
New Window	**Neues Fenster (N)**
Next	**Nächstes (N)**
Next Window	**Nächstes Fenster (N)**
No	Nein
Notepad	Notizblock
NUM LOCK	NUM
Number...	**Zahlenformat... (Z)**
Num Lock on (NUM)	NF
object	Objekt
Object...	**Objekt... (O)**
object linking & embedding (OLE)	Objekte verknüpfen und einbetten (OLE)
Object Packager	Objekt-Manager
OK	OK
OLE application	OLE-Anwendung
OLE (object linking & embedding)	Objekte verknüpfen und einbetten (OLE)
Open	**Öffnen (F)**
option button	(Rundes) Optionsfeld
Options	Optionen
Options menu	**Optionen (O)**
Orientation	Format
Overtype on (OVR)	ÜB
package	Paket
Page (Pg)	S
Pages	Seiten (S)
Page Setup	**Seite einrichten (E)**
palette	Palette
pane	Ausschnitt
Paper Size	Papiergröße (P)
Paragraph...	**Absatz... (A)**
Paste	**Einfügen (I)**
paste	Einfügen
Paste Link	**Verknüpfung einfügen (V)**
Paste Special	**Inhalte einfügen (I)**
PAUSE	PAUSE
PG DN	BILD-AB-TASTE
PG UP	BILD-AUF-TASTE
PIF Editor	PIF-Editor
point	Zeigen auf
pointer	Zeiger
Portrait	Hochformat (f)
Preferences	**Bildschirmeinstellungen (B)**
press and hold down	Gedrückt halten
Print	**Drucken (D)**
Printer	Drucker
Printer Setup	**Druckereinrichtung (E)**
Print Manager	Druck-Manager
Print Preview	**Seitenansicht (T)**

ENGLISH	GERMAN	ENGLISH	GERMAN
Print Quality	Druckqualität (u)	Search	Suchen (S)
Print Range	Druckbereich	Search	Suchen
PRINT SCREEN	DRUCK	**Search...**	**Suchen... (S)**
Print Setup...	**Druckereinrichtung... (E)**	**Search for Help on**	**Suchen (S)**
Print to File	Druckausgabe in Datei	**Section...**	**Abschnitt...(I)**
	umleiten (r)	Section (Sec)	Ab
Print Topic	**Thema drucken (D)**	select	Markieren, Auswählen
program group	Programmgruppe	select	Markieren, Auswählen, Wählen
program item	Programm	select (check box, option button)"	Aktivieren (check box),
program-item icon	Anwendungssymbol		Auswählen (Option button)
Program Manager	Programm-Manager	select (data)	Markieren
progress indicator	Statusanzeiger	select (drop-down menu)	Wählen
push button	Schaltfläche	selected command	Hervorgehobener Befehl
Quit	Beenden	Selection	Markierung (M)
radio button	Rundes Optionsfeld	selection cursor	Auswahl-Cursor
Read Only	Schreibgeschützt (S)	select (list box)	Auswählen
Record...	**Aufzeichnen... (A)**	Set	Festlegen
Recorder	Rekorder	Setup	Einrichten, Setup
Redo	Wiederherstellen, Wiederholen	SHIFT	UMSCHALTTASTE
reduce selection	Markierung verkleinern	shortcut key	Tastaturbefehl
Remove Split	**Teilung aufheben (T)**	**Short Menus**	**Kurze Menüs (M)**
Repeat	**Wiederholen (W)**	**Size**	**Größe ändern (G)**
Replace...	**Ersetzen... (E)**	size	Größe (ändern)
Replace All	Alles ersetzen (s)	size	Vergrößern/Verkleinern
Replace With	Ersetzen durch (d)	Size (font size)	Schriftgröße (g)
Reset	Zurücksetzen	sizing handle	Ziehpunkt
resize	Größe ändern	slider	Bildlauffeld
Restore	**Wiederherstellen (W)**	slider indicator	Bildlaufanzeige
restore	Wiederherstellen	small capitals	Kapitälchen
Restore button	Schaltfläche für	**Sound...**	**Klang... (k)**
	Wiederherstellen	Sound Recorder	Klangrecorder
Resume	Fortsetzen	source application	Quellanwendung
Retry	Wiederholen	source document	Quelldokument
Reverse	**Umkehren (u)**	Source (paper)	Zufuhr (Z)
Revert...	**Wiederherstellen... (w)**	SPACEBAR	LEERTASTE
right aligned	Rechtsbündig (R)	spin box	Drehfeld
RIGHT ARROW	NACH-RECHTS-TASTE	**Split**	**Teilen (T)**
right scroll arrow	Bildlaufpfeil rechts	**Split**	**Teilen (R)**
right window border	Rechter Fensterrand	split	Teilen
ruler	Lineal; Absatzlineal	split bar	Fensterteiler
Run...	**Ausführen...(A)**	split box	Teilungsfeld
Run...	**Ausführen... (U)**	StartUp	Autostart
Sample	Muster	status bar	Statusleiste
Save	**Speichern (P)**	status-bar indicator	Statusanzeige
Save All	**Alles speichern (A)**	submenu	Untermenü
Save As...	**Speichern unter... (U)**	switch	Wechseln, Umschalten
Save File as Type	Dateiformat (f)	Switch to	Wechseln zu
Scale	Skalieren, Größe ändern	**Switch To...**	**Wechseln zu... (Z)**
Scale menu	**Skala (s)**	SYS RQ	S-ABF
Scaling	Skalierung (r)	TAB	TAB
scroll	Bildlauf durchführen	Terminal	Terminal
scroll arrow	Bildlaufpfeil	text box	Textfeld
scroll bar	Bildlaufleiste	text frame	Textrahmen
scroll box	Bildlauffeld	**Tile**	**Nebeneinander (N)**
SCROLL LOCK	ROLLEN	tiled windows	Nebeneinander angeordnete
Scroll Lock on (SCRL)	RF		Fenster

ENGLISH	GERMAN	ENGLISH	GERMAN
Time	**Zeit (z)**	value set	Festgelegter Wert
title bar	Titelleiste	vertical scroll bar	Vertikale Bildlaufleiste
To	Bis (B)	vertical split bar	Vertikaler Fensterteiler
tool	Symbol	view	Anzeigen, Einsehen
toolbar	Symbolleiste	**View menu**	**Ansicht (A)**
toolbox	Toolbox	wallpaper	Hintergrundbild
Tools menu	**Extras (X)**	warning message	Warnmeldung
top window border	Oberer Fensterrand	wildcard	Stellvertreterzeichen
Tracks	**Titel (t)**	window	Fenster
Tutorial	**Lernprogramm (P)**	window background	Fensterhintergrund
type	Eingeben	window border	Fensterrand
unavailable command	Nicht verfügbarer Befehl	window corner	Fensterecke
underline	Unterstrichen (U)	window frame	Fensterrahmen
Undo	**Rückgängig (R)**	**Window menu**	**Fenster (F)**
unfreeze	Fixierung aufheben	window size	Fenstergröße
Unfreeze Panes	**Fensterfixierung aufheben (F)**	window title	Fenstertitel
Unhide...	**Einblenden... (E)**	Windows Setup	Windows-Setup
Up	Aufwärts (u)	workspace	Arbeitsbereich
UP ARROW	NACH-OBEN-TASTE	Yes	Ja
Update	**Aktualisieren (A)**	**Zoom...**	**Zoom... (Z)**
update	Aktualisieren	zoom in	Vergrößern
up scroll arrow	Bildlaufpfeil aufwärts	zoom out	Verkleinern
Utilities menu	**Extras (X)**		

CHAPTER 14

Hungarian

This chapter lists the Hungarian translations of all terms formatted in *italic* in Part 1. Terminology is listed in two ways: by category and in alphabetical order. The first section includes translations in the following categories: Window Elements, Menus, Dialog Boxes, Message Boxes, Other GUI Screen Elements, Keys, User Actions, and Applications For Microsoft Windows.

Terminology by Category

ENGLISH	HUNGARIAN	ENGLISH	HUNGARIAN
WINDOW ELEMENTS		window border	ablak széle
Main window elements		window corner	ablak sarka
active window	aktív ablak	window frame	(ablak)keret
application window	alkalmazásablak	window size	ablakméret
border	szél	window title	ablak címe
bottom window border	ablak alsó széle	workspace	munkaterület
cascading windows	lépcsőzetes elrendezésű ablakok		
desktop	munkaasztal	**Window controls**	
document window	dokumentumablak	Control-menu box	vezérlő menü (jele)
group window	csoportablak, alkalmazáscsoport-ablak	down scroll arrow	lefelé gördítő nyíl
		horizontal scroll bar	vízszintes gördítősáv
Help window	súgó ablak	horizontal split bar	vízszintes osztócsík
inactive window	inaktív ablak	left scroll arrow	balra gördítő nyíl
left window border	ablak bal széle	Maximize button	teljesméret-gomb
menu bar	menüsor	Minimize button	ikonállapot-gomb
pane	ablaktábla	Restore button	előzőméret-gomb
right window border	ablak jobb széle	right scroll arrow	jobbra gördítő nyíl
ruler	vonalzó	scroll arrow	gördítőnyíl
status bar	állapotsor	scroll bar	gördítősáv
tiled windows	mozaik elrendezésű ablakok	scroll box	gördítőcsúszka
title bar	címke	split bar	osztócsík
toolbar	ikonmenü	split box	osztócsúszka
top window border	ablak felső széle	up scroll arrow	felfelé gördítő nyíl
wallpaper	háttér	vertical scroll bar	függőleges gördítősáv
window	ablak	vertical split bar	függőleges osztócsík
window background	ablak háttere		

ENGLISH	HUNGARIAN	ENGLISH	HUNGARIAN
Pointers		Move	Áthelyez (h)
arrow	nyíl	Size	Új méret (m)
arrow pointer	nyílmutató	Minimize	Ikon állapot (i)
cross-hair pointer	szálkereszt	Maximize	Teljes méret (t)
hourglass pointer	homokóra	Next	Következő (k)
I-beam pointer	kurzormutató	Close	Bezár (z)
insertion point	kurzor	Run...	Futtat... (f)
mouse pointer	egérmutató	Switch To...	Futó programok... (p)
pointer	mutató	Split	Feloszt (o)
selection cursor	kiválasztó kurzor		
		File menu	File (f)
Icons		New...	Új... (j)
application icon	alkalmazás ikon	Open	Megnyit (n)
directory icon	könyvtár ikon	Close	Lezár (z)
disk icon	lemez ikon	Close All	Lezár mindent (r)
document file icon	dokumentumfile ikon	Save	Ment (m)
document icon	dokumentum ikon	Save As...	Ment új néven... (v)
drive icon	meghajtó ikon	Save All	Ment mindent (e)
group icon	(alkalmazás)csoport ikon	Delete	Töröl (t)
icon	ikon	Page Setup	Oldalbeállítás (o)
program-item icon	programindító ikon	Print	Nyomtat (y)
		Print Preview	Nyomtatási kép (p)
General terms		Printer Setup	Nyomtatóbeállítás (b)
access key	hívóbetű	Exit	Kilép (k)
check mark	pipa; iksz	Exit and Return to	Kilépés és ... folytatása (k)
ellipsis	három pont	Update	Frissít (f)
font	betűtípus; betűkészlet		
object	objektum	Edit menu	Szerkesztés (z)
program group	programcsoport	Undo	Visszavon (v)
program item	program	Repeat	Ismét (i)
shortcut key	gyors elérés	Cut	Kivág (k)
sizing handle	méretező pont (sarok/oldal)	Copy	Másol (m)
status-bar indicator	állapotjelző	Copy Special	Spec. másol (s)
tool	eszköz	Paste	Beilleszt (b)
unavailable command	nem elérhető parancs	Paste Link	Csatolva beilleszt (c)
		Paste Special	Spec. beilleszt (p)
MENUS		Clear	Töröl (t)
Menu elements		Clear All	Töröl mindent (r)
cascading menu	almenü	Find...	Keres... (e)
checked command	érvényben lévő parancs	Search...	Keres... (e)
command	parancs	Replace...	Cserél... (c)
command separator	a parancsokat elválasztó vonal	Go To...	Ugrás... (u)
drop-down menu	legördülő menü	Delete...	Töröl... (t)
menu	menü	Insert...	Beszúr... (z)
menu command	menüparancs	Object...	Objektum... (o)
menu name	menünév	Insert Object...	Objektum beszúrása... (e)
selected command	kiemelten megjelenő parancs		
submenu	almenü	Options menu	Egyebek (e)
		Preferences	Egyedi beállítások (e)
Menus and commands		Full Menus	Teljes menük (m)
View menu	Nézet (n)	Short Menus	Rövid menük (m)
Insert menu	Beszúrás (b)		
		Format menu	Formátum (t)
Control menu	Vezérlő menü	Character...	Betű... (b)
Restore	Előző méret (e)	Paragraph...	Bekezdés... (k)

ENGLISH	HUNGARIAN
Section...	Szakasz... (s)
Document...	Dokumentum... (d)
Number...	Szám... (z)
Alignment...	Igazítás... (i)
Utilities menu	Segédletek (g)
Tools menu	Eszközök (e)
Customize	Testre szab (t)
Macro menu	Makró (m)
Record...	Rögzít... (r)
Run...	Futtat... (f)
Edit	Szerkeszt (z)
Assign to Key	Billentyűhöz rendel (b)
Assign to Menu	Menühöz rendel (m)
Window menu	Ablak (a)
New Window	Új ablak (j)
Cascade	Lépcsőzetes elrendezés (l)
Tile	Mozaik elrendezés (m)
Next Window	Következő ablak (k)
Arrange All	Elrendez (e)
Hide	Rejt (r)
Unhide...	Felfed... (f)
Split	Feloszt (o)
Freeze Panes	Táblák rögzítése (r)
Remove Split	Felosztás eltávolítása (o)
Unfreeze Panes	Rögzítés feloldása (r)
Zoom...	Nagyítás... (a)
Help menu	Súgó (s)
Contents	Tartalom (t)
How to use Help	Használat (h)
Search for Help on	Témakör keresése (k)
Active Window	Aktív ablak (a)
Keyboard	Billentyűzet (b)
Mouse	Egér (e)
Tutorial	Tankönyv (k)
About	Névjegy (n)
Device menu	Eszköz
Scale menu	Skála
MIDI Sequencer...	MIDI sorrendvezérlő...
Sound...	Hang...
Time	Idő (i)
Tracks	Tételek (t)
Effects menu	Effektusok (e)
Revert...	Visszahoz... (s)
Insert File...	File beszúrása... (f)
Mix with File...	File rákeverése... (l)
Delete Before Current Position	Töröl az aktuális pozícióig (i)
Delete After Current Position	Töröl az aktuális pozíciótól (t)
Increase Volume (by 25%)	Hangerő növelése (25%-kal) (n)

ENGLISH	HUNGARIAN
Decrease Volume	Hangerő csökkentése (c)
Increase Speed (by 100%)	Sebesség növelése (100%-kal) (e)
Decrease Speed	Sebesség csökkentése (s)
Add Echo	Visszhangosít (v)
Reverse	Visszafelé (f)
Help application	
File menu	File (f)
Open	Megnyit (n)
Print Topic	Nyomtat (y)
Print Setup...	Nyomtatóbeállítás... (b)
Exit	Kilép (k)
Edit menu	Szerkesztés (z)
Copy...	Másol... (m)
Annotate...	Jegyzet... (j)
Bookmark menu	Könyvjelző (k)
Define...	Elhelyez/Eltávolít... (e)
Help menu	Súgó (s)
How to use Help	Használat (h)
Always on Top	Mindig látható (l)
About Help...	Névjegy... (n)
Buttons	
Contents	Tartalom (t)
Search	Keres (k)
Back	Vissza (v)
History	Előzmények (e)
Glossary	Fogalmak (o)
DIALOG BOXES	
dialog box	párbeszédpanel
wildcard	helyettesítő
Dialog box elements	
button	gomb
check box	(kiválasztó) négyzet
chevrons	bővítést jelző kettős nyíl
combo box	kombi(nált) panel
command button	parancsgomb
dialog box title	párbeszédpanel címe
drop-down combo box	legördülő kombi panel
drop-down list box	legördülő listapanel
Goto/Gosub button	új panel gomb
group box	(vezérlőelem-)csoport
label	címke
linked text and list box	csatolt beviteli mező és listapanel
list box	listapanel
option button	választókapcsoló
progress indicator	folyamatjelző
push button	nyomógomb

ENGLISH	HUNGARIAN
radio button	választókapcsoló
slider	csúszószabályzó
slider indicator	csúszka
spin box	léptetőmező
text box	itt: (adat)beviteli mező
value set	értékkészlet

Dialog box buttons

Add	Hozzáad
Apply	Alkalmaz
Cancel	Mégsem
Change	Módosít
Create	Létrehoz
Default	Alapértelmezett
Define	Megad
Done	Kész
Go To	Ugrás
Help	Súgó
More	További
No	Nem
OK	OK
Options	Egyebek
Quit	Kilép
Redo	Újra
Reset	Alaphelyzet
Resume	Tovább
Retry	Ismét
Search	Keres
Set	Beállít
Setup	Beállítás
Switch to	Átvált
Yes	Igen

Dialog box labels

All	Mind (m)
Collate copies	Sorba rendez (r)
Copies	Példányszám (p)
Direction	Irány
Directories	Az élő könyvtár (k)
Down	Le (l)
Drives	Lemezmeghajtó (l)
File Name	Filenév (n)
Find Next	Keres (k)
Find What	A keresett szöveg (v)
Font	Betűtípus (b)
Font Style	Betűtípus-jellemző (j)
From	Kezdő oldal (k)
Landscape	Fekvő (f)
List Files of Type	Listázandó filetípus (t)
Match Case	Kis- és nagybetűk megkülönböztetése (n)
Match Whole Word Only	Teljes szót keres (t)
Orientation	Tájolás
Pages	Megadott tartomány (t)
Paper Size	Papírméret (m)
Portrait	Álló (l)

ENGLISH	HUNGARIAN
Printer	Nyomtató
Print Quality	Minőség (i)
Print Range	Nyomtatandó tartomány
Print to File	File-ba nyomtat (l)
Read Only	Írásvédett (v)
Replace All	Mindet cseréli (m)
Replace With	Új szöveg (j)
Sample	Minta
Save File as Type	Formátum (f)
Scaling	Méret (m)
Selection	Kiválasztott (v)
Size (font size)	Méret (m)
Source (paper)	Forrás (r)
To	Záró oldal (z)
Up	Fel (f)

MESSAGE BOXES

critical message	hibaüzenet
message	információ
message box	üzenetpanel
message line	üzenetsor
warning message	figyelmeztetés

OTHER GUI SCREEN ELEMENTS

Graphical options

gallery	gyűjtemény
palette	paletta
text frame	szövegkeret
toolbox	eszközkészlet

Status bar abbreviations

Caps Lock on (CAPS)	CAPS
Column (Col)	Oszl (oszlop)
Extend selection on (EXT)	BŐV
Line (Ln)	Sor
Macro Recorder on (REC)	MR (makrórögzítés)
Num Lock on (NUM)	NUM
Overtype on (OVR)	ÁTÍR
Page (Pg)	Old (oldal)
Scroll Lock on (SCRL)	SCRL
Section (Sec)	Sz (szakasz)

Character formats

bold	félkövér (f)
double underline	kettős aláhúzás (e)
italic	dőlt (d)
small capitals	kis kapitális (k)
underline	aláhúzás (a)

Paragraph formats

centered	középre zárt (k)
justified	sorkizárt (s)
left aligned	balra zárt (b)
right aligned	jobbra zárt (j)

ENGLISH	HUNGARIAN
KEYS	
Shortcut keys	
CTRL+B (Bold)	CTRL+B
CTRL+C (Copy)	CTRL+C
CTRL+D (Double underline)	CTRL+D
CTRL+E (Center)	CTRL+E
CTRL+I (Italics)	CTRL+I
CTRL+J (Justify)	CTRL+J
CTRL+L (Left align)	CTRL+L
CTRL+R (Right align)	CTRL+R
CTRL+U (Underline)	CTRL+U
CTRL+V (Paste)	CTRL+V
CTRL+W (Word underline)	CTRL+W
CTRL+X (Cut)	CTRL+X
CTRL+Z (Undo)	CTRL+Z
DEL (Clear)	DEL
Keynames	
(keypad) *	SZÜRKE *
(keypad) +	SZÜRKE +
(keypad) -	SZÜRKE -
(keypad) /	SZÜRKE /
ALT	ALT
ALT GR	ALT GR
BACKSPACE	BACKSPACE
BREAK	BREAK
CAPS LOCK	CAPS LOCK
CTRL	CTRL
DEL	DELETE, DEL
DOWN ARROW	LE-NYÍL
END	END
ENTER	ENTER
ENTER (keypad)	ENTER A SZÁMBILLENTYŰZETEN
ESC	ESC
HOME	HOME
INS	INSERT, INS
LEFT ARROW	BAL-NYÍL
NUM LOCK	NUM LOCK
PAUSE	PAUSE
PG DN	PAGE DOWN, PG DN
PG UP	PAGE UP, PG DN
PRINT SCREEN	PRINT SCREEN
RIGHT ARROW	JOBB-NYÍL
SCROLL LOCK	SCROLL LOCK
SHIFT	VÁLTÓ
SPACEBAR	SZÓKÖZ
SYS RQ	SYS RQ
TAB	TAB(ULÁTOR)
UP ARROW	FEL-NYÍL
USER ACTIONS	
Keyboard actions	
enter	begépel, beír
press and hold down	lenyomva tart
type	begépel

ENGLISH	HUNGARIAN
Mouse actions	
click	kattint, rákattint
double-click	duplán kattint
drag	húz
drag-and-drop	Fogd és vidd
drop	beejt
point	rámutat
Manipulating window appearance	
arrange	elrendez
close	bezár
freeze	rögzít
hide	rejt
move	áthelyez
resize	újraméretez
restore	előző méretet visszaállítja
select	kiválaszt
size	méretez
split	feloszt
switch	átvált
unfreeze	rögzítést felold
Selecting options or content	
cancel	elvet
check	beikszel; kipipál; jelöl
choose	választ (parancsot)
clear (undo Select)	töröl (pipát, ikszet, négyzetet); visszavon (pipát, ikszet)
extend selection	bővíti a kijelölést
reduce selection	szűkíti a kijelölést
select	kiválaszt, választ
select (check box, option button)	beikszel, jelöl (négyzetet); bekapcsol, választ (kapcsolót)
select (data)	kijelöl (egy adatot)
select (drop-down menu)	kibont (egy legördülő menüt)
select (list box)	kibont (egy listát)
Viewing content	
autoscroll	automatikus görgetés
browse	tallóz
collapse	tömörít, bezár
expand	részletez, kifejt
scroll	gördít
view	megmutat
zoom in	közelít
zoom out	távolít
Removing content	
clear	töröl; tartalmat töröl
copy	másol
cut	kivág
delete	töröl; eltávolít
paste	beilleszt

ENGLISH	HUNGARIAN	ENGLISH	HUNGARIAN
Manipulating objects		source document	forrásdokumentum
arrange	elrendez	update	frissít
automatic link	automatikus csatolás		
Clipboard	Vágólap	**APPLICATIONS FOR**	
container application	fogadó alkalmazás	**MICROSOFT WINDOWS**	
container document	fogadó dokumentum		
copy	másol	Accessories	Kellékek
crop	méretre vág	Applications	Alkalmazások
destination application	célalkalmazás	Calculator	Számológép
destination document	céldokumentum	Calendar	Naptár
drag-and-drop	Fogd és vidd	Cardfile	Kartoték
embed	beágyaz	Character Map	Karaktertábla
embedded object	beágyazott objektum	Clipboard Viewer	Vágólap-megjelenítő
group	csoport	Clock	Óra
link	csatol	Control Panel	Vezérlőpult
linked object	csatolt objektum	File Manager	Filekezelő
main application	főalkalmazás	Games	Játékok
main document	fődokumentum	Main	Rendszer
manual link	kézi csatolás	Media Player	Médialejátszó
object	objektum	MS-DOS Prompt	MS-DOS
object linking & embedding	objektumcsatolás és	Notepad	Jegyzettömb
(OLE)	-beágyazás (OLE)	Object Packager	Objektumcsomagoló,
OLE (object linking &	OLE (objektumcsatolás		Csomagoló
embedding)	és -beágyazás; object linking	PIF Editor	PIF-szerkesztő
	& embedding)	Print Manager	Nyomtatásvezérlő
OLE application	OLE alkalmazás	Program Manager	Programkezelő
package	csomag	Recorder	Makrórögzítő
paste	beilleszt	Sound Recorder	Hangrögzítő
scale	átméretez, beilleszt	StartUp	Automatikus indítás
size	átméretez, beilleszt	Terminal	Terminál
source application	forrásalkalmazás	Windows Setup	Windows Telepítő

Terminology by Alphabet

Notes:
1. All terms formatted in **bold** refer to menu names or command names.
2. All characters between parentheses are preferred access keys.

ENGLISH	HUNGARIAN	ENGLISH	HUNGARIAN
(keypad) *	SZÜRKE *	cascading menu	almenü
(keypad) +	SZÜRKE +	cascading windows	lépcsőzetes elrendezésű ablakok
(keypad) -	SZÜRKE -	centered	középre zárt (k)
(keypad) /	SZÜRKE /	Change	Módosít
About	**Névjegy (n)**	**Character...**	**Betű... (b)**
About Help...	**Névjegy... (n)**	Character Map	Karaktertábla
access key	hívóbetű	check	beikszel; kipipál; jelöl
Accessories	Kellékek	check box	(kiválasztó) négyzet
active window	aktív ablak	checked command	érvényben lévő parancs
Active Window	**Aktív ablak (a)**	check mark	pipa; iksz
Add	Hozzáad	chevrons	bővítést jelző kettős nyíl
Add Echo	**Visszhangosít (v)**	choose	választ (parancsot)
Alignment...	**Igazítás... (i)**	**Clear**	**Töröl (t)**
All	Mind (m)	clear	töröl; tartalmat töröl
ALT	ALT	**Clear All**	**Töröl mindent (r)**
ALT GR	ALT GR	clear (undo Select)	töröl (pipát, ikszet, négyzetet);
Always on Top	**Mindig látható (l)**		visszavon (pipát, ikszet)
Annotate...	**Jegyzet... (j)**	click	kattint, rákattint
application icon	alkalmazás ikon	Clipboard	Vágólap
Applications	Alkalmazások	Clipboard Viewer	Vágólap-megjelenítő
application window	alkalmazásablak	Clock	Óra
Apply	Alkalmaz	Close	Bezár (z)
arrange	elrendez	**Close**	**Lezár (z)**
Arrange All	**Elrendez (e)**	close	bezár
arrow	nyíl	**Close All**	**Lezár mindent (r)**
arrow pointer	nyílmutató	collapse	tömörít, bezár
Assign to Key	**Billentyűhöz rendel (b)**	Collate copies	Sorba rendez (r)
Assign to Menu	**Menühöz rendel (m)**	Column (Col)	Oszl (oszlop)
automatic link	automatikus csatolás	combo box	kombi(nált) panel
autoscroll	automatikus görgetés	command	parancs
Back	Vissza (v)	command button	parancsgomb
BACKSPACE	BACKSPACE	command separator	a parancsokat elválasztó
bold	félkövér (f)		vonal
Bookmark menu	**Könyvjelző (k)**	container application	fogadó alkalmazás
border	szél	container document	fogadó dokumentum
bottom window border	ablak alsó széle	**Contents**	**Tartalom (t)**
BREAK	BREAK	Contents	Tartalom (t)
browse	tallóz	**Control menu**	**Vezérlő menü**
button	gomb	Control-menu box	vezérlő menü (jele)
Calculator	Számológép	Control Panel	Vezérlőpult
Calendar	Naptár	Copies	Példányszám (p)
Cancel	Mégsem	**Copy**	**Másol (m)**
cancel	elvet	copy	másol
CAPS LOCK	CAPS LOCK	**Copy...**	**Másol... (m)**
Caps Lock on (CAPS)	CAPS	**Copy Special**	**Spec. másol (s)**
Cardfile	Kartoték	Create	Létrehoz
Cascade	**Lépcsőzetes elrendezés (l)**	critical message	hibaüzenet

ENGLISH	HUNGARIAN	ENGLISH	HUNGARIAN
crop	méretre vág	drop-down combo box	legördülő kombi panel
cross-hair pointer	szálkereszt	drop-down list box	legördülő listapanel
CTRL	CTRL	drop-down menu	legördülő menü
CTRL+B (Bold)	CTRL+B	**Edit**	**Szerkeszt (z)**
CTRL+C (Copy)	CTRL+C	**Edit menu**	**Szerkesztés (z)**
CTRL+D (Double underline)	CTRL+D	**Effects menu**	**Effektusok (e)**
CTRL+E (Center)	CTRL+E	ellipsis	három pont
CTRL+I (Italics)	CTRL+I	embed	beágyaz
CTRL+J (Justify)	CTRL+J	embedded object	beágyazott objektum
CTRL+L (Left align)	CTRL+L	END	END
CTRL+R (Right align)	CTRL+R	ENTER	ENTER
CTRL+U (Underline)	CTRL+U	enter	begépel, beír
CTRL+V (Paste)	CTRL+V	ENTER (keypad)	ENTER A
CTRL+W (Word underline)	CTRL+W		SZÁMBILLENTYŰZETEN
CTRL+X (Cut)	CTRL+X	ESC	ESC
CTRL+Z (Undo)	CTRL+Z	**Exit**	**Kilép (k)**
Customize	**Testre szab (t)**	**Exit and Return to**	**Kilépés és ... folytatása (k)**
Cut	**Kivág (k)**	expand	részletez, kifejt
cut	kivág	extend selection	bővíti a kijelölést
Decrease Speed	**Sebesség csökkentése (s)**	Extend selection on (EXT)	BŐV
Decrease Volume	**Hangerő csökkentése (c)**	File Manager	Filekezelő
Default	Alapértelmezett	**File menu**	**File (f)**
Define	Megad	File Name	Filenév (n)
Define...	**Elhelyez/Eltávolít... (e)**	**Find...**	**Keres... (e)**
DEL	DELETE, DEL	Find Next	Keres (k)
DEL (Clear)	DEL	Find What	A keresett szöveg (v)
Delete	**Töröl (t)**	font	betűtípus; betűkészlet
delete	töröl; eltávolít	Font	Betűtípus (b)
Delete...	**Töröl... (t)**	Font Style	Betűtípus-jellemző (j)
Delete After Current Position	**Töröl az aktuális pozíciótól (t)**	**Format menu**	**Formátum (t)**
		freeze	rögzít
Delete Before Current Position	**Töröl az aktuális pozícióig (i)**	**Freeze Panes**	**Táblák rögzítése (r)**
		From	Kezdő oldal (k)
desktop	munkaasztal	**Full Menus**	**Teljes menük (m)**
destination application	célalkalmazás	gallery	gyűjtemény
destination document	céldokumentum	Games	Játékok
Device menu	**Eszköz**	Glossary	Fogalmak (o)
dialog box	párbeszédpanel	Go To	Ugrás
dialog box title	párbeszédpanel címe	**Go To...**	**Ugrás... (u)**
Direction	Irány	Goto/Gosub button	új panel gomb
Directories	Az élő könyvtár (k)	group	csoport
directory icon	könyvtár ikon	group box	(vezérlőelem-)csoport
disk icon	lemez ikon	group icon	(alkalmazás)csoport ikon
Document...	**Dokumentum... (d)**	group window	csoportablak,
document file icon	dokumentumfile ikon		alkalmazáscsoport-ablak
document icon	dokumentum ikon	Help	Súgó
document window	dokumentumablak	**Help menu**	**Súgó (s)**
Done	Kész	Help window	súgó ablak
double-click	duplán kattint	**Hide**	**Rejt (r)**
double underline	kettős aláhúzás (e)	hide	rejt
Down	Le (l)	History	Előzmények (e)
DOWN ARROW	LE-NYÍL	HOME	HOME
down scroll arrow	lefelé gördítő nyíl	horizontal scroll bar	vízszintes gördítősáv
drag	húz	horizontal split bar	vízszintes osztócsík
drag-and-drop	Fogd és vidd	hourglass pointer	homokóra
drive icon	meghajtó ikon	**How to use Help**	**Használat (h)**
Drives	Lemezmeghajtó (l)	I-beam pointer	kurzormutató
drop	beejt	icon	ikon

ENGLISH	HUNGARIAN	ENGLISH	HUNGARIAN
inactive window	inaktív ablak	Next	Következő (k)
Increase Speed (by 100%)	**Sebesség növelése**	**Next Window**	**Következő ablak (k)**
	(100%-kal) (e)	No	Nem
Increase Volume (by 25%)	**Hangerő növelése**	Notepad	Jegyzettömb
	(25%-kal) (n)	**Number...**	**Szám... (z)**
INS	INSERT, INS	NUM LOCK	NUM LOCK
Insert...	**Beszúr... (z)**	Num Lock on (NUM)	NUM
Insert File...	**File beszúrása... (f)**	object	objektum
insertion point	kurzor	**Object...**	**Objektum... (o)**
Insert menu	**Beszúrás (b)**	object linking & embedding	objektumcsatolás és
Insert Object...	**Objektum beszúrása... (e)**	(OLE)	-beágyazás (OLE)
italic	dőlt (d)	Object Packager	Objektumcsomagoló,
justified	sorkizárt (s)		Csomagoló
Keyboard	**Billentyűzet (b)**	OK	OK
label	címke	OLE application	OLE alkalmazás
Landscape	Fekvő (f)	OLE (object linking &	OLE (objektumcsatolás és
left aligned	balra zárt (b)	embedding)	-beágyazás; object linking &
LEFT ARROW	BAL-NYÍL		embedding)
left scroll arrow	balra gördítő nyíl	**Open**	**Megnyit (n)**
left window border	ablak bal széle	option button	választókapcsoló
Line (Ln)	Sor	Options	Egyebek
link	csatol	**Options menu**	**Egyebek (e)**
linked object	csatolt objektum	Orientation	Tájolás
linked text and list box	csatolt beviteli mező és	Overtype on (OVR)	ÁTÍR
	listapanel	package	csomag
list box	listapanel	Page (Pg)	Old (oldal)
List Files of Type	Listázandó filetípus (t)	Pages	Megadott tartomány (t)
Macro menu	**Makró (m)**	**Page Setup**	**Oldalbeállítás (o)**
Macro Recorder on (REC)	MR (makrórögzítés)	Pages	Megadott tartomány (t)
Main	Rendszer	palette	paletta
main application	főalkalmazás	pane	ablaktábla
main document	fődokumentum	Paper Size	Papírméret (m)
manual link	kézi csatolás	**Paragraph...**	**Bekezdés... (k)**
Match Case	Kis- és nagybetűk	**Paste**	**Beilleszt (b)**
	megkülönböztetése (n)	paste	beilleszt
Match Whole Word Only	Teljes szót keres (t)	**Paste Link**	**Csatolva beilleszt (c)**
Maximize	**Teljes méret (t)**	**Paste Special**	**Spec. beilleszt (p)**
Maximize button	teljesméret-gomb	PAUSE	PAUSE
Media Player	Médialejátszó	PG DN	PAGE DOWN, PG DN
menu	menü	PG UP	PAGE UP, PG DN
menu bar	menüsor	PIF Editor	PIF-szerkesztő
menu command	menüparancs	point	rámutat
menu name	menünév	pointer	mutató
message	információ	Portrait	Álló (l)
message box	üzenetpanel	**Preferences**	**Egyedi beállítások (e)**
message line	üzenetsor	press and hold down	lenyomva tart
MIDI Sequencer...	**MIDI sorrendvezérlő...**	**Print**	**Nyomtat (y)**
Minimize	**Ikon állapot (i)**	Printer	Nyomtató
Minimize button	ikonállapot-gomb	**Printer Setup**	**Nyomtatóbeállítás (b)**
Mix with File...	**File rákeverése... (l)**	Print Manager	Nyomtatásvezérlő
More	További	**Print Preview**	**Nyomtatási kép (p)**
Mouse	**Egér (e)**	Print Quality	Minőség (i)
mouse pointer	egérmutató	Print Range	Nyomtatandó tartomány
Move	**Áthelyez (h)**	PRINT SCREEN	PRINT SCREEN
move	áthelyez	**Print Setup...**	**Nyomtatóbeállítás... (b)**
MS-DOS Prompt	MS-DOS	Print to File	File-ba nyomtat (l)
New...	**Új... (j)**	**Print Topic**	**Nyomtat (y)**
New Window	**Új ablak (j)**	program group	programcsoport

ENGLISH	HUNGARIAN	ENGLISH	HUNGARIAN
program item	program	select (drop-down menu)	kibont (egy legördülő menüt)
program-item icon	programindító ikon	selected command	kiemelten megjelenő parancs
Program Manager	Programkezelő	Selection	Kiválasztott (v)
progress indicator	folyamatjelző	selection cursor	kiválasztó kurzor
push button	nyomógomb	select (list box)	kibont (egy listát)
Quit	Kilép	Set	Beállít
radio button	választókapcsoló	Setup	Beállítás
Read Only	Írásvédett (v)	SHIFT	VÁLTÓ
Record...	**Rögzít... (r)**	**Short Menus**	**Rövid menük (m)**
Recorder	Makrórögzítő	shortcut key	gyors elérés
Redo	Újra	**Size**	**Új méret (m)**
reduce selection	szűkíti a kijelölést	size	méretez
Remove Split	**Felosztás eltávolítása (o)**	size	átméretez, beilleszt
Repeat	**Ismét (i)**	Size (font size)	Méret (m)
Replace...	**Cserél... (c)**	sizing handle	méretező pont (sarok/oldal)
Replace All	Mindet cseréli (m)	slider	csúszószabályzó
Replace With	Új szöveg (j)	slider indicator	csúszka
Reset	Alaphelyzet	small capitals	kis kapitális (k)
resize	újraméretez	**Sound...**	**Hang...**
Restore	**Előző méret (e)**	Sound Recorder	Hangrögzítő
restore	előző méretet visszaállítja	source application	forrásalkalmazás
Restore button	előzőméret-gomb	source document	forrásdokumentum
Resume	Tovább	Source (paper)	Forrás (r)
Retry	Ismét	SPACEBAR	SZÓKÖZ
Reverse	**Visszafelé (f)**	spin box	léptetőmező
Revert...	**Visszahoz... (s)**	**Split**	**Feloszt (o)**
right aligned	jobbra zárt (j)	split	feloszt
RIGHT ARROW	JOBB-NYÍL	split bar	osztócsík
right scroll arrow	jobbra gördítő nyíl	split box	osztócsúszka
right window border	ablak jobb széle	StartUp	Automatikus indítás
ruler	vonalzó	status bar	állapotsor
Run...	**Futtat... (f)**	status-bar indicator	állapotjelző
Sample	Minta	submenu	almenü
Save	**Ment (m)**	switch	átvált
Save All	**Ment mindent (e)**	Switch to	Átvált
Save As...	**Ment új néven... (v)**	**Switch To...**	**Futó programok... (p)**
Save File as Type	Formátum (f)	SYS RQ	SYS RQ
scale	átméretez, beilleszt	TAB	TAB(ULÁTOR)
Scale menu	**Skála**	Terminal	Terminál
Scaling	Méret (m)	text box	itt: (adat)beviteli mező
scroll	gördít	text frame	szövegkeret
scroll arrow	gördítőnyíl	**Tile**	**Mozaik elrendezés (m)**
scroll bar	gördítősáv	tiled windows	mozaik elrendezésű ablakok
scroll box	gördítőcsúszka	**Time**	**Idő (i)**
SCROLL LOCK	SCROLL LOCK	title bar	címke
Scroll Lock on (SCRL)	SCRL	To	Záró oldal (z)
Search	Keres (k)	tool	eszköz
Search	Keres	toolbar	ikonmenü
Search...	**Keres... (e)**	toolbox	eszközkészlet
Search for Help on	**Témakör keresése (k)**	**Tools menu**	**Eszközök (e)**
Section...	**Szakasz... (s)**	top window border	ablak felső széle
Section (Sec)	Sz (szakasz)	**Tracks**	**Tételek (t)**
select	kiválaszt	**Tutorial**	**Tankönyv (k)**
select	kiválaszt, választ	type	begépel
select (check box, option button)	beikszel, jelöl (négyzetet); bekapcsol, választ (kapcsolót)	unavailable command	nem elérhető parancs
		underline	aláhúzás (a)
		Undo	**Visszavon (v)**
select (data)	kijelöl (egy adatot)	unfreeze	rögzítést felold

ENGLISH	HUNGARIAN	ENGLISH	HUNGARIAN
Unfreeze Panes	**Rögzítés feloldása (r)**	wildcard	helyettesítő
Unhide...	**Felfed... (f)**	window	ablak
Up	Fel (f)	window background	ablak háttere
UP ARROW	FEL-NYÍL	window border	ablak széle
up scroll arrow	felfelé gördítő nyíl	window corner	ablak sarka
Update	**Frissít (f)**	window frame	(ablak)keret
update	frissít	**Window menu**	**Ablak (a)**
Utilities menu	**Segédletek (g)**	window size	ablakméret
value set	értékkészlet	window title	ablak címe
vertical scroll bar	függőleges gördítősáv	Windows Setup	Windows Telepítő
vertical split bar	függőleges osztócsík	workspace	munkaterület
view	megmutat	Yes	Igen
View menu	**Nézet (n)**	**Zoom...**	**Nagyítás... (a)**
wallpaper	háttér	zoom in	közelít
warning message	figyelmeztetés	zoom out	távolít

CHAPTER 15

Italian

This chapter lists the Italian translations of all terms formatted in *italic* in Part 1. Terminology is listed in two ways: by category and in alphabetical order. The first section includes translations in the following categories: Window Elements, Menus, Dialog Boxes, Message Boxes, Other GUI Screen Elements, Keys, User Actions, and Applications For Microsoft Windows.

Terminology by Category

ENGLISH	ITALIAN	ENGLISH	ITALIAN
WINDOW ELEMENTS		window frame	cornice della finestra
Main window elements		window size	dimensioni della finestra
active window	finestra attiva	window title	titolo della finestra
application window	finestra dell'applicazione	workspace	area di lavoro
border	bordo		
bottom window border	bordo inferiore della finestra	**Window controls**	
cascading windows	finestre sovrapposte	Control-menu box	casella del menu di controllo
desktop	desktop	down scroll arrow	freccia di scorrimento Giù
document window	finestra del documento	horizontal scroll bar	barra di scorrimento
group window	finestra del gruppo		orizzontale
Help window	finestra della Guida	horizontal split bar	barra di divisione orizzontale
inactive window	finestra inattiva	left scroll arrow	freccia di scorrimento Sinistra
left window border	bordo sinistro della finestra	Maximize button	pulsante di ingrandimento
menu bar	barra dei menu	Minimize button	pulsante di riduzione a icona
pane	riquadro	Restore button	pulsante di ripristino
right window border	bordo destro della finestra	right scroll arrow	freccia di scorrimento Destra
ruler	righello	scroll arrow	freccia di scorrimento
status bar	barra di stato	scroll bar	barra di scorrimento
tiled windows	finestra affiancata	scroll box	casella di scorrimento
title bar	barra del titolo	split bar	barra di divisione
toolbar	barra degli strumenti	split box	casella di divisione
top window border	bordo superiore della finestra	up scroll arrow	freccia di scorrimento Su
wallpaper	sfondo	vertical scroll bar	barra di scorrimento verticale
window	finestra	vertical split bar	barra di divisione verticale
window background	sfondo della finestra		
window border	bordo della finestra		
window corner	angolo della finestra		

ENGLISH	ITALIAN	ENGLISH	ITALIAN
Pointers		Control menu	Menu di controllo
arrow	freccia	Restore	Ripristina (r)
arrow pointer	puntatore a freccia	Move	Sposta (s)
cross-hair pointer	mirino	Size	Ridimensiona (d)
hourglass pointer	clessidra	Minimize	Riduci a icona (i)
I-beam pointer	cursore	Maximize	Ingrandisci (n)
insertion point	punto di inserimento	Next	Successivo (u)
mouse pointer	puntatore del mouse	Close	Chiudi (c)
pointer	puntatore	Run...	Esegui... (e)
selection cursor	cursore di selezione	Switch To...	Passa a... (p)
		Split	Dividi (v)
Icons			
application icon	icona dell'applicazione	File menu	File (f)
directory icon	icona della directory	New...	Nuovo... (n)
disk icon	icona del disco	Open	Apri (a)
document file icon	icona del file del documento	Close	Chiudi (c)
document icon	icona del documento	Close All	Chiudi tutto (c)
drive icon	icona dell'unità disco	Save	Salva (s)
group icon	icona del gruppo	Save As...	Salva con nome... (v)
icon	icona	Save All	Salva tutto (t)
program-item icon	icona del programma	Delete	Elimina (l)
		Page Setup	Imposta pagina (p)
General terms		Print	Stampa (m)
access key	tasto di scelta	Print Preview	Anteprima di stampa (d)
check mark	segno di spunta	Printer Setup	Imposta stampante (i)
ellipsis	puntini di sospensione	Exit	Esci (e)
font	tipo di carattere	Exit and Return to	Esci e ritorna (r)
object	oggetto	Update	Aggiorna (g)
program group	gruppo di programmi		
program item	programma	Edit menu	Modifica (m)
shortcut key	tasto di scelta rapida	Undo	Annulla (a)
sizing handle	quadratino di ridimensionamento	Repeat	Ripeti (r)
		Cut	Taglia (g)
status-bar indicator	indicatore della barra di stato	Copy	Copia (p)
tool	strumento	Copy Special	Copia speciale (o)
unavailable command	comando non disponibile	Paste	Incolla (n)
		Paste Link	Incolla collegamento (m)
MENUS		Paste Special	Incolla speciale (s)
Menu elements		Clear	Cancella (c)
cascading menu	menu sovrapposto	Clear All	Cancella tutto (c)
checked command	comando spuntato	Find...	Trova... (t)
command	comando	Search...	Cerca... (e)
command separator	segno di separazione dei comandi	Replace...	Sostituisci... (u)
		Go To...	Vai a... (v)
drop-down menu	menu a discesa	Delete...	Elimina... (l)
menu	menu	Insert...	Inserisci... (i)
menu command	comando del menu	Object...	Oggetto... (o)
menu name	nome del menu	Insert Object...	Inserisci oggetto... (o)
selected command	comando selezionato		
submenu	sottomenu	Options menu	Opzioni (p)
		Preferences	Preferenze (p)
Menus and commands		Full Menus	Menu completi (m)
View menu	Visualizza (v)	Short Menus	Menu brevi (m)
Insert menu	Inserisci (i)		

ENGLISH	ITALIAN
Format menu	Formato (o)
Character...	Carattere... (c)
Paragraph...	Paragrafo... (p)
Section...	Sezione... (s)
Document...	Documento... (d)
Number...	Numero... (n)
Alignment...	Allineamento... (a)
Utilities menu	Varie (r)
Tools menu	Strumenti (s)
Customize	Personalizza (p)
Macro menu	Macro (a)
Record...	Registra... (r)
Run...	Esegui... (e)
Edit	Modifica (o)
Assign to Key	Assegna al tasto (t)
Assign to Menu	Assegna al menu (m)
Window menu	Finestra (n)
New Window	Nuova finestra (f)
Cascade	Sovrapponi (p)
Tile	Affianca (a)
Next Window	Finestra successiva (u)
Arrange All	Disponi tutto (d)
Hide	Nascondi (n)
Unhide...	Scopri... (s)
Split	Dividi (v)
Freeze Panes	Blocca riquadri (b)
Remove Split	Rimuovi divisione (v)
Unfreeze Panes	Sblocca riquadri (b)
Zoom...	Zoom... (z)
Help menu	?
Contents	Sommario (s)
How to use Help	Uso della Guida (u)
Search for Help on	Cerca argomento (c)
Active Window	Finestra attiva (f)
Keyboard	Tastiera (t)
Mouse	Mouse (m)
Tutorial	Esercitazione (e)
About	Informazioni su (i)
Device menu	Periferica (p)
Scale menu	Scala (s)
MIDI Sequencer...	MIDI Sequencer...
Sound...	Suono... (s)
Time	Tempo (t)
Tracks	Piste (p)
Effects menu	Effetti (e)
Revert...	Ripristina... (r)
Insert File...	Inserisci file... (i)
Mix with File...	Missaggio con file... (m)
Delete Before Current Position	Elimina prima della posizione corrente (l)

ENGLISH	ITALIAN
Delete After Current Position	Elimina dopo la posizione corrente (d)
Increase Volume (by 25%)	Alza il volume (25%) (a)
Decrease Volume	Abbassa il volume (b)
Increase Speed (by 100%)	Aumenta la velocità (100%) (v)
Decrease Speed	Diminuisci la velocità (d)
Add Echo	Eco (e)
Reverse	Riproduci al contrario (c)
Help application	
File menu	File (f)
Open	Apri (a)
Print Topic	Stampa argomento (s)
Print Setup...	Imposta stampante... (i)
Exit	Esci (e)
Edit menu	Modifica (m)
Copy...	Copia... (p)
Annotate...	Annota... (a)
Bookmark menu	Segnalibro (s)
Define...	Definisci... (d)
Help menu	?
How to use Help	Uso della Guida (u)
Always on Top	Sempre in primo piano (s)
About Help...	Informazioni su... (i)
Buttons	
Contents	Sommario (o)
Search	Cerca (e)
Back	Precedente (p)
History	Cronologia (c)
Glossary	Glossario (g)
DIALOG BOXES	
dialog box	finestra di dialogo
wildcard	carattere jolly
Dialog box elements	
button	pulsante
check box	casella di controllo
chevrons	virgolette acute
combo box	casella combinata
command button	pulsante di comando
dialog box title	nome della finestra di dialogo
drop-down combo box	casella combinata a discesa
drop-down list box	casella di riepilogo a discesa
Goto/Gosub button	pulsante di avanzamento
group box	casella di gruppo
label	etichetta
linked text and list box	casella di modifica e riepilogo collegata
list box	casella di riepilogo

ENGLISH	ITALIAN
option button	pulsante di opzione
progress indicator	indicatore di avanzamento
push button	pulsante di comando
radio button	pulsante di scelta
slider	dispositivo di scorrimento
slider indicator	indicatore di scorrimento
spin box	casella di selezione
text box	casella di testo
value set	insieme di valori

Dialog box buttons

Add	Aggiungi
Apply	Applica
Cancel	Annulla
Change	Cambia
Create	Crea
Default	Predefinito
Define	Definisci
Done	Chiudi
Go To	Vai a
Help	? (question mark)
More	Altro
No	No
OK	OK
Options	Opzioni
Quit	Esci
Redo	Ripeti
Reset	Reimposta
Resume	Riprendi
Retry	Riprova
Search	Cerca
Set	Imposta
Setup	Imposta
Switch to	Passa a
Yes	Sì

Dialog box labels

All	Tutto (t)
Collate copies	Fascicola copie (c)
Copies	Numero copie (n)
Direction	Direzione
Directories	Directory (d)
Down	Giù (g)
Drives	Unità (u)
File Name	Nome file (n)
Find Next	Trova successivo (r)
Find What	Trova (t)
Font	Tipo (t)
Font Style	Stile (i)
From	Da (d)
Landscape	Orizzontale (o)
List Files of Type	Tipo file (t)
Match Case	Maiuscole/minuscole (m)
Match Whole Word Only	Parola intera (p)
Orientation	Orientamento
Pages	Pagine (p)

ENGLISH	ITALIAN
Paper Size	Dimensioni foglio (d)
Portrait	Verticale (v)
Printer	Stampante
Print Quality	Qualità stampa (q)
Print Range	Intervallo di stampa
Print to File	Stampa su file (m)
Read Only	Sola lettura (l)
Replace All	Sostituisci tutto
Replace With	Sostituisci con (s)
Sample	Esempio (e)
Save File as Type	Tipo file (t)
Scaling	Proporzioni (z)
Selection	Selezione (s)
Size (font size)	Dimensione (d)
Source (paper)	Alimentazione (a)
To	A (a)
Up	Su (s)

MESSAGE BOXES

critical message	messaggio critico
message	messaggio
message box	finestra di messaggio
message line	barra dei messaggi
warning message	messaggio di avviso

OTHER GUI SCREEN ELEMENTS

Graphical options

gallery	modelli
palette	tavolozza (Paintbrush); pannello (strumenti)
text frame	cornice di testo
toolbox	casella degli strumenti

Status bar abbreviations

Caps Lock on (CAPS)	MA
Column (Col)	Col
Extend selection on (EXT)	EST
Line (Ln)	Ri
Macro Recorder on (REC)	REG
Num Lock on (NUM)	NUM
Overtype on (OVR)	SSC
Page (Pg)	Pg
Scroll Lock on (SCRL)	BS
Section (Sec)	Sez

Character formats

bold	grassetto (g)
double underline	sottolineato doppio (d)
italic	corsivo (c)
small capitals	maiuscoletto (m)
underline	sottolineato (s)

ENGLISH	ITALIAN	ENGLISH	ITALIAN
Paragraph formats		TAB	TAB
centered	centrato (a)	UP ARROW	freccia SU
justified	giustificato (f)		
left aligned	allineato a sinistra (t)	**USER ACTIONS**	
right aligned	allineato a destra (r)		
		Keyboard actions	
KEYS		enter	immettere
		press and hold down	premere e tenere premuto
Shortcut keys		type	digitare
CTRL+B (Bold)	CTRL+G		
CTRL+C (Copy)	CTRL+C	**Mouse actions**	
CTRL+D (Double underline)	CTRL+D	click	fare clic su
CTRL+E (Center)	CTL+A	double-click	fare doppio clic su
CTRL+I (Italics)	CTRL+I	drag	trascinare
CTRL+J (Justify)	CTRL+F	drag-and-drop	trascinare selezione
CTRL+L (Left align)	CTRL+T	drop	rilasciare
CTRL+R (Right align)	CTRL+R	point	puntare su
CTRL+U (Underline)	CTRL+S		
CTRL+V (Paste)	CTRL+V	**Manipulating window**	
CTRL+W (Word underline)	CTRL+P	**appearance**	
CTRL+X (Cut)	CTRL+X	arrange	disporre (finestre, icone)
CTRL+Z (Undo)	CTRL+Z	close	chiudere
DEL (Clear)	DEL	freeze	bloccare
		hide	nascondere
Keynames		move	spostare
(keypad) *	* (Tn)	resize	ridimensionare
(keypad) +	+ (Tn)	restore	ripristinare
(keypad) -	- (Tn)	select	selezionare
(keypad) /	/ (Tn)	size	ridimensionare
ALT	ALT	split	dividere
ALT GR	ALT GR	switch	passare a
BACKSPACE	BACKSPACE	unfreeze	sbloccare
BREAK	INTER		
CAPS LOCK	BLOC MAIUSC	**Selecting options or content**	
CTRL	CTRL	cancel	annullare
DEL	CANC	check	spuntare
DOWN ARROW	freccia GIÙ	choose	scegliere
END	FINE	clear (undo Select)	disattivare
ENTER	INVIO	extend selection	estendere la selezione
ENTER (keypad)	INVIO (Tn)	reduce selection	ridurre la selezione
ESC	ESC	select	selezionare
HOME	HOME	select (check box, option button)	attivare (casella di controllo);
INS	INS		scegliere (pulsante)
LEFT ARROW	freccia SINISTRA	select (data)	selezionare (dati)
NUM LOCK	BLOC NUM	select (drop-down menu)	scegliere (menu a discesa)
PAUSE	PAUSA	select (list box)	selezionare (casella di
PG DN	PGGIÙ		riepilogo)
PG UP	PGSU		
PRINT SCREEN	STAMP	**Viewing content**	
RIGHT ARROW	freccia DESTRA	autoscroll	scorrimento automatico
SCROLL LOCK	BLOC SCORR	browse	sfogliare
SHIFT	MAIUSC	collapse	comprimere
SPACEBAR	BARRA SPAZIATRICE	expand	espandere
SYS RQ	RSIST		

ENGLISH	ITALIAN	ENGLISH	ITALIAN
scroll	scorrere/far scorrere	OLE application	applicazione OLE
view	visualizzare	package	package
zoom in	zoom avanti	paste	incollare
zoom out	zoom indietro	scale	cambiare proporzioni
		size	ridimensionare
Removing content		source application	applicazione di origine
clear	cancellare	source document	documento di origine
copy	copiare	update	aggiornare
cut	tagliare		
delete	eliminare	**APPLICATIONS FOR**	
paste	incollare	**MICROSOFT WINDOWS**	
		Accessories	Accessori
Manipulating objects		Applications	Applicazioni
arrange	disporre (finestre, icone)	Calculator	Calcolatrice
automatic link	collegamento automatico	Calendar	Agenda
Clipboard	Clipboard	Cardfile	Schedario
container application	applicazione client	Character Map	Mappa caratteri
container document	documento client	Clipboard Viewer	Visualizzatore Appunti
copy	copiare	Clock	Orologio
crop	ritagliare	Control Panel	Pannello di controllo
destination application	applicazione di destinazione	File Manager	File Manager
destination document	documento di destinazione	Games	Giochi
drag-and-drop	trascinare selezione	Main	Principale
embed	incorporare	Media Player	Lettore multimediale
embedded object	oggetto incorporato	MS-DOS Prompt	Prompt di MS-DOS
group	raggruppare	Notepad	Blocco note
link	collegare	Object Packager	Packager
linked object	oggetto collegato	PIF Editor	PIF Editor
main application	applicazione principale	Print Manager	Print Manager
main document	documento principale	Program Manager	Program Manager
manual link	collegamento manuale	Recorder	Registratore
object	oggetto	Sound Recorder	Registratore di suoni
object linking & embedding (OLE)	collegamento ed incorporamento di oggetti (OLE)	StartUp	Avvio
		Terminal	Terminale
OLE (object linking & embedding)	OLE (collegamento ed incorporamento di oggetti, object linking and embedding)	Windows Setup	Setup di Windows

Terminology by Alphabet

Notes:
1. All terms formatted in **bold** refer to menu names or command names.
2. All characters between parentheses are preferred access keys.

ENGLISH	ITALIAN	ENGLISH	ITALIAN
(keypad) *	* (Tn)	CAPS LOCK	BLOC MAIUSC
(keypad) +	+ (Tn)	Caps Lock on (CAPS)	MA
(keypad) -	- (Tn)	Cardfile	Schedario
(keypad) /	/ (Tn)	**Cascade**	**Sovrapponi (p)**
About	**Informazioni su (i)**	cascading menu	menu sovrapposto
About Help...	**Informazioni su... (i)**	cascading windows	finestre sovrapposte
access key	tasto di scelta	centered	centrato (a)
Accessories	Accessori	Change	Cambia
active window	finestra attiva	**Character...**	**Carattere... (c)**
Active Window	**Finestra attiva (f)**	Character Map	Mappa caratteri
Add	Aggiungi	check	spuntare
Add Echo	**Eco (e)**	check box	casella di controllo
Alignment...	**Allineamento... (a)**	checked command	comando spuntato
All	Tutto (t)	check mark	segno di spunta
ALT	ALT	chevrons	virgolette acute
ALT GR	ALT GR	choose	scegliere
Always on Top	**Sempre in primo piano (s)**	**Clear**	**Cancella (c)**
		clear	cancellare
Annotate...	**Annota... (a)**	**Clear All**	**Cancella tutto (c)**
application icon	icona dell'applicazione	clear (undo Select)	disattivare
Applications	Applicazioni	click	fare clic su
application window	finestra dell'applicazione	Clipboard	Clipboard
Apply	Applica	Clipboard Viewer	Visualizzatore Appunti
arrange	disporre (finestre, icone)	Clock	Orologio
Arrange All	**Disponi tutto (d)**	**Close**	**Chiudi (c)**
arrow	freccia	close	chiudere
arrow pointer	puntatore a freccia	**Close All**	**Chiudi tutto (c)**
Assign to Key	**Assegna al tasto (t)**	collapse	comprimere
Assign to Menu	**Assegna al menu (m)**	Collate copies	Fascicola copie (c)
automatic link	collegamento automatico	Column (Col)	Col
autoscroll	scorrimento automatico	combo box	casella combinata
Back	Precedente (p)	command	comando
BACKSPACE	BACKSPACE	command button	pulsante di comando
bold	grassetto (g)	command separator	segno di separazione dei comandi
Bookmark menu	**Segnalibro (s)**		
border	bordo	container application	applicazione client
bottom window border	bordo inferiore della finestra	container document	documento client
		Contents	**Sommario (s)**
BREAK	INTER	Contents	Sommario (o)
browse	sfogliare	**Control menu**	**Menu di controllo**
button	pulsante	Control-menu box	casella del menu di controllo
Calculator	Calcolatrice	Control Panel	Pannello di controllo
Calendar	Agenda	Copies	Numero copie (n)
Cancel	Annulla	**Copy**	**Copia (p)**
cancel	annullare	copy	copiare

ENGLISH	ITALIAN	ENGLISH	ITALIAN
Copy...	**Copia... (p)**	down scroll arrow	freccia di scorrimento Giù
Copy Special	**Copia speciale (o)**	drag	trascinare
Create	Crea	drag-and-drop	trascinare selezione
critical message	messaggio critico	drive icon	icona dell'unità disco
crop	ritagliare	Drives	Unità (u)
cross-hair pointer	mirino	drop	rilasciare
CTRL	CTRL	drop-down combo box	casella combinata a
CTRL+B (Bold)	CTRL+G		discesa
CTRL+C (Copy)	CTRL+C	drop-down list box	casella di riepilogo a
CTRL+D (Double underline)	CTRL+D		discesa
CTRL+E (Center)	CTL+A	drop-down menu	menu a discesa
CTRL+I (Italics)	CTRL+I	**Edit**	**Modifica (o)**
CTRL+J (Justify)	CTRL+F	**Edit menu**	**Modifica (m)**
CTRL+L (Left align)	CTRL+T	**Effects menu**	**Effetti (e)**
CTRL+R (Right align)	CTRL+R	ellipsis	puntini di sospensione
CTRL+U (Underline)	CTRL+S	embed	incorporare
CTRL+V (Paste)	CTRL+V	embedded object	oggetto incorporato
CTRL+W (Word underline)	CTRL+P	END	FINE
CTRL+X (Cut)	CTRL+X	ENTER	INVIO
CTRL+Z (Undo)	CTRL+Z	enter	immettere
Customize	**Personalizza (p)**	ENTER (keypad)	INVIO (Tn)
Cut	**Taglia (g)**	ESC	ESC
cut	tagliare	**Exit**	**Esci (e)**
Decrease Speed	**Diminuisci la velocità (d)**	**Exit and Return to**	**Esci e ritorna (r)**
Decrease Volume	**Abbassa il volume (b)**	expand	espandere
Default	Predefinito	extend selection	estendere la selezione
Define	Definisci	Extend selection on (EXT)	EST
Define...	**Definisci... (d)**	File Manager	File Manager
DEL	CANC	**File menu**	**File (f)**
DEL (Clear)	DEL	File Name	Nome file (n)
Delete	**Elimina (l)**	**Find...**	**Trova... (t)**
delete	eliminare	Find Next	Trova successivo (r)
Delete...	**Elimina... (l)**	Find What	Trova (t)
Delete After Current Position	**Elimina dopo la**	font	tipo di carattere
	posizione corrente (d)	Font	Tipo (t)
Delete Before Current Position	**Elimina prima della**	Font Style	Stile (i)
	posizione corrente (l)	**Format menu**	**Formato (o)**
desktop	desktop	freeze	bloccare
destination application	applicazione di destinazione	**Freeze Panes**	**Blocca riquadri (b)**
destination document	documento di destinazione	From	Da (d)
Device menu	**Periferica (p)**	**Full Menus**	**Menu completi (m)**
dialog box	finestra di dialogo	gallery	modelli
dialog box title	nome della finestra di dialogo	Games	Giochi
Direction	Direzione	Glossary	Glossario (g)
Directories	Directory (d)	Go To	Vai a
directory icon	icona della directory	**Go To...**	**Vai a... (v)**
disk icon	icona del disco	Goto/Gosub button	pulsante di avanzamento
Document...	**Documento... (d)**	group	raggruppare
document file icon	icona del file del documento	group box	casella di gruppo
document icon	icona del documento	group icon	icona del gruppo
document window	finestra del documento	group window	finestra del gruppo
Done	Chiudi	Help	? (question mark)
double-click	fare doppio clic su	**Help menu**	**?**
double underline	sottolineato doppio (d)	Help window	finestra della Guida
Down	Giù (g)	**Hide**	**Nascondi (n)**
DOWN ARROW	freccia GIÙ	hide	nascondere

ENGLISH	ITALIAN	ENGLISH	ITALIAN
History	Cronologia (c)	Minimize	Riduci a icona (i)
HOME	HOME	Minimize button	pulsante di riduzione a
horizontal scroll bar	barra di scorrimento		icona
	orizzontale	Mix with File...	Missaggio con file... (m)
horizontal split bar	barra di divisione orizzontale	More	Altro
hourglass pointer	clessidra	Mouse	Mouse (m)
How to use Help	Uso della Guida (u)	mouse pointer	puntatore del mouse
I-beam pointer	cursore	Move	Sposta (s)
icon	icona	move	spostare
inactive window	finestra inattiva	MS-DOS Prompt	Prompt di MS-DOS
Increase Speed (by 100%)	Aumenta la velocità	New...	Nuovo... (n)
	(100%) (v)	New Window	Nuova finestra (f)
Increase Volume (by 25%)	Alza il volume (25%) (a)	Next	Successivo (u)
INS	INS	Next Window	Finestra successiva (u)
Insert...	Inserisci... (i)	No	No
Insert File...	Inserisci file... (i)	Notepad	Blocco note
insertion point	punto di inserimento	Number...	Numero... (n)
Insert menu	Inserisci (i)	NUM LOCK	BLOC NUM
Insert Object...	Inserisci oggetto... (o)	Num Lock on (NUM)	NUM
italic	corsivo (c)	object	oggetto
justified	giustificato (f)	Object...	Oggetto... (o)
Keyboard	Tastiera (t)	object linking & embedding	collegamento ed
label	etichetta	(OLE)	incorporamento di oggetti
Landscape	Orizzontale (o)		(OLE)
left aligned	allineato a sinistra (t)	Object Packager	Packager
LEFT ARROW	freccia SINISTRA	OK	OK
left scroll arrow	freccia di scorrimento	OLE application	applicazione OLE
	Sinistra	OLE (object linking &	OLE (collegamento ed
left window border	bordo sinistro della finestra	embedding)	incorporamento di oggetti,
Line (Ln)	Ri		object linking and
link	collegare		embedding)
linked object	oggetto collegato	Open	Apri (a)
linked text and list box	casella di modifica e	option button	pulsante di opzione
	riepilogo collegata	Options	Opzioni
list box	casella di riepilogo	Options menu	Opzioni (p)
List Files of Type	Tipo file (t)	Orientation	Orientamento
Macro menu	Macro (a)	Overtype on (OVR)	SSC
Macro Recorder on (REC)	REG	package	package
Main	Principale		
main application	applicazione principale	Page (Pg)	Pg
main document	documento principale	Pages	Pagine (p)
manual link	collegamento manuale	Page Setup	Imposta pagina (p)
Match Case	Maiuscole/minuscole (m)	palette	tavolozza (Paintbrush);
Match Whole Word Only	Parola intera (p)		pannello (strumenti)
Maximize	Ingrandisci (n)	pane	riquadro
Maximize button	pulsante di ingrandimento	Paper Size	Dimensioni foglio (d)
Media Player	Lettore multimediale	Paragraph...	Paragrafo... (p)
menu	menu	Paste	Incolla (n)
menu bar	barra dei menu	paste	incollare
menu command	comando del menu	Paste Link	Incolla collegamento (m)
menu name	nome del menu	Paste Special	Incolla speciale (s)
message	messaggio	PAUSE	PAUSA
message box	finestra di messaggio	PG DN	PGGIÙ
message line	barra dei messaggi	PG UP	PGSU
MIDI Sequencer...	MIDI Sequencer...		

ENGLISH	ITALIAN	ENGLISH	ITALIAN
PIF Editor	PIF Editor	**Scale menu**	**Scala (s)**
point	puntare su	Scaling	Proporzioni (z)
pointer	puntatore	scroll	scorrere/far scorrere
Portrait	Verticale (v)	scroll arrow	freccia di scorrimento
Preferences	**Preferenze (p)**	scroll bar	barra di scorrimento
press and hold down	premere e tenere premuto	scroll box	casella di scorrimento
Print	**Stampa (m)**	SCROLL LOCK	BLOC SCORR
Printer	Stampante	Scroll Lock on (SCRL)	BS
Printer Setup	**Imposta stampante (i)**	Search	Cerca (e)
Print Manager	Print Manager	Search	Cerca
Print Preview	**Anteprima di stampa (d)**	**Search...**	**Cerca... (e)**
Print Quality	Qualità stampa (q)	**Search for Help on**	**Cerca argomento (c)**
Print Range	Intervallo di stampa	**Section...**	**Sezione... (s)**
PRINT SCREEN	STAMP	Section (Sec)	Sez
Print Setup...	**Imposta stampante... (i)**	select	selezionare
Print to File	Stampa su file (m)	select (check box, option button)	attivare (casella di controllo);
Print Topic	**Stampa argomento (s)**		scegliere (pulsante)
program group	gruppo di programmi	select (data)	selezionare (dati)
program item	programma	select (drop-down menu)	scegliere (menu a discesa)
program-item icon	icona del programma	selected command	comando selezionato
Program Manager	Program Manager	Selection	Selezione (s)
progress indicator	indicatore di avanzamento	selection cursor	cursore di selezione
push button	pulsante di comando	select (list box)	selezionare (casella di
Quit	Esci		riepilogo)
radio button	pulsante di scelta	Set	Imposta
Read Only	Sola lettura (l)	Setup	Imposta
Record...	**Registra... (r)**	SHIFT	MAIUSC
Recorder	Registratore	shortcut key	tasto di scelta rapida
Redo	Ripeti	**Short Menus**	**Menu brevi (m)**
reduce selection	ridurre la selezione	**Size**	**Ridimensiona (d)**
Remove Split	**Rimuovi divisione (v)**	size	ridimensionare
Repeat	**Ripeti (r)**	Size (font size)	Dimensione (d)
Replace...	**Sostituisci... (u)**	sizing handle	quadratino di
Replace All	Sostituisci tutto		ridimensionamento
Replace With	Sostituisci con (s)	slider	dispositivo di scorrimento
Reset	Reimposta	slider indicator	indicatore di scorrimento
resize	ridimensionare	small capitals	maiuscoletto (m)
Restore	**Ripristina (r)**	**Sound...**	**Suono... (s)**
restore	ripristinare	Sound Recorder	Registratore di suoni
Restore button	pulsante di ripristino	source application	applicazione di origine
Resume	Riprendi	source document	documento di origine
Retry	Riprova	Source (paper)	Alimentazione (a)
Reverse	**Riproduci al contrario (c)**	SPACEBAR	BARRA SPAZIATRICE
Revert...	**Ripristina... (r)**	spin box	casella di selezione
right aligned	allineato a destra (r)	**Split**	**Dividi (v)**
RIGHT ARROW	freccia DESTRA	split	dividere
right scroll arrow	freccia di scorrimento Destra	split bar	barra di divisione
right window border	bordo destro della finestra	split box	casella di divisione
ruler	righello	StartUp	Avvio
Run...	**Esegui... (e)**	status bar	barra di stato
Sample	Esempio (e)	status-bar indicator	indicatore della barra
Save	**Salva (s)**		di stato
Save All	**Salva tutto (t)**	submenu	sottomenu
Save As...	**Salva con nome... (v)**	switch	passare a
Save File as Type	Tipo file (t)	Switch to	Passa a
scale	cambiare proporzioni	**Switch To...**	**Passa a... (p)**

ENGLISH	ITALIAN	ENGLISH	ITALIAN
SYS RQ	RSIST	**Update**	**Aggiorna (g)**
TAB	TAB	update	aggiornare
Terminal	Terminale	up scroll arrow	freccia di scorrimento Su
text box	casella di testo	**Utilities menu**	**Varie (r)**
text frame	cornice di testo	value set	insieme di valori
Tile	**Affianca (a)**	vertical scroll bar	barra di scorrimento verticale
tiled windows	finestra affiancata	vertical split bar	barra di divisione verticale
Time	**Tempo (t)**	view	visualizzare
title bar	barra del titolo	**View menu**	**Visualizza (v)**
To	A (a)	wallpaper	sfondo
tool	strumento	warning message	messaggio di avviso
toolbar	barra degli strumenti	wildcard	carattere jolly
toolbox	casella degli strumenti	window	finestra
Tools menu	**Strumenti (s)**	window background	sfondo della finestra
top window border	bordo superiore della finestra	window border	bordo della finestra
Tracks	**Piste (p)**	window corner	angolo della finestra
Tutorial	**Esercitazione (e)**	window frame	cornice della finestra
type	digitare	**Window menu**	**Finestra (n)**
unavailable command	comando non disponibile	window size	dimensioni della finestra
underline	sottolineato (s)	window title	titolo della finestra
Undo	**Annulla (a)**	Windows Setup	Setup di Windows
unfreeze	sbloccare	workspace	area di lavoro
Unfreeze Panes	**Sblocca riquadri (b)**	Yes	Sì
Unhide...	**Scopri... (s)**	**Zoom...**	**Zoom... (z)**
Up	Su (s)	zoom in	zoom avanti
UP ARROW	freccia SU	zoom out	zoom indietro

CHAPTER 16

Norwegian

This chapter lists the Norwegian translations of all terms formatted in *italic* in Part 1. Terminology is listed in two ways: by category and in alphabetical order. The first section includes translations in the following categories: Window Elements, Menus, Dialog Boxes, Message Boxes, Other GUI Screen Elements, Keys, User Actions, and Applications For Microsoft Windows.

Terminology by Category

ENGLISH	NORWEGIAN	ENGLISH	NORWEGIAN
WINDOW ELEMENTS		window corner	vindushjørne
Main window elements		window frame	vindusramme
active window	aktivt vindu	window size	vindusstørrelse
application window	programvindu	window title	vindustittel
border	ramme	workspace	arbeidsområde
bottom window border	nedre vindusramme		
cascading windows	overlappende vinduer	**Window controls**	
desktop	skrivebord	Control-menu box	systemmenyboks
document window	dokumentvindu	down scroll arrow	rullepil ned
group window	gruppevindu	horizontal scroll bar	vannrett rullefelt
Help window	hjelpevindu	horizontal split bar	vannrett delelinje
inactive window	passivt vindu	left scroll arrow	rullepil venstre
left window border	venstre vindusramme	Maximize button	maksimeringsknapp
menu bar	menylinje	Minimize button	minimeringsknapp
pane	rute	Restore button	gjenopprettingsknapp
right window border	høyre vindusramme	right scroll arrow	rullepil høyre
ruler	linjal	scroll arrow	rullepil
status bar	statuslinje	scroll bar	rullefelt
tiled windows	vinduer side ved side	scroll box	rulleboks
title bar	tittellinje	split bar	delelinje
toolbar	verktøylinje	split box	deleboks
top window border	øvre vindusramme	up scroll arrow	rullepil opp
wallpaper	bakgrunn	vertical scroll bar	loddrett rullefelt
window	vindu	vertical split bar	loddrett delelinje
window background	vindusbakgrunn		
window border	vindusramme		

ENGLISH	NORWEGIAN	ENGLISH	NORWEGIAN
Pointers		Move	Flytt (f)
arrow	pil	Size	Endre størrelse (e)
arrow pointer	pilkryss	Minimize	Minimer (m)
cross-hair pointer	tråkors	Maximize	Maksimer (a)
hourglass pointer	timeglass	Next	Neste (n)
I-beam pointer	tekstmarkør	Close	Lukk (l)
insertion point	innsettingspunkt	Run...	Kjør... (k)
mouse pointer	muspeker	Switch To...	Bytt til... (b)
pointer	peker	Split	Del (d)
selection cursor	markør		
		File menu	Fil (f)
Icons		New...	Ny... (n)
application icon	programikon	Open	Åpne (p)
directory icon	katalogikon	Close	Lukk (l)
disk icon	diskikon	Close All	Lukk alle (l)
document file icon	dokumentfilikon	Save	Lagre (g)
document icon	dokumentikon	Save As...	Lagre som... (s)
drive icon	stasjonsikon	Save All	Lagre alle (g)
group icon	gruppeikon	Delete	Slett (e)
icon	ikon	Page Setup	Utskriftsformat (i)
program-item icon	programobjektikon	Print	Skriv ut (u)
		Print Preview	Forhåndsvisning (v)
General terms		Printer Setup	Skriveroppsett (o)
access key	hurtigtast	Exit	Avslutt (a)
check mark	hake	Exit and Return to	Avslutt og gå tilbake (v)
ellipsis	ellipse	Update	Oppdater (o)
font	skrift		
object	objekt	Edit menu	Rediger (r)
program group	programgruppe	Undo	Angre (a)
program item	programobjekt	Repeat	Gjenta (g)
shortcut key	snarvei/(hurtig om taster)	Cut	Klipp ut (u)
sizing handle	skaleringshåndtak	Copy	Kopier (k)
status-bar indicator	statusindikator	Copy Special	Kopier utvalg (o)
tool	verktøy	Paste	Lim inn (l)
unavailable command	utilgjengelig kommando	Paste Link	Lim inn kobling (i)
		Paste Special	Lim inn utvalg (t)
MENUS		Clear	Fjern (f)
Menu elements		Clear All	Fjern alle (f)
cascading menu	overlappende meny	Find...	Finn... (i)
checked command	valgt kommando	Search...	Søk... (s)
command	kommando	Replace...	Erstatt...(r)
command separator	menyskillelinje	Go To...	Gå til... (å)
drop-down menu	rullegardinmeny	Delete...	Slett... (e)
menu	meny	Insert...	Sett inn... (n)
menu command	menykommando	Object...	Objekt... (k)
menu name	menynavn	Insert Object...	Sett inn objekt... (o)
selected command	uthevet kommando		
submenu	undermeny	Options menu	Alternativer (a)
		Preferences	Innstillinger (i)
Menus and commands		Full Menus	Fullstendige menyer (m)
View menu	Vis (v)	Short Menus	Korte menyer (m)
Insert menu	Sett inn (i)		
		Format menu	Format (o)
Control menu	Systemmeny	Character...	Tegn... (t)
Restore	Gjenopprett (g)	Paragraph...	Avsnitt... (a)

ENGLISH	NORWEGIAN
Section...	Inndeling... (d)
Document...	Dokument... (d)
Number...	Tall... (l)
Alignment...	Justering... (j)
Utilities menu	Tilbehør (t)
Tools menu	Verktøy (e)
Customize	Tilpass (t)
Macro menu	Makro (m)
Record...	Registrer... (r)
Run...	Kjør... (k)
Edit	Rediger (d)
Assign to Key	Tilordne tast (t)
Assign to Menu	Tilordne meny (m)
Window menu	Vindu (n)
New Window	Nytt vindu (n)
Cascade	Overlappet/overlappe (l)
Tile	Side ved side (v)
Next Window	Neste vindu (e)
Arrange All	Ordne alle (o)
Hide	Skjul (s)
Unhide...	Ta frem... (t)
Split	Del (d)
Freeze Panes	Frys (f)
Remove Split	Fjern vindusdeling (d)
Unfreeze Panes	Frigi (f)
Zoom...	Zoom... (z)
Help menu	Hjelp (h)
Contents	Innhold (i)
How to use Help	Hvordan bruke Hjelp (h)
Search for Help on	Søk etter hjelp om (s)
Active Window	Aktivt vindu (a)
Keyboard	Tastatur (t)
Mouse	Mus (m)
Tutorial	Opplæring (p)
About	Om (o)
Device menu	Enhet (e)
Scale menu	Skala (s)
MIDI Sequencer...	MIDI Sequencer...
Sound...	Lyd... (l)
Time	Tid (t)
Tracks	Spor (s)
Effects menu	Effekter (e)
Revert...	Gjenopprett... (j)
Insert File...	Sett inn fil... (i)
Mix with File...	Slå sammen med fil... (s)
Delete Before Current Position	Slett før gjeldende posisjon (l)
Delete After Current Position	Slett etter gjeldende posisjon (e)
Increase Volume (by 25%)	Høyere volum (25 %) (h)
Decrease Volume	Lavere volum (l)

ENGLISH	NORWEGIAN
Increase Speed (by 100%)	Høyere hastighet (100 %) (a)
Decrease Speed	Lavere hastighet (s)
Add Echo	Legg til ekko (e)
Reverse	Snu (n)
Help application	
File menu	Fil (f)
Open	Åpne (p)
Print Topic	Skriv ut emne (u)
Print Setup...	Skriveroppsett... (o)
Exit	Avslutt (a)
Edit menu	Rediger (r)
Copy...	Kopier... (k)
Annotate...	Merknad... (a)
Bookmark menu	Bokmerke (o)
Define...	Definer... (d)
Help menu	Hjelp (h)
How to use Help	Hvordan bruke Hjelp (h)
Always on Top	Alltid øverst (a)
About Help...	Om... (o)
Buttons	
Contents	Innhold (i)
Search	Søk (s)
Back	Tilbake (t)
History	Logg (l)
Glossary	Ordliste (o)
DIALOG BOXES	
dialog box	dialogboks
wildcard	jokertegn
Dialog box elements	
button	knapp
check box	avkrysningsboks
chevrons	«-tegn
combo box	kombinasjonsboks
command button	kommandoknapp
dialog box title	dialogbokstittel
drop-down combo box	kombinasjonsboks
drop-down list box	rullegardinliste
Goto/Gosub button	dialogknapp
group box	gruppeboks
label	etikett
linked text and list box	koblet redigerings- og listeboks
list box	listeboks
option button	alternativknapp
progress indicator	fremgangsindikator
push button	trykk-knapp
radio button	alternativknapp
slider	glidebryterpanel
slider indicator	glidebryter

ENGLISH	NORWEGIAN
spin box	verdisettingsboks
text box	tekstboks
value set	verdisett

Dialog box buttons

ENGLISH	NORWEGIAN
Add	Legg til
Apply	Bruk
Cancel	Avbryt
Change	Endre
Create	Lag
Default	Standard
Define	Definer
Done	Utført
Go To	Gå til
Help	Hjelp
More	Mer
No	Nei
OK	OK
Options	Alternativer
Quit	Avslutt
Redo	Gjenta
Reset	Tilbakestill
Resume	Fortsett
Retry	Prøv igjen
Search	Søk
Set	Sett/Aktiver/Still/Angi
Setup	Oppsett
Switch to	Bytt til
Yes	Ja

Dialog box labels

ENGLISH	NORWEGIAN
All	Alt (a)
Collate copies	Sorter kopier (r)
Copies	Kopier (k)
Direction	Retning
Directories	Kataloger (k)
Down	Ned (n)
Drives	Stasjoner (s)
File Name	Filnavn (f)
Find Next	Søk etter neste (e)
Find What	Søk etter (s)
Font	Skrift (s)
Font Style	Skriftstil (k)
From	Fra (f)
Landscape	Liggende (l)
List Files of Type	Liste over filtypen (l)
Match Case	Skill mellom store/små bokstaver (b)
Match Whole Word Only	Bare hele ord (h)
Orientation	Retning
Pages	Sider (s)
Paper Size	Størrelse (r)
Portrait	Stående (t)
Printer	Skriver
Print Quality	Utskriftskvalitet (u)
Print Range	Utskriftsområde

ENGLISH	NORWEGIAN
Print to File	Skriv til fil (v)
Read Only	Skrivebeskyttet (v)
Replace All	Erstatt alle
Replace With	Erstatt med (e)
Sample	Eksempel
Save File as Type	Lagre som filtypen (l)
Scaling	Skalering (r)
Selection	Merket område (o)
Size (font size)	Størrelse (r)
Source (paper)	Kilde (k)
To	Til (t)
Up	Opp (o)

MESSAGE BOXES

ENGLISH	NORWEGIAN
critical message	kritisk situasjon
message	informasjonsmelding
message box	meldingsboks
message line	meldingslinje
warning message	advarsel

OTHER GUI SCREEN ELEMENTS

Graphical options

ENGLISH	NORWEGIAN
gallery	galleri
palette	palett
text frame	tekstramme
toolbox	verktøykasse

Status bar abbreviations

ENGLISH	NORWEGIAN
Caps Lock on (CAPS)	CAPS
Column (Col)	Kol
Extend selection on (EXT)	UTV
Line (Ln)	Li
Macro Recorder on (REC)	REG
Num Lock on (NUM)	NUM
Overtype on (OVR)	OVER
Page (Pg)	Si
Scroll Lock on (SCRL)	SCRL
Section (Sec)	Innd

Character formats

ENGLISH	NORWEGIAN
bold	fet (f)
double underline	dobbel understreking (d)
italic	kursiv (k)
small capitals	kapitéler (e)
underline	understreking (u)

Paragraph formats

ENGLISH	NORWEGIAN
centered	midtstilt (m)
justified	blokkjustert (b)
left aligned	venstrejustert (v)
right aligned	høyrejustert (h)

ENGLISH	NORWEGIAN	ENGLISH	NORWEGIAN
KEYS		**Mouse actions**	
Shortcut keys		click	klikke
CTRL+B (Bold)	CTRL+F	double-click	dobbeltklikke
CTRL+C (Copy)	CTRL+C	drag	dra
CTRL+D (Double underline)	CTRL+D	drag-and-drop	dra og slippe
CTRL+E (Center)	CTRL+E	drop	slippe
CTRL+I (Italics)	CTRL+K	point	peke på
CTRL+J (Justify)	CTRL+J		
CTRL+L (Left align)	CTRL+L	**Manipulating window**	
CTRL+R (Right align)	CTRL+R	**appearance**	
CTRL+U (Underline)	CTRL+U	arrange	ordne
CTRL+V (Paste)	CTRL+V	close	lukke
CTRL+W (Word underline)	CTRL+W	freeze	fryse
CTRL+X (Cut)	CTRL+X	hide	skjule
CTRL+Z (Undo)	CTRL+Z	move	flytte
DEL (Clear)	DEL	resize	endre størrelse
		restore	gjenopprette
Keynames		select	merke
(keypad) *	NUM *	size	endre størrelse
(keypad) +	NUM PLUSS	split	dele
(keypad) -	NUM MINUS	switch	bytte
(keypad) /	NUM /	unfreeze	frigi
ALT	ALT		
ALT GR	ALT GR	**Selecting options or content**	
BACKSPACE	TILBAKE	cancel	avbryte
BREAK	BREAK	check	krysse av
CAPS LOCK	CAPS LOCK	choose	velge
CTRL	CTRL	clear (undo Select)	oppheve valg
DEL	DEL	extend selection	utvide merking
DOWN ARROW	PIL NED	reduce selection	krympe merking
END	END	select	merke
ENTER	ENTER	select (check box, option button)	markere (avkrysningsboks,
ENTER (keypad)	NUM ENTER		alternativknapp)
ESC	ESC	select (data)	merke (data)
HOME	HOME	select (drop-down menu)	velge (rullegardinmeny)
INS	INS	select (list box)	merke (liste)
LEFT ARROW	PIL VENSTRE		
NUM LOCK	NUM LOCK	**Viewing content**	
PAUSE	PAUSE	autoscroll	automatisk rulling
PG DN	PGDN	browse	bla gjennom
PG UP	PGUP	collapse	fjerne/undertrykke
PRINT SCREEN	PRINTSCRN	expand	vise/utvide
RIGHT ARROW	PIL HØYRE	scroll	rulle
SCROLL LOCK	SCROLL LOCK	view	vise
SHIFT	SKIFT	zoom in	zoome inn
SPACEBAR	MELLOMROM	zoom out	zoome ut
SYS RQ	SYS RQ		
TAB	TAB	**Removing content**	
UP ARROW	PIL OPP	clear	fjerne
		copy	kopiere
USER ACTIONS		cut	klippe ut
Keyboard actions		delete	slette
enter	skrive inn	paste	lime inn
press and hold down	trykke og holde nede		
type	skrive		

ENGLISH	NORWEGIAN
Manipulating objects	
arrange	ordne
automatic link	automatisk kobling
Clipboard	Utklippstavle
container application	klientprogram
container document	klientdokument
copy	kopiere
crop	beskjære
destination application	målprogram
destination document	måldokument
drag-and-drop	dra og slippe
embed	innebygge
embedded object	innebygd objekt
group	gruppere
link	koble
linked object	koblet objekt
main application	hovedprogram
main document	hoveddokument
manual link	manuell kobling
object	objekt
object linking & embedding (OLE)	objektkobling og innebygging (OLE)
OLE (object linking & embedding)	OLE (Object Linking & Embedding)
OLE application	OLE-program
package	pakke
paste	lime inn
scale	skala/skalere
size	endre størrelse
source application	kildeprogram

ENGLISH	NORWEGIAN
source document	kildedokument
update	oppdatere
APPLICATIONS FOR MICROSOFT WINDOWS	
Accessories	Tilbehør
Applications	Programmer
Calculator	Kalkulator
Calendar	Kalender
Cardfile	Kartotek
Character Map	Tegnkart
Clipboard Viewer	Utklippstavle
Clock	Klokke
Control Panel	Kontrollpanel
File Manager	Filbehandling
Games	Spill
Main	Hovedgruppe
Media Player	Mediaavspilling
MS-DOS Prompt	MS-DOS-ledetekst
Notepad	Notisblokk
Object Packager	Objektinnpakking
PIF Editor	PIF-redigering
Print Manager	Utskriftsbehandling
Program Manager	Programbehandling
Recorder	Innspilling
Sound Recorder	Lydinnspilling
StartUp	Oppstart
Terminal	Terminal
Windows Setup	Installere Windows

Terminology by Alphabet

Notes:
1. All terms formatted in **bold** refer to menu names or command names.
2. All characters between parentheses are preferred access keys.

ENGLISH	NORWEGIAN	ENGLISH	NORWEGIAN
(keypad) *	NUM *	Cardfile	Kartotek
(keypad) +	NUM PLUSS	**Cascade**	**Overlappet/overlappe (l)**
(keypad) -	NUM MINUS	cascading menu	overlappende meny
(keypad) /	NUM /	cascading windows	overlappende vinduer
About	**Om (o)**	centered	midtstilt (m)
About Help...	**Om... (o)**	Change	Endre
access key	hurtigtast	**Character...**	**Tegn... (t)**
Accessories	Tilbehør	Character Map	Tegnkart
active window	aktivt vindu	check	krysse av
Active Window	**Aktivt vindu (a)**	check box	avkrysningsboks
Add	Legg til	check mark	hake
Add Echo	**Legg til ekko (e)**	checked command	valgt kommando
Alignment...	**Justering... (j)**	chevrons	«-tegn
All	Alt (a)	choose	velge
ALT	ALT	clear	fjerne
ALT GR	ALT GR	clear (undo Select)	oppheve valg
Always on Top	**Alltid øverst (a)**	**Clear**	**Fjern (f)**
Annotate...	**Merknad... (a)**	**Clear All**	**Fjern alle (f)**
application icon	programikon	click	klikke
application window	programvindu	Clipboard	Utklippstavle
Applications	Programmer	Clipboard Viewer	Utklippstavle
Apply	Bruk	Clock	Klokke
arrange	ordne	**Close**	**Lukk (l)**
Arrange All	**Ordne alle (o)**	close	lukke
arrow	pil	**Close All**	**Lukk alle (l)**
arrow pointer	pilkryss	collapse	fjerne/undertrykke
Assign to Key	**Tilordne tast (t)**	Collate copies	Sorter kopier (r)
Assign to Menu	**Tilordne meny (m)**	Column (Col)	Kol
automatic link	automatisk kobling	combo box	kombinasjonsboks
autoscroll	automatisk rulling	command	kommando
Back	Tilbake (t)	command button	kommandoknapp
BACKSPACE	TILBAKE	command separator	menyskillelinje
bold	fet (f)	container application	klientprogram
Bookmark menu	**Bokmerke (o)**	container document	klientdokument
border	ramme	**Contents**	**Innhold (i)**
bottom window border	nedre vindusramme	Contents	Innhold (i)
BREAK	BREAK	**Control menu**	**Systemmeny**
browse	bla gjennom	Control-menu box	systemmenyboks
button	knapp	Control Panel	Kontrollpanel
Calculator	Kalkulator	Copies	Kopier (k)
Calendar	Kalender	copy	kopiere
Cancel	Avbryt	**Copy**	**Kopier (k)**
cancel	avbryte	**Copy...**	**Kopier... (k)**
CAPS LOCK	CAPS LOCK	**Copy Special**	**Kopier utvalg (o)**
Caps Lock on (CAPS)	CAPS	Create	Lag

ENGLISH	NORWEGIAN	ENGLISH	NORWEGIAN
critical message	kritisk situasjon	drive icon	stasjonsikon
crop	beskjære	Drives	Stasjoner (s)
cross-hair pointer	tråkors	drop	slippe
CTRL	CTRL	drop-down combo box	kombinasjonsboks
CTRL+B (Bold)	CTRL+F	drop-down list box	rullegardinliste
CTRL+C (Copy)	CTRL+C	drop-down menu	rullegardinmeny
CTRL+D (Double underline)	CTRL+D	**Edit**	**Rediger (d)**
CTRL+E (Center)	CTRL+E	**Edit menu**	**Rediger (r)**
CTRL+I (Italics)	CTRL+K	**Effects menu**	**Effekter (e)**
CTRL+J (Justify)	CTRL+J	ellipsis	ellipse
CTRL+L (Left align)	CTRL+L	embed	innebygge
CTRL+R (Right align)	CTRL+R	embedded object	innebygd objekt
CTRL+U (Underline)	CTRL+U	END	END
CTRL+V (Paste)	CTRL+V	ENTER	ENTER
CTRL+W (Word underline)	CTRL+W	enter	skrive inn
CTRL+X (Cut)	CTRL+X	ENTER (keypad)	NUM ENTER
CTRL+Z (Undo)	CTRL+Z	ESC	ESC
Customize	**Tilpass (t)**	**Exit**	**Avslutt (a)**
Cut	**Klipp ut (u)**	**Exit and Return to**	**Avslutt og gå tilbake (v)**
cut	klippe ut	expand	vise/utvide
Decrease Speed	**Lavere hastighet (s)**	extend selection	utvide merking
Decrease Volume	**Lavere volum (l)**	Extend selection on (EXT)	UTV
Default	Standard	File Manager	Filbehandling
Define	Definer	**File menu**	**Fil (f)**
Define...	**Definer... (d)**	File Name	Filnavn (f)
DEL	DEL	**Find...**	**Finn... (i)**
DEL (Clear)	DEL	Find Next	Søk etter neste (e)
Delete	**Slett (e)**	Find What	Søk etter (s)
Delete...	**Slett... (e)**	font	skrift
delete	slette	Font	Skrift (s)
Delete After Current Position	**Slett etter gjeldende posisjon (e)**	Font Style	Skriftstil (k)
Delete Before Current Position	**Slett før gjeldende posisjon (l)**	**Format menu**	**Format (o)**
		freeze	fryse
desktop	skrivebord	**Freeze Panes**	**Frys (f)**
destination application	målprogram	From	Fra (f)
destination document	måldokument	**Full Menus**	**Fullstendige menyer (m)**
Device menu	**Enhet (e)**	gallery	galleri
dialog box	dialogboks	Games	Spill
dialog box title	dialogbokstittel	Glossary	Ordliste (o)
Direction	Retning	Go To	Gå til
Directories	Kataloger (k)	**Go To...**	**Gå til... (å)**
directory icon	katalogikon	Goto/Gosub button	dialogknapp
disk icon	diskikon	group	gruppere
Document...	**Dokument... (d)**	group box	gruppeboks
document file icon	dokumentfilikon	group icon	gruppeikon
document icon	dokumentikon	group window	gruppevindu
document window	dokumentvindu	Help	Hjelp
Done	Utført	**Help menu**	**Hjelp (h)**
double-click	dobbeltklikke	Help window	hjelpevindu
double underline	dobbel understreking (d)	**Hide**	**Skjul (s)**
Down	Ned (n)	hide	skjule
DOWN ARROW	PIL NED	History	Logg (l)
down scroll arrow	rullepil ned	HOME	HOME
drag	dra	horizontal scroll bar	vannrett rullefelt
drag-and-drop	dra og slippe	horizontal split bar	vannrett delelinje
		hourglass pointer	timeglass

ENGLISH	NORWEGIAN	ENGLISH	NORWEGIAN
How to use Help	**Hvordan bruke Hjelp (h)**	**New...**	**Ny... (n)**
I-beam pointer	tekstmarkør	**New Window**	**Nytt vindu (n)**
icon	ikon	**Next**	**Neste (n)**
inactive window	passivt vindu	**Next Window**	**Neste vindu (e)**
Increase Speed (by 100%)	**Høyere hastighet (100 %) (a)**	No	Nei
Increase Volume (by 25%)	**Høyere volum (25 %) (h)**	Notepad	Notisblokk
INS	INS	**Number...**	**Tall... (l)**
Insert...	**Sett inn... (n)**	NUM LOCK	NUM LOCK
Insert File...	**Sett inn fil... (i)**	Num Lock on (NUM)	NUM
insertion point	innsettingspunkt	object	objekt
Insert menu	**Sett inn (i)**	**Object...**	**Objekt... (k)**
Insert Object...	**Sett inn objekt... (o)**	object linking & embedding (OLE)	objektkobling og innebygging (OLE)
italic	kursiv (k)	Object Packager	Objektinnpakking
justified	blokkjustert (b)	OK	OK
Keyboard	**Tastatur (t)**	OLE application	OLE-program
label	etikett	OLE (object linking & embedding)	OLE (Object Linking & Embedding)
Landscape	Liggende (l)	**Open**	**Åpne (p)**
left aligned	venstrejustert (v)	option button	alternativknapp
LEFT ARROW	PIL VENSTRE	Options	Alternativer
left scroll arrow	rullepil venstre	**Options menu**	**Alternativer (a)**
left window border	venstre vindusramme	Orientation	Retning
Line (Ln)	Li	Overtype on (OVR)	OVER
link	koble	package	pakke
linked object	koblet objekt	Page (Pg)	Si
linked text and list box	koblet redigerings- og listeboks	Pages	Sider (s)
list box	listeboks	**Page Setup**	**Utskriftsformat (i)**
List Files of Type	Liste over filtypen (l)	palette	palett
Macro	**Makro (m)**	pane	rute
Macro Recorder on (REC)	REG	Paper Size	Størrelse (r)
Main	Hovedgruppe	**Paragraph...**	**Avsnitt... (a)**
main application	hovedprogram	**Paste**	**Lim inn (l)**
main document	hoveddokument	paste	lime inn
manual link	manuell kobling	**Paste Link**	**Lim inn kobling (i)**
Match Case	Skill mellom store/små bokstaver (b)	**Paste Special**	**Lim inn utvalg (t)**
Match Whole Word Only	Bare hele ord (h)	PAUSE	PAUSE
Maximize	**Maksimer (a)**	PG DN	PGDN
Maximize button	maksimeringsknapp	PG UP	PGUP
Media Player	Mediaavspilling	PIF Editor	PIF-redigering
menu	meny	point	peke på
menu bar	menylinje	pointer	peker
menu command	menykommando	Portrait	Stående (t)
menu name	menynavn	**Preferences**	**Innstillinger (i)**
message	informasjonsmelding	press and hold down	trykke og holde nede
message box	meldingsboks	**Print**	**Skriv ut (u)**
message line	meldingslinje	Printer	Skriver
MIDI Sequencer...	**MIDI Sequencer...**	**Printer Setup**	**Skriveroppsett (o)**
Minimize	**Minimer (m)**	Print Manager	Utskriftsbehandling
Minimize button	minimeringsknapp	**Print Preview**	**Forhåndsvisning (v)**
Mix with File...	**Slå sammen med fil... (s)**	Print Quality	Utskriftskvalitet (u)
More	Mer	Print Range	Utskriftsområde
Mouse	**Mus (m)**	PRINT SCREEN	PRINTSCRN
mouse pointer	muspeker	**Print Setup...**	**Skriveroppsett... (o)**
Move	**Flytt (f)**	Print to File	Skriv til fil (v)
move	flytte	**Print Topic**	**Skriv ut emne (u)**
MS-DOS Prompt	MS-DOS-ledetekst		

ENGLISH	NORWEGIAN	ENGLISH	NORWEGIAN
program group	programgruppe	select (data)	merke (data)
program item	programobjekt	select (drop-down menu)	velge (rullegardinmeny)
program-item icon	programobjektikon	selected command	uthevet kommando
Program Manager	Programbehandling	Selection	Merket område (o)
progress indicator	fremgangsindikator	selection cursor	markør
push button	trykk-knapp	select (list box)	merke (liste)
Quit	Avslutt	Set	Sett/Aktiver/Still/Angi
radio button	alternativknapp	Setup	Oppsett
Read Only	Skrivebeskyttet (v)	SHIFT	SKIFT
Record...	**Registrer... (r)**	shortcut key	snarvei/(hurtig om taster)
Recorder	Innspilling	**Short Menus**	**Korte menyer (m)**
Redo	Gjenta	**Size**	**Endre størrelse (e)**
reduce selection	krympe merking	size	endre størrelse
Remove Split	**Fjern vindusdeling (d)**	Size (font size)	Størrelse (r)
Repeat	**Gjenta (g)**	sizing handle	skaleringshåndtak
Replace...	**Erstatt...(r)**	slider	glidebryterpanel
Replace All	Erstatt alle	slider indicator	glidebryter
Replace With	Erstatt med (e)	small capitals	kapitéler (e)
Reset	Tilbakestill	**Sound...**	**Lyd... (l)**
resize	endre størrelse	Sound Recorder	Lydinnspilling
Restore	**Gjenopprett (g)**	source application	kildeprogram
restore	gjenopprette	source document	kildedokument
Restore button	gjenopprettingsknapp	Source (paper)	Kilde (k)
Resume	Fortsett	SPACEBAR	MELLOMROM
Retry	Prøv igjen	spin box	verdisettingsboks
Reverse	**Snu (n)**	**Split**	**Del (d)**
Revert...	**Gjenopprett... (j)**	split	dele
right aligned	høyrejustert (h)	split bar	delelinje
RIGHT ARROW	PIL HØYRE	split box	deleboks
right scroll arrow	rullepil høyre	StartUp	Oppstart
right window border	høyre vindusramme	status bar	statuslinje
ruler	linjal	status-bar indicator	statusindikator
Run...	**Kjør... (k)**	submenu	undermeny
Sample	Eksempel	switch	bytte
Save	**Lagre (g)**	Switch to	Bytt til
Save All	**Lagre alle (g)**	**Switch To...**	**Bytt til... (b)**
Save As...	**Lagre som... (s)**	SYS RQ	SYS RQ
Save File as Type	Lagre som filtypen (l)	TAB	TAB
scale	skala/skalere	Terminal	Terminal
Scale menu	**Skala (s)**	text box	tekstboks
Scaling	Skalering (r)	text frame	tekstramme
scroll	rulle	**Tile**	**Side ved side (v)**
scroll arrow	rullepil	tiled windows	vinduer side ved side
scroll bar	rullefelt	**Time**	**Tid (t)**
scroll box	rulleboks	title bar	tittellinje
SCROLL LOCK	SCROLL LOCK	To	Til (t)
Scroll Lock on (SCRL)	SCRL	tool	verktøy
Search	Søk (s)	toolbar	verktøylinje
Search	Søk	toolbox	verktøykasse
Search...	**Søk... (s)**	**Tools menu**	**Verktøy (e)**
Search for Help on	**Søk etter hjelp om (s)**	top window border	øvre vindusramme
Section...	**Inndeling... (d)**	**Tracks**	**Spor (s)**
Section (Sec)	Innd	**Tutorial**	**Opplæring (p)**
select	merke	type	skrive
select (check box, option button)	markere (avkrysningsboks, alternativknapp)	unavailable command	utilgjengelig kommando
		underline	understreking (u)

ENGLISH	NORWEGIAN	ENGLISH	NORWEGIAN
Undo	**Angre (a)**	warning message	advarsel
unfreeze	frigi	wildcard	jokertegn
Unfreeze Panes	**Frigi (f)**	window	vindu
Unhide...	**Ta frem... (t)**	window background	vindusbakgrunn
Up	Opp (o)	window border	vindusramme
UP ARROW	PIL OPP	window corner	vindushjørne
up scroll arrow	rullepil opp	window frame	vindusramme
Update	**Oppdater (o)**	**Window menu**	**Vindu (n)**
update	oppdatere	window size	vindusstørrelse ⸰
Utilities menu	**Tilbehør (t)**	Windows Setup	Installere Windows
value set	verdisett	window title	vindustittel
vertical scroll bar	loddrett rullefelt	workspace	arbeidsområde
vertical split bar	loddrett delelinje	Yes	Ja
view	vise	**Zoom...**	**Zoom... (z)**
View menu	**Vis (v)**	zoom in	zoome inn
wallpaper	bakgrunn	zoom out	zoome ut

C H A P T E R   1 7

Polish

This chapter lists the Polish translations of all terms formatted in *italic* in Part 1. Terminology is listed in two ways: by category and in alphabetical order. The first section includes translations in the following categories: Window Elements, Menus, Dialog Boxes, Message Boxes, Other GUI Screen Elements, Keys, User Actions, and Applications For Microsoft Windows.

Terminology by Category

ENGLISH	POLISH	ENGLISH	POLISH
WINDOW ELEMENTS			
Main window elements			
active window	okno aktywne	window frame	ramka okna
application window	okno aplikacji	window size	rozmiar okna
border	krawędź	window title	tytuł okna
bottom window border	dolna krawędź okna	workspace	obszar roboczy
cascading windows	kaskada okien		
desktop	pulpit	**Window controls**	
document window	okno dokumentu	Control-menu box	pole menu sterowania
group window	okno grupy	down scroll arrow	strzałka przewijania w dół
Help window	okno pomocy	horizontal scroll bar	pasek przewijania poziomego
inactive window	okno nieaktywne	horizontal split bar	linia podziału poziomego
left window border	lewa krawędź okna	left scroll arrow	strzałka przewijania w lewo
menu bar	pasek menu	Maximize button	przycisk "Pełny ekran"
pane	okienko	Minimize button	przycisk "Do ikony"
right window border	prawa krawędź okna	Restore button	przycisk przywracający
ruler	linijka		poprzedni rozmiar
status bar	pasek stanu	right scroll arrow	strzałka przewijania w prawo
tiled windows	okna sąsiadujące	scroll arrow	strzałka przewijania
title bar	pasek tytułu	scroll bar	pasek przewijania
toolbar	pasek narzędzi	scroll box	suwak przewijania
top window border	górna krawędź okna	split bar	linia podziału
wallpaper	tapeta	split box	pole podziału
window	okno	up scroll arrow	strzałka przewijania w górę
window background	tło okna	vertical scroll bar	pasek przewijania pionowego
window border	krawędź okna	vertical split bar	linia podziału pionowego
window corner	róg okna		

ENGLISH	POLISH	ENGLISH	POLISH
Pointers		Minimize	Do ikony (i)
arrow	strzałka	Maximize	Pełny ekran (e)
arrow pointer	strzałka	Next	Następne (n)
cross-hair pointer	celownik	Close	Zamknij (z)
hourglass pointer	klepsydra	Run...	Uruchom... (u)
I-beam pointer	kursor tekstowy	Switch to...	Przełącz na... (c)
insertion point	punkt wstawiania	Split	Podziel (d)
mouse pointer	wskaźnik myszy		
pointer	wskaźnik	File menu	Plik (p)
selection cursor	kursor wyboru	New...	Nowy... (n)
		Open	Otwórz (o)
Icons		Close	Zamknij (z)
application icon	ikona aplikacji	Close All	Zamknij wszystkie (a)
directory icon	ikona katalogu	Save	Zachowaj (h)
disk icon	ikona dysku	Save As...	Zachowaj jako... (j)
document file icon	ikona dokumentu	Save All	Zachowaj wszystkie (w)
document icon	ikona dokumentu	Delete	Usuń (u)
drive icon	ikona stacji dysków	Page Setup	Układ strony (s)
group icon	ikona grupy	Print	Drukuj (d)
icon	ikona	Print Preview	Podgląd wydruku (g)
program-item icon	ikona elementu grupy	Printer Setup	Ustawienie drukarki (t)
		Exit	Koniec (k)
General terms		Exit and Return to	Koniec i powrót do (k)
access key	klawisz szybkiego dostępu	Update	Aktualizuj (a)
check mark	znacznik		
ellipsis	wielokropek (...)	Edit menu	Edycja (e)
font	czcionka	Undo	Cofnij (c)
object	obiekt	Repeat	Powtórz (p)
program group	grupa (programów)	Cut	Wytnij (n)
program item	element grupy	Copy	Kopiuj (k)
shortcut key	klawisz skrótu	Copy Special	Kopiuj wybiórczo (o)
sizing handle	uchwyt zmiany rozmiaru	Paste	Wklej (w)
status-bar indicator	wskaźnik paska stanu	Paste Link	Wklej połączenie (e)
tool	narzędzie	Paste Special	Wklej wybiórczo (l)
unavailable command	polecenie niedostępne	Clear	Wyczyść (y)
		Clear All	Wyczyść wszystko (t)
MENUS		Find...	Znajdź... (z)
Menu elements		Search...	Szukaj... (u)
cascading menu	menu kaskadowe	Replace...	Zamień... (a)
checked command	polecenie wybrane	Go To...	Idź do... (i)
command	polecenie	Delete...	Usuń... (u)
command separator	separator poleceń	Insert...	Wstaw... (s)
drop-down menu	menu rozwijane	Object...	Obiekt... (o)
menu	menu	Insert Object...	Wstaw obiekt... (s)
menu command	polecenie menu		
menu name	nazwa menu	Options menu	Opcje (o)
selected command	polecenie wybrane	Preferences	Preferencje (r)
submenu	podmenu	Full Menus	Pełne menu (p)
		Short Menus	Skrócone menu (s)
Menus and commands			
View menu	Widok (w)	Format menu	Format (f)
Insert menu	Wstaw (s)	Character...	Znak... (z)
		Paragraph...	Akapit... (a)
Control menu	Menu sterowania	Section...	Sekcja... (s)
Restore	Przywróć (p)	Document...	Dokument... (d)
Move	Przesuń (s)	Number...	Liczba... (l)
Size	Rozmiar (r)	Alignment...	Wyrównanie... (w)

ENGLISH	POLISH	ENGLISH	POLISH
Utilities menu	Narzędzia (n)	Print Topic	Drukuj (d)
Tools menu	Narzędzia (n)	Print Setup...	Ustawienie drukarki... (u)
Customize	Dopasuj (d)	Exit	Koniec pomocy (k)
Macro menu	Makro (m)	Edit menu	Edycja (e)
Record...	Nagraj... (n)	Copy...	Kopiuj... (k)
Run...	Uruchom... (u)	Annotate...	Skomentuj... (s)
Edit	Modyfikuj (o)		
Assign to Key	Przypisz do klawisza (p)	Bookmark menu	Zakładka (z)
Assign to Menu	Przypisz do menu (r)	Define...	Załóż... (a)
Window menu	Okno (k)	Help menu	Pomoc (c)
New Window	Nowe okno (n)	How to use Help	Korzystanie z (k)
Cascade	Kaskada (a)	Always on Top	Zawsze na wierzchu (z)
Tile	Sąsiadująco (s)	About Help...	O Pomocy... (o)
Next Window	Następne okno (t)		
Arrange All	Uporządkuj (p)	**Buttons**	
Hide	Ukryj (u)	Contents	Spis treści (t)
Unhide...	Odkryj... (o)	Search	Szukaj (s)
Split	Podziel (d)	Back	Wstecz (w)
Freeze Panes	Zablokuj (z)	History	Historia (h)
Remove Split	Usuń podział (i)	Glossary	Słowniczek (o)
Unfreeze Panes	Odblokuj (b)		
Zoom...	Powiększ... (w)	**DIALOG BOXES**	
		dialog box	pole dialogu
Help menu	Pomoc (c)	wildcard	wieloznacznik
Contents	Spis treści (t)		
How to use Help	Korzystanie z (k)	**Dialog box elements**	
Search for Help on	Pomoc na temat (p)	button	przycisk
Active Window	Aktywne okno (a)	check box	pole wyboru, kratka
Keyboard	Klawiatura (l)	chevrons	znak >>
Mouse	Mysz (m)	combo box	lista rozwijana z możliwością
Tutorial	Samouczek (u)		edycji
About	O (o)	command button	przycisk polecenia
		dialog box title	tytuł pola dialogu
Device menu	Urządzenie (u)	drop-down combo box	lista rozwijana z możliwością
Scale menu	Skala (s)		edycji
MIDI Sequencer...	Sekwenser MIDI...	drop-down list box	lista rozwijana
Sound...	Dźwięk...	Goto/Gosub button	idź do
Time	Czas (c)	group box	pole grupy
Tracks	Ścieżki (i)	label	etykieta
		linked text and list box	pole powiązanej listy i edycji
Effects menu	Efekty (f)	list box	pole listy
Revert...	Przywróć... (p)	option button	przycisk opcji
Insert File...	Wstaw plik... (w)	progress indicator	wskaźnik zaawansowania
Mix with File...	Miksuj z plikiem... (i)	push button	przycisk
Delete Before Current Position	Skasuj do bieżącej pozycji (d)	radio button	przycisk radiowy
Delete After Current Position	Skasuj od bieżącej pozycji (o)	slider	suwak
Increase Volume (by 25%)	Głośniej (o 25 %) (g)	slider indicator	wskaźnik suwakowy
Decrease Volume	Ciszej (c)	spin box	pole pokrętła
Increase Speed (by 100%)	Szybciej (o 100 %) (s)	text box	pole tekstu
Decrease Speed	Wolniej (w)	value set	zbiór wartości
Add Echo	Dodaj echo (d)		
Reverse	Wstecz (t)	**Dialog box buttons**	
		Add	Dodaj
Help application		Apply	Użyj
File menu	Plik (p)		
Open	Otwórz (o)		

ENGLISH	POLISH
Cancel	Anuluj
Change	Zmień
Create	Utwórz
Default	Domyślny
Define	Zdefiniuj
Done	Gotowe
Go To	Idź do
Help	Pomoc
More	Więcej
No	Nie
OK	OK
Options	Opcje
Quit	Porzuć
Redo	Powtórz
Reset	Przywróć
Resume	Wznów
Retry	Ponów próbę
Search	Szukaj
Set	Ustaw
Setup	Ustawienie
Switch to	Przełącz do
Yes	Tak

Dialog box labels

All	Wszystko (w)
Collate Copies	Sortuj kopie (k)
Copies	Liczba (l)
Direction	Kierunek
Directories	Katalogi (k)
Down	W dół (d)
Drives	Stacje dysków (s)
File Name	Nazwa pliku (n)
Find Next	Znajdź następny (n)
Find What	Znajdź (z)
Font	Czcionka (z)
Font Style	Styl (czcionki) (s)
From	Od (o)
Landscape	W poziomie (z)
List Files of Type	Wyświetl pliki typu (w)
Match Case	Uwzględnij wielkość liter (u)
Match Whole Word Only	Uwzględnij tylko całe wyrazy (t)
Orientation	Orientacja
Pages	Strony (s)
Paper Size	Rozmiar papieru (r)
Portrait	W pionie (i)
Printer	Drukarka
Print Quality	Jakość wydruku (j)
Print Range	Zakres wydruku
Print to File	Drukuj do pliku (d)
Read Only	Tylko do odczytu (t)
Replace All	Zamień wszystkie (w)
Replace With	Zamień na (a)
Sample	Przykład
Save File as Type	Zachowaj plik w formacie (z)
Scaling	Skalowanie
Selection	Wybór (b)
Size (font size)	Rozmiar (czcionki) (r)

ENGLISH	POLISH
Source (paper)	Podajnik (papieru) (p)
To	Do (d)
Up	W górę (w)

MESSAGE BOXES

critical message	ostrzeżenie alarmowe
message	komunikat
message box	pole komunikatu
message line	wiersz komunikatu
warning message	ostrzeżenie

OTHER GUI SCREEN ELEMENTS

Graphical options

gallery	galeria
palette	paleta
text frame	ramka tekstu
toolbox	zestaw narzędzi

Status bar abbreviations

Caps Lock on (CAPS)	WER
Column (Col)	kol
Extend selection on (EXT)	WYB
Line (Ln)	wrs
Macro Recorder on (REC)	MAK
Num Lock on (NUM)	NUM
Overtype on (OVR)	NAD
Page (Pg)	str
Scroll Lock on (SCRL)	SUW
Section (Sec)	sek

Character formats

bold	pogrubiony (g)
double underline	podwójne podkreślenie (d)
italic	kursywa (k)
small capitals	kapitaliki (a)
underline	podkreślenie (p)

Paragraph formats

centered	wyśrodkowany (y)
justified	wyjustowany (j)
left aligned	wyrównany do lewej (l)
right aligned	wyrównany do prawej (r)

KEYS

Shortcut keys

CTRL+B (Bold)	CTRL+B
CTRL+C (Copy)	CTRL+C
CTRL+D (Double underline)	CTRL+D
CTRL+E (Center)	CTRL+E
CTRL+I (Italics)	CTRL+I
CTRL+J (Justify)	CTRL+J
CTRL+L (Left align)	CTRL+L
CTRL+R (Right align)	CTRL+R

ENGLISH	POLISH	ENGLISH	POLISH
		Manipulating window appearance	
CTRL+U (Underline)	CTRL+U	arrange	rozmieścić
CTRL+V (Paste)	CTRL+V	close	zamknąć
CTRL+W (Word underline)	CTRL+W	freeze	zablokować
CTRL+X (Cut)	CTRL+X	hide	ukryć
CTRL+Z (Undo)	CTRL+Z	move	przesunąć
DEL (Clear)	DEL	resize	zmienić rozmiar
		restore	przywrócić
Keynames		select	wybrać
(keypad) *	SZARA*	size	zmienić rozmiar
(keypad) +	SZARY+	split	podzielić
(keypad) -	SZARY -	switch	przełączyć
(keypad) /	SZARY/	unfreeze	odblokować
ALT	ALT		
ALT GR	ALT GR	**Selecting options or content**	
BACKSPACE	BACKSPACE	cancel	anulować
BREAK	BREAK	check	zaznaczyć
CAPS LOCK	CAPS LOCK	choose	wybrać
CTRL	CTRL	clear (undo Select)	usunąć znacznik
DEL	DEL	extend selection	rozszerzyć wybór
DOWN ARROW	strzałka w dół	reduce selection	ograniczyć wybór
END	END	select	wybrać, zaznaczyć
ENTER	ENTER	select (check box, option button)	wybrać
ENTER (keypad)	SZARY ENTER	select (data)	zaznaczyć
ESC	ESC	select (drop-down menu)	otworzyć
HOME	HOME	select (list box)	otworzyć
INS	INS		
LEFT ARROW	strzałka w lewo	**Viewing content**	
NUM LOCK	NUM LOCK	autoscroll	przewijać automatycznie
PAUSE	PAUSE	browse	przeglądać
PG DN	PG DN	collapse	zwinąć
PG UP	PG UP	expand	rozwinąć
PRINT SCREEN	PRINT SCREEN	scroll	przewinąć
RIGHT ARROW	strzałka w prawo	view	obejrzeć
SCROLL LOCK	SCROLL LOCK	zoom in	powiększyć
SHIFT	SHIFT	zoom out	pomniejszyć
SPACEBAR	SPACJA		
SYS RQ	SYS RQ	**Removing content**	
TAB	TAB	clear	wyczyścić
UP ARROW	strzałka w górę	copy	kopiować
		cut	wyciąć
USER ACTIONS		delete	usunąć
		paste	wkleić
Keyboard actions			
enter	wprowadzić	**Manipulating objects**	
press and hold down	przytrzymać naciśnięty	arrange	rozmieścić
type	wpisać	automatic link	połączenie automatyczne
		Clipboard	Schowek
Mouse actions		container application	aplikacja zawierająca
click	kliknąć	container document	dokument zawierający
double-click	kliknąć dwukrotnie	copy	kopiować
drag	ciągnąć, przemieścić	crop	przyciąć
drag-and-drop	przemieścić i upuścić	destination application	aplikacja docelowa
drop	upuścić	destination document	dokument docelowy
point	wskazać	drag-and-drop	przemieścić i upuścić

ENGLISH	POLISH
embed	osadzić
embedded object	obiekt osadzony
group	grupa
link	połączyć
linked object	obiekt połączony
main application	aplikacja główna
main document	dokument główny
manual link	połączenie ręczne
object	obiekt
object linking & embedding (OLE)	Łączenie i osadzanie obiektów (OLE)
OLE (object linking & embedding)	Łączenie i osadzanie obiektów (OLE)
OLE application	aplikacja OLE
package	pakiet
paste	wkleić
scale	zmienić rozmiar
size	zmienić rozmiar
source application	aplikacja źródłowa
source document	dokument źródłowy
update	aktualizować

APPLICATIONS FOR MICROSOFT WINDOWS

Accessories	Akcesoria
Applications	Aplikacje

ENGLISH	POLISH
Calculator	Kalkulator
Calendar	Kalendarz
Cardfile	Kartoteka
Character Map	Tablica znaków
Clipboard Viewer	Schowek
Clock	Zegar
Control Panel	Panel sterowania
File Manager	Menedżer plików
Games	Gry
Main	Grupa główna
Media Player	Media
MS-DOS Prompt	MS-DOS
Notepad	Notatnik
Object Packager	Pakowarka
PIF Editor	Edytor PIF
Print Manager	Menedżer wydruku
Program Manager	Menedżer programów
Recorder	Rejestrator
Sound Recorder	Rejestrator dźwięku
StartUp	Autostart
Terminal	Terminal
Windows Setup	Program instalacyjny Windows

Terminology by Alphabet

Notes:

1. All terms formatted in **bold** refer to menu names or command names.
2. All characters between parentheses are preferred access keys.

ENGLISH	POLISH	ENGLISH	POLISH
(keypad) *	SZARA*	**Cascade**	**Kaskada (a)**
(keypad) +	SZARY+	cascading menu	menu kaskadowe
(keypad) -	SZARY -	cascading windows	kaskada okien
(keypad) /	SZARY/	centered	wyśrodkowany (y)
About	**O (o)**	Change	Zmień
About Help...	**O Pomocy... (o)**	**Character...**	**Znak... (z)**
access key	klawisz szybkiego dostępu	Character Map	Tablica znaków
Accessories	Akcesoria	check	zaznaczyć
active window	okno aktywne	check box	pole wyboru, kratka
Active Window	**Aktywne okno (a)**	check mark	znacznik
Add	Dodaj	checked command	polecenie wybrane
Add Echo	**Dodaj echo (d)**	chevrons	znak >>
Alignment...	**Wyrównanie... (w)**	choose	wybrać
All	Wszystko (w)	**Clear**	**Wyczyść (y)**
ALT	ALT	clear	wyczyścić
ALT GR	ALT GR	**Clear All**	**Wyczyść wszystko (t)**
Always on Top	**Zawsze na wierzchu (z)**	clear (undo Select)	usunąć znacznik
Annotate...	**Skomentuj... (s)**	click	kliknąć
application icon	ikona aplikacji	Clipboard	Schowek
application window	okno aplikacji	Clipboard Viewer	Schowek
Applications	Aplikacje	Clock	Zegar
Apply	Użyj	**Close**	**Zamknij (z)**
arrange	rozmieścić	close	zamknąć
Arrange All	**Uporządkuj (p)**	**Close All**	**Zamknij wszystkie (a)**
arrow	strzałka	collapse	zwinąć
arrow pointer	strzałka	Collate Copies	Sortuj kopie (k)
Assign to Key	**Przypisz do klawisza (p)**	Column (Col)	kol
Assign to Menu	**Przypisz do menu (r)**	combo box	lista rozwijana z możliwością
automatic link	połączenie automatyczne		edycji
autoscroll	przewijać automatycznie	command	polecenie
Back	Wstecz (w)	command button	przycisk polecenia
BACKSPACE	BACKSPACE	command separator	separator poleceń
bold	pogrubiony (g)	container application	aplikacja zawierająca
Bookmark menu	**Zakładka (z)**	container document	dokument zawierający
border	krawędź	**Contents**	**Spis treści (t)**
bottom window border	dolna krawędź okna	Contents	Spis treści (t)
BREAK	BREAK	**Control menu**	**Menu sterowania**
browse	przeglądać	Control-menu box	pole menu sterowania
button	przycisk	Control Panel	Panel sterowania
Calculator	Kalkulator	Copies	Liczba (l)
Calendar	Kalendarz	**Copy**	**Kopiuj (k)**
Cancel	Anuluj	copy	kopiować
cancel	anulować	**Copy...**	**Kopiuj... (k)**
CAPS LOCK	CAPS LOCK	**Copy Special**	**Kopiuj wybiórczo (o)**
Caps Lock on (CAPS)	WER	Create	Utwórz
Cardfile	Kartoteka	critical message	ostrzeżenie alarmowe

ENGLISH	POLISH	ENGLISH	POLISH
crop	przyciąć	drop-down combo box	lista rozwijana z możliwością edycji
cross-hair pointer	celownik	drop-down list box	lista rozwijana
CTRL	CTRL	drop-down menu	menu rozwijane
CTRL+B (Bold)	CTRL+B	**Edit**	**Modyfikuj (o)**
CTRL+C (Copy)	CTRL+C	**Edit menu**	**Edycja (e)**
CTRL+D (Double underline)	CTRL+D	**Effects menu**	**Efekty (f)**
CTRL+E (Center)	CTRL+E	ellipsis	wielokropek (...)
CTRL+I (Italics)	CTRL+I	embed	osadzić
CTRL+J (Justify)	CTRL+J	embedded object	obiekt osadzony
CTRL+L (Left align)	CTRL+L	END	END
CTRL+R (Right align)	CTRL+R	ENTER	ENTER
CTRL+U (Underline)	CTRL+U	enter	wprowadzić
CTRL+V (Paste)	CTRL+V	ENTER (keypad)	SZARY ENTER
CTRL+W (Word underline)	CTRL+W	ESC	ESC
CTRL+X (Cut)	CTRL+X	Exit	Koniec (k)
CTRL+Z (Undo)	CTRL+Z	**Exit**	**Koniec pomocy (k)**
Customize	**Dopasuj (d)**	**Exit and Return to**	**Koniec i powrót do (k)**
Cut	**Wytnij (n)**	expand	rozwinąć
cut	wyciąć	extend selection	rozszerzyć wybór
Decrease Speed	**Wolniej (w)**	Extend selection on (EXT)	WYB
Decrease Volume	**Ciszej (c)**	File Manager	Menedżer plików
Default	Domyślny	**File menu**	**Plik (p)**
Define	Zdefiniuj	File Name	Nazwa pliku (n)
Define...	**Załóż... (a)**	**Find...**	**Znajdź... (z)**
DEL	DEL	Find Next	Znajdź następny (n)
DEL (Clear)	DEL	Find What	Znajdź (z)
Delete	**Usuń (u)**	font	czcionka
delete	usunąć	Font	Czcionka (z)
Delete...	**Usuń... (u)**	Font Style	Styl (czcionki) (s)
Delete After Current Position	**Skasuj od bieżącej pozycji (o)**	**Format menu**	**Format (f)**
		freeze	zablokować
Delete Before Current Position	**Skasuj do bieżącej pozycji (d)**	**Freeze Panes**	**Zablokuj (z)**
		From	Od (o)
desktop	pulpit	**Full Menus**	**Pełne menu (p)**
destination application	aplikacja docelowa	gallery	galeria
destination document	dokument docelowy	Games	Gry
Device menu	**Urządzenie (u)**	Glossary	Słowniczek (o)
dialog box	pole dialogu	Go To	Idź do
dialog box title	tytuł pola dialogu	**Go To...**	**Idź do... (i)**
Direction	Kierunek	Goto/Gosub button	idź do
Directories	Katalogi (k)	group	grupa
directory icon	ikona katalogu	group box	pole grupy
disk icon	ikona dysku	group icon	ikona grupy
Document...	**Dokument... (d)**	group window	okno grupy
document file icon	ikona dokumentu	Help	Pomoc
document icon	ikona dokumentu	**Help menu**	**Pomoc (c)**
document window	okno dokumentu	Help window	okno pomocy
Done	Gotowe	**Hide**	**Ukryj (u)**
double-click	kliknąć dwukrotnie	hide	ukryć
double underline	podwójne podkreślenie (d)	History	Historia (h)
Down	W dół (d)	HOME	HOME
DOWN ARROW	strzałka w dół	horizontal scroll bar	pasek przewijania poziomego
down scroll arrow	strzałka przewijania w dół	horizontal split bar	linia podziału poziomego
drag	ciągnąć, przemieścić	hourglass pointer	klepsydra
drag-and-drop	przemieścić i upuścić	**How to use Help**	**Korzystanie z (k)**
drive icon	ikona stacji dysków	I-beam pointer	kursor tekstowy
Drives	Stacje dysków (s)	icon	ikona
drop	upuścić		

ENGLISH	POLISH	ENGLISH	POLISH
inactive window	okno nieaktywne	Notepad	Notatnik
Increase Speed (by 100%)	**Szybciej (o 100 %) (s)**	**Number...**	**Liczba... (l)**
Increase Volume (by 25%)	**Głośniej (o 25 %) (g)**	NUM LOCK	NUM LOCK
INS	INS	Num Lock on (NUM)	NUM
Insert...	**Wstaw... (s)**	object	obiekt
Insert File...	**Wstaw plik... (w)**	**Object...**	**Obiekt... (o)**
insertion point	punkt wstawiania	object linking & embedding	Łączenie i osadzanie obiektów
Insert menu	**Wstaw (s)**	(OLE)	(OLE)
Insert Object...	**Wstaw obiekt... (s)**	Object Packager	Pakowarka
italic	kursywa (k)	OK	OK
justified	wyjustowany (j)	OLE application	aplikacja OLE
Keyboard	**Klawiatura (l)**	OLE (object linking &	Łączenie i osadzanie obiektów
label	etykieta	embedding)	(OLE)
Landscape	W poziomie (z)	**Open**	**Otwórz (o)**
left aligned	wyrównany do lewej (l)	option button	przycisk opcji
LEFT ARROW	strzałka w lewo	Options	Opcje
left scroll arrow	strzałka przewijania w lewo	**Options menu**	**Opcje (o)**
left window border	lewa krawędź okna	Orientation	Orientacja
Line (Ln)	wrs	Overtype on (OVR)	NAD
link	połączyć	package	pakiet
linked object	obiekt połączony	Page (Pg)	str
linked text and list box	pole powiązanej listy i edycji	Pages	Strony (s)
list box	pole listy	**Page Setup**	**Układ strony (s)**
List Files of Type	Wyświetl pliki typu (w)	palette	paleta
Macro menu	**Makro (m)**	pane	okienko
Macro Recorder on (REC)	MAK	Paper Size	Rozmiar papieru (r)
Main	Grupa główna	**Paragraph...**	**Akapit... (a)**
main application	aplikacja główna	**Paste**	**Wklej (w)**
main document	dokument główny	paste	wkleić
manual link	połączenie ręczne	**Paste Link**	**Wklej połączenie (e)**
Match Case	Uwzględnij wielkość liter (u)	**Paste Special**	**Wklej wybiórczo (l)**
Match Whole Word Only	Uwzględnij tylko całe	PAUSE	PAUSE
	wyrazy (t)	PG DN	PG DN
Maximize	**Pełny ekran (e)**	PG UP	PG UP
Maximize button	przycisk "Pełny ekran"	PIF Editor	Edytor PIF
Media Player	Media	point	wskazać
menu	menu	pointer	wskaźnik
menu bar	pasek menu	Portrait	W pionie (i)
menu command	polecenie menu	**Preferences**	**Preferencje (r)**
menu name	nazwa menu	press and hold down	przytrzymać naciśnięty
message	komunikat	**Print**	**Drukuj (d)**
message box	pole komunikatu	Printer	Drukarka
message line	wiersz komunikatu	**Printer Setup**	**Ustawienie drukarki (t)**
MIDI Sequencer...	**Sekwenser MIDI...**	Print Manager	Menedżer wydruku
Minimize	**Do ikony (i)**	**Print Preview**	**Podgląd wydruku (g)**
Minimize button	przycisk "Do ikony"	Print Quality	Jakość wydruku (j)
Mix with File...	**Miksuj z plikiem... (i)**	Print Range	Zakres wydruku
More	Więcej	PRINT SCREEN	PRINT SCREEN
Mouse	**Mysz (m)**	**Print Setup...**	**Ustawienie drukarki... (u)**
mouse pointer	wskaźnik myszy	Print to File	Drukuj do pliku (d)
Move	**Przesuń (s)**	**Print Topic**	**Drukuj (d)**
move	przesunąć	program group	grupa (programów)
MS-DOS Prompt	MS-DOS	program item	element grupy
New...	**Nowy... (n)**	program-item icon	ikona elementu grupy
New Window	**Nowe okno (n)**	Program Manager	Menedżer programów
Next	**Następne (n)**	progress indicator	wskaźnik zaawansowania
Next Window	**Następne okno (t)**	push button	przycisk
No	Nie	Quit	Porzuć

ENGLISH	POLISH
radio button	przycisk radiowy
Read Only	Tylko do odczytu (t)
Record...	**Nagraj... (n)**
Recorder	Rejestrator
Redo	Powtórz
reduce selection	ograniczyć wybór
Remove Split	**Usuń podział (i)**
Repeat	**Powtórz (p)**
Replace...	**Zamień... (a)**
Replace All	Zamień wszystkie (w)
Replace With	Zamień na (a)
Reset	Przywróć
resize	zmienić rozmiar
Restore	Przywróć (p)
restore	przywrócić
Restore button	przycisk przywracający poprzedni rozmiar
Resume	Wznów
Retry	Ponów próbę
Reverse	**Wstecz (t)**
Revert...	**Przywróć... (p)**
right aligned	wyrównany do prawej (r)
RIGHT ARROW	strzałka w prawo
right scroll arrow	strzałka przewijania w prawo
right window border	prawa krawędź okna
ruler	linijka
Run...	**Uruchom... (u)**
Sample	Przykład
Save	**Zachowaj (h)**
Save All	**Zachowaj wszystkie (w)**
Save As...	**Zachowaj jako... (j)**
Save File as Type	Zachowaj plik w formacie (z)
scale	zmienić rozmiar
Scale menu	**Skala (s)**
Scaling	Skalowanie
scroll	przewinąć
scroll arrow	strzałka przewijania
scroll bar	pasek przewijania
scroll box	suwak przewijania
SCROLL LOCK	SCROLL LOCK
Scroll Lock on (SCRL)	SUW
Search	Szukaj (s)
Search	Szukaj
Search...	**Szukaj... (u)**
Search for Help on	**Pomoc na temat (p)**
Section...	**Sekcja... (s)**
Section (Sec)	sek
select	wybrać
select	wybrać, zaznaczyć
select (check box, option button)	wybrać
select (data)	zaznaczyć
select (drop-down menu)	otworzyć
selected command	polecenie wybrane
Selection	Wybór (b)
selection cursor	kursor wyboru
select (list box)	otworzyć
Set	Ustaw
Setup	Ustawienie

ENGLISH	POLISH
SHIFT	SHIFT
shortcut key	klawisz skrótu
Short Menus	**Skrócone menu (s)**
Size	**Rozmiar (r)**
size	zmienić rozmiar
Size (font size)	Rozmiar (czcionki) (r)
sizing handle	uchwyt zmiany rozmiaru
slider	suwak
slider indicator	wskaźnik suwakowy
small capitals	kapitaliki (a)
Sound...	**Dźwięk...**
Sound Recorder	Rejestrator dźwięku
source application	aplikacja źródłowa
source document	dokument źródłowy
Source (paper)	Podajnik (papieru) (p)
SPACEBAR	SPACJA
spin box	pole pokrętła
Split	**Podziel (d)**
split	podzielić
split bar	linia podziału
split box	pole podziału
StartUp	Autostart
status bar	pasek stanu
status-bar indicator	wskaźnik paska stanu
submenu	podmenu
switch	przełączyć
Switch to	Przełącz do
Switch to...	**Przełącz na... (c)**
SYS RQ	SYS RQ
TAB	TAB
Terminal	Terminal
text box	pole tekstu
text frame	ramka tekstu
Tile	**Sąsiadująco (s)**
tiled windows	okna sąsiadujące
Time	**Czas (c)**
title bar	pasek tytułu
To	Do (d)
tool	narzędzie
toolbar	pasek narzędzi
toolbox	zestaw narzędzi
Tools menu	**Narzędzia (n)**
top window border	górna krawędź okna
Tracks	**Ścieżki (i)**
Tutorial	**Samouczek (u)**
type	wpisać
unavailable command	polecenie niedostępne
underline	podkreślenie (p)
Undo	**Cofnij (c)**
unfreeze	odblokować
Unfreeze Panes	**Odblokuj (b)**
Unhide...	**Odkryj... (o)**
Up	W górę (w)
UP ARROW	strzałka w górę
up scroll arrow	strzałka przewijania w górę
Update	**Aktualizuj (a)**
update	aktualizować
Utilities menu	**Narzędzia (n)**

ENGLISH	POLISH	ENGLISH	POLISH
value set	zbiór wartości	window corner	róg okna
vertical scroll bar	pasek przewijania pionowego	window frame	ramka okna
vertical split bar	linia podziału pionowego	**Window menu**	**Okno (k)**
view	obejrzeć	window size	rozmiar okna
View menu	**Widok (w)**	window title	tytuł okna
wallpaper	tapeta	Windows Setup	Program instalacyjny Windows
warning message	ostrzeżenie	workspace	obszar roboczy
wildcard	wieloznacznik	Yes	Tak
window	okno	**Zoom...**	**Powiększ... (w)**
window background	tło okna	zoom in	powiększyć
window border	krawędź okna	zoom out	pomniejszyć

CHAPTER 18

Portuguese

This chapter lists the Portuguese translations of all terms formatted in *italic* in Part 1. Terminology is listed in two ways: by category and in alphabetical order. The first section includes translations in the following categories: Window Elements, Menus, Dialog Boxes, Message Boxes, Other GUI Screen Elements, Keys, User Actions, and Applications For Microsoft Windows.

The terminology in this chapter is based on the Brazilian Portuguese version of Windows and is adapted to suit the European Portuguese market.

Terminology by Category

ENGLISH	PORTUGUESE	ENGLISH	PORTUGUESE
WINDOW ELEMENTS		window background	fundo da janela
Main window elements		window border	contorno da janela
active window	janela activa	window corner	canto da janela
application window	janela de aplicação	window frame	moldura da janela
border	contorno	window size	tamanho da janela
bottom window border	contorno inferior da janela	window title	título da janela
cascading windows	janelas em cascata	workspace	área de trabalho
desktop	área de trabalho		
document window	janela de documento	**Window controls**	
group window	janela de grupo	Control-menu box	caixa do menu de controlo
Help window	janela de Ajuda	down scroll arrow	seta de elevadores abaixo
inactive window	janela inactiva	horizontal scroll bar	barra de elevadores horizontal
left window border	borda esquerda da janela	horizontal split bar	barra de divisão horizontal
menu bar	barra de menus	left scroll arrow	seta de elevadores esquerda
pane	ecrã	Maximize button	botão maximizar
right window border	contorno direito da janela	Minimize button	botão minimizar
ruler	régua	Restore button	botão restaurar
status bar	barra de status	right scroll arrow	seta de elevadores direita
tiled windows	janelas lado a lado	scroll arrow	seta de elevadores
title bar	barra de título	scroll bar	barra de elevadores
toolbar	barra de ferramentas	scroll box	elevador
top window border	contorno superior da janela	split bar	barra de divisão
wallpaper	papel de parede		
window	janela		

ENGLISH	PORTUGUESE
split box	caixa de divisão
up scroll arrow	seta de elevadores acima
vertical scroll bar	barra de elevadores vertical
vertical split bar	barra de divisão vertical
Pointers	
arrow	seta
arrow pointer	seta de quatro pontas
cross-hair pointer	em forma de mira
hourglass pointer	ampulheta
I-beam pointer	cursor em forma de I
insertion point	ponto de inserção
mouse pointer	ponteiro do rato
pointer	cursor
selection cursor	cursor de selecção
Icons	
application icon	símbolo da aplicação
directory icon	símbolo do directório
disk icon	símbolo do disco
document file icon	símbolo do ficheiro de documento
document icon	símbolo de documento
drive icon	símbolo da unidade
group icon	símbolo de grupo
icon	símbolo
program-item icon	símbolo do item de programa
General terms	
access key	teclas de acesso
check mark	marca
ellipsis	reticências
font	fonte
object	objecto
program group	grupo de programa
program item	item de programa
shortcut key	atalho
sizing handle	gestor de dimensionamento
status-bar indicator	indicador da barra de status
tool	ferramenta
unavailable command	comando não disponível
MENUS	
Menu elements	
cascading menu	menu em cascata
checked command	comando marcado
command	comando
command separator	separador de comando
drop-down menu	menu de cortina
menu	menu
menu command	comando do menu
menu name	nome do menu
selected command	comando realçado
submenu	submenu

ENGLISH	PORTUGUESE
Menus and commands	
View menu	Exibir (e)
Insert menu	Inserir (i)
Control menu	Menu Controlo
Restore	Restaurar (r)
Move	Mover (m)
Size	Tamanho (t)
Minimize	Minimizar (n)
Maximize	Maximizar (x)
Next	Próximo (p)
Close	Fechar (f)
Run...	Executar... (e)
Switch to...	Alternar Para... (a)
Split	Dividir (d)
File menu	Ficheiro (f)
New...	Novo... (n)
Open	Abrir (a)
Close	Fechar (f)
Close All	Fechar Tudo (u)
Save	Guardar (g)
Save As...	Guardar Como... (c)
Save All	Guardar Tudo (t)
Delete	Eliminar (e)
Page Setup	Definição de Página (p)
Print	Imprimir (i)
Print Preview	Visualizar Impressão (u)
Printer Setup	Definição de Impressora (m)
Exit	Sair (r)
Exit and Return to	Sair e Retornar Para (r)
Update	Atualizar (a)
Edit menu	Editar (e)
Undo	Desfazer (d)
Repeat	Repetir (t)
Cut	Cortar (r)
Copy	Copiar (c)
Copy Special	Copiar Especial (s)
Paste	Colar (c)
Paste Link	Colar Vínculo (o)
Paste Special	Colar Especial (s)
Clear	Limpar (p)
Clear All	Limpar Tudo (t)
Find...	Encontrar...(e)
Search...	Procurar... (p)
Replace...	Substituir... (s)
Go To...	Ir Para... (i)
Delete...	Eliminar... (e)
Insert...	Inserir... (i)
Object...	Objecto... (b)
Insert Object...	Inserir Objecto... (j)
Options menu	Opções (o)
Preferences	Preferências (p)

ENGLISH	PORTUGUESE	ENGLISH	PORTUGUESE
Full Menus	Menus Completos (m)	Insert File...	Inserir Arquivo... (i)
Short Menus	Menus Resumidos (m)	Mix with File...	Combinar com o Arquivo... (o)
		Delete Before Current Position	Apagar Antes da Posição Atual (n)
Format menu	Formatar (f)	Delete After Current Position	Apagar Após a Posição Atual (a)
Character...	Carácter... (c)		
Paragraph...	Parágrafo... (p)	Increase Volume (by 25%)	Aumentar o Volume (em 25%) (a)
Section...	Secção... (s)		
Document...	Documento... (d)	Decrease Volume	Diminuir o Volume (d)
Number...	Número... (n)	Increase Speed (by 100%)	Aumentar a Velocidade (em 100%) (u)
Alignment...	Alinhamento... (a)		
		Decrease Speed	Diminuir a Velocidade (m)
Utilities menu	Utilitários (u)	Add Echo	Adicionar Eco (e)
Tools menu	Ferramentas (f)	Reverse	Inverter (i)
Customize	Personalisar (p)		
		Help application	
Macro menu	Macro (m)	File menu	Ficheiro (f)
Record...	Gravar... (g)	Open	Abrir (a)
Run...	Executar... (x)	Print Topic	Imprimir Tópico (i)
Edit	Editar (e)	Print Setup...	Definição de Impressora... (m)
Assign to Key	Atribuir Combinação de Teclas (t)	Exit	Sair (r)
Assign to Menu	Atribuir ao Menu (m)	Edit menu	Editar (e)
		Copy...	Copiar... (c)
Window menu	Janela (j)	Annotate...	Anotar... (a)
New Window	Nova Janela (n)		
Cascade	Em Cascata (c)	Bookmark menu	Marcador de Posição (m)
Tile	Lado a Lado (l)	Define...	Definir... (d)
Next Window	Próxima Janela (p)		
Arrange All	Dispor Todas (o)	Help menu	?
Hide	Ocultar (c)	How to use Help	Como Usar a Ajuda (m)
Unhide...	Descobrir... (r)	Always on Top	Sempre Visível (s)
Split	Dividir (d)	About Help...	Acerca de... (a)
Freeze Panes	Congelar Ecrãs (c)		
Remove Split	Remover Divisão (d)	**Buttons**	
Unfreeze Panes	Descongelar Ecrãs (c)	Contents	Conteúdo (c)
Zoom...	Zoom... (z)	Search	Localizar (l)
		Back	Voltar (v)
Help menu	?	History	Histórico (h)
Contents	Conteúdo (c)	Glossary	Glossário (g)
How to use Help	Como Usar a Ajuda (m)		
Search for Help on	Procurar Ajuda Sobre (p)	**DIALOG BOXES**	
Active Window	Janela Activa (j)	dialog box	caixa de diálogo
Keyboard	Teclado (t)	wildcard	curinga
Mouse	Rato (r)		
Tutorial	Tutorial (u)	**Dialog box elements**	
About	Acerca de (a)	button	botão
		check box	caixa de verificação
Device menu	Dispositivo (d)	chevrons	divisas
Scale menu	Escala (e)	combo box	caixa combinada
MIDI Sequencer...	Seqüenciador de MIDI...	command button	botão de comando
Sound...	Som... (s)	dialog box title	título da caixa de diálogo
Time	Tempo (t)	drop-down combo box	caixa combinada de cortina
Tracks	Trilhas (r)	drop-down list box	caixa de listagem de cortina
		Goto/Gosub button	botão ir para
Effects menu	Efeitos (f)		
Revert...	Restaurar... (e)		

ENGLISH	PORTUGUESE
group box	caixa de grupo
label	rótulo
linked text and list box	caixa de edição/listagem vinculada
list box	caixa de listagem
option button	botão de opção
progress indicator	indicador de avanço
push button	botão de acção
radio button	botão de selecção
slider	elevador
slider indicator	indicador do elevador
spin box	caixa de rotação
text box	caixa de texto
value set	conjunto de valores

Dialog box buttons

Add	Adicionar
Apply	Aplicar
Cancel	Cancelar
Change	Alterar
Create	Criar
Default	Padrão
Define	Definir
Done	Pronto
Go To	Ir para
Help	Ajuda
More	Mais
No	Não
OK	OK
Options	Opções
Quit	Sair
Redo	Refazer
Reset	Reiniciar/Redefinir
Resume	Retornar
Retry	Tentar novamente
Search	Localizar
Set	Definir
Setup	Configurar
Switch to	Mudar para
Yes	Sim

Dialog box labels

All	Tudo (t)
Collate Copies	Cópias agrupadas (g)
Copies	Cópias (c)
Direction	Direcção
Directories	Directórios (d)
Down	Abaixo (b)
Drives	Unidades (u)
File Name	Nome do ficheiro (n)
Find Next	Encontrar a próxima (x)
Find What	Encontrar (n)
Font	Fonte (f)
Font Style	Estilo da fonte (e)
From	De (d)
Landscape	Paisagem (p)

ENGLISH	PORTUGUESE
List Files of Type	Listar ficheiros do tipo (l)
Match Case	Maiúscula/Minúscula (m)
Match Whole Word Only	Somente palavra inteira (p)
Orientation	Orientação (o)
Pages	Páginas (p)
Paper Size	Tamanho do papel (m)
Portrait	Retrato (r)
Printer	Impressora
Print Quality	Qualidade de impressão (q)
Print Range	Intervalo de impressão
Print to File	Imprimir para ficheiro (m)
Read Only	Somente para leitura (s)
Replace All	Substituir todas
Replace With	Substituir por (s)
Sample	Exemplo (e)
Save File as Type	Guardar ficheiros como tipo (s)
Scaling	Escala (e)
Selection	selecção (s)
Size (font size)	Tamanho (fonte) (t)
Source (paper)	Origem (papel) (r)
To	Para (p)
Up	Acima (a)

MESSAGE BOXES

critical message	mensagem crítica
message	mensagem de informação
message box	caixa de informação
message line	linha de mensagens
warning message	mensagem de advertência

OTHER GUI SCREEN ELEMENTS

Graphical options

gallery	galeria
palette	paleta
text frame	estrutura do texto
toolbox	barra de ferramentas

Status bar abbreviations

Caps Lock on (CAPS)	CAPS
Column (Col)	Col
Extend selection on (EXT)	EXT
Line (Ln)	Li
Macro Recorder on (REC)	GM
Num Lock on (NUM)	NUM
Overtype on (OVR)	SE
Page (Pg)	Pág
Scroll Lock on (SCRL)	SCRL
Section (Sec)	Sec

Character formats

bold	negrito (n)
double underline	duplo sublinhado (l)
italic	itálico (i)

ENGLISH	PORTUGUESE
small capitals	maiúsculas menores (k)
underline	sublinhado (s)

Paragraph formats

centered	centrado (w)
justified	justificado (j)
left aligned	alinhado à esquerda (e)
right aligned	alinhado à direita (d)

KEYS

Shortcut keys

CTRL+B (Bold)	CTRL+N
CTRL+C (Copy)	CTRL+C
CTRL+D (Double underline)	CTRL+L
CTRL+E (Center)	CTRL+W
CTRL+I (Italics)	CTRL+I
CTRL+J (Justify)	CTRL+J
CTRL+L (Left align)	CTRL+E
CTRL+R (Right align)	CTRL+D
CTRL+U (Underline)	CTRL+S
CTRL+V (Paste)	CTRL+V
CTRL+W (Word underline)	CTRL+B
CTRL+X (Cut)	CTRL+X
CTRL+Z (Undo)	CTRL+Z
DEL (Clear)	DEL

Keynames

(keypad) *	MULTIPLICAÇÃO (TECLADO NUMÉRICO)
(keypad) +	ADIÇÃO (TECLADO NUMÉRICO)
(keypad) -	SUBTRAÇÃO (TECLADO NUMÉRICO)
(keypad) /	DIVISÃO (TECLADO NUMÉRICO)
ALT	ALT
ALT GR	ALT GR
BACKSPACE	BACKSPACE
BREAK	BREAK
CAPS LOCK	CAPS LOCK
CTRL	CTRL
DEL	DELETE (DEL)
DOWN ARROW	SETA ABAIXO
END	END
ENTER	ENTER
ENTER (keypad)	NUMPAD ENTER
ESC	ESC
HOME	HOME
INS	INSERT (INS)
LEFT ARROW	SETA À ESQUERDA
NUM LOCK	NUM LOCK
PAUSE	PAUSE
PG DN	PAGE DOWN (PG DN)
PG UP	PAGE UP (PG UP)
PRINT SCREEN	PRINT SCREEN

ENGLISH	PORTUGUESE
RIGHT ARROW	SETA À DIREITA
SCROLL LOCK	SCROLL LOCK
SHIFT	SHIFT
SPACEBAR	SPACEBAR
SYS RQ	SYS RQ
TAB	TAB
UP ARROW	SETA ACIMA

USER ACTIONS

Keyboard actions

enter	Inserir
press and hold down	prima e mantenha premida
type	digite

Mouse actions

click	prima o botão do rato
double-click	prima duas vezes o botão do rato
drag	arrastar
drag-and-drop	arrastar e soltar
drop	soltar
point	apontar para

Manipulating window appearance

arrange	organizar
close	fechar
freeze	congelar
hide	ocultar
move	mover
resize	redimensionar
restore	restaurar
select	seleccionar
size	tamanho
split	dividir
switch	alternar
unfreeze	descongelar

Selecting options or content

cancel	cancelar
check	seleccionar
choose	escolha
clear (undo Select)	desactivar
extend selection	estender a selecção
reduce selection	reduzir selecção
select	seleccionar
select (check box, option button)	seleccionar (caixa de verificação, botão de opções)
select (data)	seleccionar (dados)
select (drop-down menu)	seleccionar (menu de cortina)
select (list box)	seleccionar (caixa de listagem)

Viewing content

autoscroll	rolamento automático
browse	movimentar

ENGLISH	PORTUGUESE	ENGLISH	PORTUGUESE
collapse	recolher/contrair/exibir subníveis	OLE application	aplicação OLE
expand	expandir	package	pacote
scroll	rolar	paste	colar
view	visualizar	scale	escala
zoom in	mais zoom	size	tamanho
zoom out	menos zoom	source application	aplicação de origem
		source document	documento de origem
		update	atualizar

Removing content

ENGLISH	PORTUGUESE
clear	limpar
copy	copiar
cut	recortar
delete	excluir
paste	colar

Manipulating objects

ENGLISH	PORTUGUESE
arrange	organizar
automatic link	vínculo automático
Clipboard	Área de Transferência
container application	aplicação container
container document	documento container
copy	copiar
crop	recortar
destination application	aplicação de destino
destination document	documento de destino
drag-and-drop	arrastar e soltar
embed	incorporar
embedded object	objeto incorporado
group	agrupar (v) / grupo (n)
link	vincular
linked object	objeto vinculado
main application	aplicação principal
main document	documento principal
manual link	vínculo manual
object	objeto
object linking & embedding (OLE)	vinculação e incorporação de objetos (OLE)
OLE (object linking & embedding)	OLE (vinculação e incorporação de objetos)

APPLICATIONS FOR MICROSOFT WINDOWS

ENGLISH	PORTUGUESE
Accessories	Acessórios
Applications	Aplicações
Calculator	Calculadora
Calendar	Agenda
Cardfile	Ficheiro de Fichas
Character Map	Mapa de Caracteres
Clipboard Viewer	Área de Transferência
Clock	Relógio
Control Panel	Painel de Controlo
File Manager	Gerenciador de Ficheiros
Games	Jogos
Main	Principal
Media Player	Controlador de Mídia
MS-DOS Prompt	Aviso do MS-DOS
Notepad	Bloco de Notas
Object Packager	Gestor de Objeto
PIF Editor	Editor PIF
Print Manager	Gestor de Impressão
Program Manager	Gestor de Programas
Recorder	Gravador
Sound Recorder	Gravador de Som
StartUp	Iniciar
Terminal	Terminal
Windows Setup	Config do Windows

Terminology by Alphabet

Notes:
1. All terms formatted in **bold** refer to menu names or command names.
2. All characters between parentheses are preferred access keys.

ENGLISH	PORTUGUESE	ENGLISH	PORTUGUESE
(keypad) *	MULTIPLICAÇÃO (TECLADO NUMÉRICO)	Calendar	Agenda
(keypad) +	ADIÇÃO (TECLADO NUMÉRICO)	Cancel	Cancelar
(keypad) -	SUBTRAÇÃO (TECLADO NUMÉRICO)	cancel	cancelar
		CAPS LOCK	CAPS LOCK
(keypad) /	DIVISÃO (TECLADO NUMÉRICO)	Caps Lock on (CAPS)	CAPS
		Cardfile	Ficheiro de Fichas
About	**Acerca de (a)**	**Cascade**	**Em Cascata (c)**
About Help...	**Acerca de... (a)**	cascading menu	menu em cascata
access key	teclas de acesso	cascading windows	janelas em cascata
Accessories	Acessórios	centered	centrado (w)
active window	janela activa	Change	Alterar
Active Window	**Janela Activa (j)**	**Character...**	**Carácter... (c)**
Add	Adicionar	Character Map	Mapa de Caracteres
Add Echo	**Adicionar Eco (e)**	check	seleccionar
Alignment...	**Alinhamento... (a)**	check box	caixa de verificação
All	Tudo (t)	checked command	comando marcado
ALT	ALT	check mark	marca
ALT GR	ALT GR	chevrons	divisas
Always on Top	**Sempre Visível (s)**	choose	escolha
Annotate...	**Anotar... (a)**	**Clear**	**Limpar (p)**
application icon	símbolo da aplicação	clear	limpar
application window	janela de aplicação	**Clear All**	**Limpar Tudo (t)**
Applications	Aplicações	clear (undo Select)	desactivar
Apply	Aplicar	click	prima o botão do rato
arrange	organizar	Clipboard	Área de Transferência
Arrange All	**Dispor Todas (o)**	Clipboard Viewer	Área de Transferência
arrow	seta	Clock	Relógio
arrow pointer	seta de quatro pontas	**Close**	**Fechar (f)**
Assign to Key	**Atribuir Combinação de Teclas (t)**	close	fechar
		Close All	**Fechar Tudo (u)**
Assign to Menu	**Atribuir ao Menu (m)**	collapse	recolher/contrair/exibir subníveis
automatic link	vínculo automático	Collate Copies	Cópias agrupadas (g)
autoscroll	rolamento automático	Column (Col)	Col
Back	Voltar (v)	combo box	caixa combinada
BACKSPACE	BACKSPACE	command	comando
bold	negrito (n)	command button	botão de comando
Bookmark menu	**Marcador de Posição (m)**	command separator	separador de comando
border	contorno	container application	aplicação container
bottom window border	contorno inferior da janela	container document	documento container
BREAK	BREAK	**Contents**	**Conteúdo (c)**
browse	movimentar	Contents	Conteúdo (c)
button	botão	**Control menu**	**Menu Controlo**
Calculator	Calculadora	Control-menu box	caixa do menu de controlo
		Control Panel	Painel de Controlo

ENGLISH	PORTUGUESE	ENGLISH	PORTUGUESE
Copies	Cópias (c)	double-click	prima duas vezes o botão do rato
Copy	**Copiar (c)**		
copy	copiar	double underline	duplo sublinhado (l)
Copy...	**Copiar... (c)**	Down	Abaixo (b)
Copy Special	**Copiar Especial (s)**	DOWN ARROW	SETA ABAIXO
Create	Criar	down scroll arrow	seta de elevadores abaixo
critical message	mensagem crítica	drag	arrastar
crop	recortar	drag-and-drop	arrastar e soltar
cross-hair pointer	em forma de mira	drive icon	símbolo da unidade
CTRL	CTRL	Drives	Unidades (u)
CTRL+B (Bold)	CTRL+N	drop	soltar
CTRL+C (Copy)	CTRL+C	drop-down combo box	caixa combinada de cortina
CTRL+D (Double underline)	CTRL+L	drop-down list box	caixa de listagem de cortina
CTRL+E (Center)	CTRL+W	drop-down menu	menu de cortina
CTRL+I (Italics)	CTRL+I	**Edit**	**Editar (e)**
CTRL+J (Justify)	CTRL+J	**Edit menu**	**Editar (e)**
CTRL+L (Left align)	CTRL+E	**Effects menu**	**Efeitos (f)**
CTRL+R (Right align)	CTRL+D	ellipsis	reticências
CTRL+U (Underline)	CTRL+S	embed	incorporar
CTRL+V (Paste)	CTRL+V	embedded object	objecto incorporado
CTRL+W (Word underline)	CTRL+B	END	END
CTRL+X (Cut)	CTRL+X	ENTER	ENTER
CTRL+Z (Undo)	CTRL+Z	enter	Inserir
Customize	**Personalisar (p)**	ENTER (keypad)	NUMPAD ENTER
Cut	**Cortar (r)**	ESC	ESC
cut	recortar	**Exit**	**Sair (r)**
Decrease Speed	**Diminuir a Velocidade (m)**	**Exit and Return to**	**Sair e Retornar Para (r)**
Decrease Volume	**Diminuir o Volume (d)**	expand	expandir
Default	Padrão	extend selection	estender a selecção
Define	Definir	Extend selection on (EXT)	EXT
Define...	**Definir... (d)**	File Manager	Gerenciador de Arquivos
DEL	DELETE (DEL)	**File menu**	**Ficheiro (f)**
DEL (Clear)	DEL	File Name	Nome do ficheiro (n)
Delete	Eliminar (e)	**Find...**	**Encontrar...(e)**
delete	excluir	Find Next	Encontrar a próxima (x)
Delete...	**Eliminar... (e)**	Find What	Encontrar (n)
Delete After Current Position	**Apagar Após a Posição Atual (a)**	font	fonte
		Font	Fonte (f)
Delete Before Current Position	**Apagar Antes da Posição Atual (n)**	Font Style	Estilo da fonte (e)
		Format menu	**Formatar (f)**
desktop	área de trabalho	freeze	congelar
destination application	aplicação de destino	**Freeze Panes**	**Congelar Ecrãs (c)**
destination document	documento de destino	From	De (d)
Device menu	**Dispositivo (d)**	**Full Menus**	**Menus Completos (m)**
dialog box	caixa de diálogo	gallery	galeria
dialog box title	título da caixa de diálogo	Games	Jogos
Direction	Direcção	Glossary	Glossário (g)
Directories	Directórios (d)	Go To	Ir para
directory icon	símbolo do directório	**Go To...**	**Ir Para... (i)**
disk icon	símbolo do disco	Goto/Gosub button	botão ir para
Document...	**Documento... (d)**	group	agrupar (v) / grupo (n)
document file icon	símbolo do ficheiro de documento	group box	caixa de grupo
		group icon	símbolo de grupo
document icon	símbolo de documento	group window	janela de grupo
document window	janela de documento	Help	Ajuda
Done	Pronto	**Help menu**	**?**

ENGLISH	PORTUGUESE	ENGLISH	PORTUGUESE
Help window	janela de Ajuda	MIDI Sequencer...	Seqüenciador de MIDI...
Hide	**Ocultar (c)**	**Minimize**	**Minimizar (n)**
hide	ocultar	Minimize button	botão minimizar
History	Histórico (h)	**Mix with File...**	**Combinar com o**
HOME	HOME		**Arquivo... (o)**
horizontal scroll bar	barra de elevadores horizontal	More	Mais
horizontal split bar	barra de divisão horizontal	**Mouse**	**Rato (r)**
hourglass pointer	ampulheta	mouse pointer	ponteiro do rato
How to use Help	**Como Usar a Ajuda (m)**	**Move**	**Mover (m)**
I-beam pointer	cursor em forma de I	move	mover
icon	símbolo	MS-DOS Prompt	Aviso do MS-DOS
inactive window	janela inactiva	**New...**	**Novo... (n)**
Increase Speed (by 100%)	**Aumentar a Velocidade**	New Window	Nova Janela (n)
	(em 100%) (u)	Next	Próximo (p)
Increase Volume (by 25%)	**Aumentar o Volume**	Next Window	Próxima Janela (p)
	(em 25%) (a)	No	Não
INS	INSERT (INS)	Notepad	Bloco de Notas
Insert...	**Inserir... (i)**	**Number...**	**Número... (n)**
Insert File...	**Inserir Arquivo... (i)**	NUM LOCK	NUM LOCK
insertion point	ponto de inserção	Num Lock on (NUM)	NUM
Insert menu	**Inserir (i)**	object	objecto
Insert Object...	**Inserir Objecto... (j)**	**Object...**	**Objecto... (b)**
italic	itálico (i)	object linking & embedding	vinculação e incorporação de
justified	justificado (j)	(OLE)	objectos (OLE)
Keyboard	**Teclado (t)**	Object Packager	Gestor de Objeto
label	rótulo	OK	OK
Landscape	Paisagem (p)	OLE application	aplicação OLE
left aligned	alinhado à esquerda (e)	OLE (object linking &	OLE (vinculação e incorporação
LEFT ARROW	SETA À ESQUERDA	embedding)	de objectos)
left scroll arrow	seta de elevadores esquerda	**Open**	**Abrir (a)**
left window border	borda esquerda da janela	option button	botão de opção
Line (Ln)	Li	Options	Opções
link	vincular	**Options menu**	**Opções (o)**
linked object	objecto vinculado	Orientation	Orientação (o)
linked text and list box	caixa de edição/listagem	Overtype on (OVR)	SE
	vinculada	package	pacote
list box	caixa de listagem	Page (Pg)	Pág
List Files of Type	Listar ficheiros do tipo (l)	Pages	Páginas (p)
Macro menu	**Macro (m)**	**Page Setup**	**Definição de Página (p)**
Macro Recorder on (REC)	GM	palette	paleta
Main	Principal	pane	ecrã
main application	aplicação principal	Paper Size	Tamanho do papel (m)
main document	documento principal	**Paragraph...**	**Parágrafo... (p)**
manual link	vínculo manual	**Paste**	**Colar (c)**
Match Case	Maiúscula/Minúscula (m)	paste	colar
Match Whole Word Only	Somente palavra inteira (p)	**Paste Link**	**Colar Vínculo (o)**
Maximize	**Maximizar (x)**	**Paste Special**	**Colar Especial (s)**
Maximize button	botão maximizar	PAUSE	PAUSE
Media Player	Controlador de Mídia	PG DN	PAGE DOWN (PG DN)
menu	menu	PG UP	PAGE UP (PG UP)
menu bar	barra de menus	PIF Editor	Editor PIF
menu command	comando do menu	point	apontar para
menu name	nome do menu	pointer	cursor
message	mensagem de informação	Portrait	Retrato (r)
message box	caixa de informação	**Preferences**	**Preferências (p)**
message line	linha de mensagens	press and hold down	prima e mantenha premida

ENGLISH	PORTUGUESE	ENGLISH	PORTUGUESE
Print	**Imprimir (i)**	scroll arrow	seta de elevadores
Printer	Impressora	scroll bar	barra de elevadores
Printer Setup	**Definição de Impressora (m)**	scroll box	elevador
		SCROLL LOCK	SCROLL LOCK
Print Manager	Gestor de Impressão	Scroll Lock on (SCRL)	SCRL
Print Preview	**Visualizar Impressão (u)**	Search	Localizar (l)
Print Quality	Qualidade de impressão (q)	Search	Localizar
Print Range	Intervalo de impressão	**Search...**	**Procurar... (p)**
PRINT SCREEN	PRINT SCREEN	**Search for Help on**	**Procurar Ajuda Sobre (p)**
Print Setup...	**Definição de Impressora... (m)**	**Section...**	**Secção... (s)**
		Section (Sec)	Sec
Print to File	Imprimir para ficheiro (m)	select	seleccionar
Print Topic	**Imprimir Tópico (i)**	select (check box, option button)	seleccionar (caixa de verificação, botão de opções)
program group	grupo de programa		
program item	item de programa	select (data)	seleccionar (dados)
program-item icon	símbolo do item de programa	select (drop-down menu)	seleccionar (menu de cortina)
Program Manager	Gestor de Programas	selected command	comando realçado
progress indicator	indicador de avanço	Selection	selecção (s)
push button	botão de acção	selection cursor	cursor de selecção
Quit	Sair	select (list box)	seleccionar (caixa de listagem)
radio button	botão de selecção	Set	Definir
Read Only	Somente para leitura (s)	Setup	Configurar
Record...	**Gravar... (g)**	SHIFT	SHIFT
Recorder	Gravador	**Short Menus**	**Menus Resumidos (m)**
Redo	Refazer	shortcut key	atalho
reduce selection	reduzir selecção	**Size**	**Tamanho (t)**
Remove Split	**Remover Divisão (d)**	size	tamanho
Repeat	**Repetir (t)**	Size (font size)	Tamanho (fonte) (t)
Replace...	**Substituir... (s)**	sizing handle	gestor de dimensionamento
Replace All	Substituir todas	slider	elevador
Replace With	Substituir por (s)	slider indicator	indicador do elevador
Reset	Reiniciar/Redefinir	small capitals	maiúsculas menores (k)
resize	redimensionar	**Sound...**	**Som... (s)**
Restore	**Restaurar (r)**	Sound Recorder	Gravador de Som
restore	restaurar	source application	aplicação de origem
Restore button	botão restaurar	source document	documento de origem
Resume	Retornar	Source (paper)	Origem (papel) (r)
Retry	Tentar novamente	SPACEBAR	SPACEBAR
Reverse	**Inverter (i)**	spin box	caixa de rotação
Revert...	**Restaurar... (e)**	**Split**	**Dividir (d)**
right aligned	alinhado à direita (d)	split	dividir
RIGHT ARROW	SETA À DIREITA	split bar	barra de divisão
right scroll arrow	seta de elevadores direita	split box	caixa de divisão
right window border	contorno direito da janela	StartUp	Iniciar
ruler	régua	status bar	barra de status
Run...	**Executar... (e)**	status-bar indicator	indicador da barra de status
Run...	**Executar... (x)**	submenu	submenu
Sample	Exemplo (e)	switch	alternar
Save	**Guardar (g)**	Switch to	Mudar para
Save All	**Guardar Tudo (t)**	**Switch to...**	**Alternar Para... (a)**
Save As...	**Guardar Como... (c)**	SYS RQ	SYS RQ
Save File as Type	Guardar ficheiros como tipo (s)	TAB	TAB
scale	escala	Terminal	Terminal
Scale menu	**Escala (e)**	text box	caixa de texto
Scaling	Escala (e)	text frame	estrutura do texto
scroll	rolar	**Tile**	**Lado a Lado (l)**

ENGLISH	PORTUGUESE	ENGLISH	PORTUGUESE
tiled windows	janelas lado a lado	**Utilities menu**	**Utilitários (u)**
Time	**Tempo (t)**	value set	conjunto de valores
title bar	barra de título	vertical scroll bar	barra de elevadores vertical
To	Para (p)	vertical split bar	barra de divisão vertical
tool	ferramenta	view	visualizar
toolbar	barra de ferramentas	**View menu**	**Exibir (e)**
toolbox	barra de ferramentas	wallpaper	papel de parede
Tools menu	**Ferramentas (f)**	warning message	mensagem de advertência
top window border	contorno superior da janela	wildcard	curinga
Tracks	**Trilhas (r)**	window	janela
Tutorial	**Tutorial (u)**	window background	fundo da janela
type	digite	window border	contorno da janela
unavailable command	comando não disponível	window corner	canto da janela
underline	sublinhado (s)	window frame	moldura da janela
Undo	**Desfazer (d)**	**Window menu**	**Janela (j)**
unfreeze	descongelar	window size	tamanho da janela
Unfreeze Panes	**Descongelar Ecrãs (c)**	window title	título da janela
Unhide...	**Descobrir... (r)**	Windows Setup	Config do Windows
Up	Acima (a)	workspace	área de trabalho
UP ARROW	SETA ACIMA	Yes	Sim
up scroll arrow	seta de elevadores acima	**Zoom...**	**Zoom... (z)**
Update	**Atualizar (a)**	zoom in	mais zoom
update	atualizar	zoom out	menos zoom

CHAPTER 19

Russian

This chapter lists the Russian translations of all terms formatted in *italic* in Part 1. Terminology is listed in two ways: by category and in alphabetical order. The first section includes translations in the following categories: Window Elements, Menus, Dialog Boxes, Message Boxes, Other GUI Screen Elements, Keys, User Actions, and Applications For Microsoft Windows.

Terminology by Category

ENGLISH	RUSSIAN	ENGLISH	RUSSIAN
WINDOW ELEMENTS		window border	граница окна
Main window elements		window corner	угол окна
active window	активное окно	window frame	рамка окна
application window	окно приложения	window size	размер окна
border	граница	window title	заголовок окна
bottom window border	нижняя граница окна	workspace	рабочая область
cascading windows	окна каскадом		
desktop	оформление	**Window controls**	
document window	окно документа	Control-menu box	кнопка Системного меню
group window	окно группы	down scroll arrow	стрелка прокрутки вниз
Help window	окно справки	horizontal scroll bar	горизонтальная линейка просмотра
inactive window	неактивное окно		
left window border	левая граница окна	horizontal split bar	горизонтальная линия разбиения
menu bar	строка меню		
pane	подокно	left scroll arrow	стрелка прокрутки влево
right window border	правая граница окна	Maximize button	кнопка Развернуть
ruler	линейка	Minimize button	кнопка Свернуть
status bar	строка состояния	Restore button	кнопка Восстановить
tiled windows	окна мозаикой	right scroll arrow	стрелка прокрутки вправо
title bar	строка заголовка	scroll arrow	стрелка прокрутки
toolbar	панель инструментов	scroll bar	линейка просмотра
top window border	верхняя граница окна	scroll box	бегунок
wallpaper	обои	split bar	линия разбиения
window	окно		
window background	фон окна		

ENGLISH	RUSSIAN
split box	маркер разбиения
up scroll arrow	стрелка прокрутки вверх
vertical scroll bar	вертикальная линейка просмотра
vertical split bar	вертикальная линия разбиения

Pointers

arrow	стрелка
arrow pointer	указатель стрелка
cross-hair pointer	указатель прицел
hourglass pointer	указатель песочные часы
I-beam pointer	указатель луч
insertion point	место ввода / позиция ввода
mouse pointer	указатель мыши
pointer	указатель
selection cursor	курсор выбора

Icons

application icon	значок приложения / значок прикладной программы
directory icon	значок каталога
disk icon	значок диска
document file icon	значок файла документа
document icon	значок документа
drive icon	значок устройства
group icon	значок группы
icon	значок
program-item icon	значок программного элемента

General terms

access key	клавиша доступа
check mark	галочка
ellipsis	многоточие
font	шрифт
object	объект
program group	группа программ
program item	программный элемент
shortcut key	быстрая клавиша
sizing handle	ручка изменения размера
status-bar indicator	индикатор строки состояния
tool	инструмент
unavailable command	недоступная команда

MENUS

Menu elements

cascading menu	меню каскад
checked command	отмеченная команда
command	команда
command separator	разделитель команд
drop-down menu	раскрывающееся меню

ENGLISH	RUSSIAN
menu	меню
menu command	команда меню
menu name	имя меню
selected command	выбранная команда
submenu	подменю

Menus and commands

View menu	Просмотр
Insert menu	Поместить
Control menu	Системное меню
Restore	Восстановить (В)
Move	Переместить (П)
Size	Размер (Р)
Minimize	Свернуть (С)
Maximize	Развернуть (А)
Next	Следующий (Л)
Close	Закрыть (З)
Run...	Выполнить...
Switch To...	Переключиться в... (Е)
Split	Разбить (Б)
File menu	Файл (Ф)
New...	Создать... (З)
Open	Открыть (О)
Close	Закрыть
Close All	Закрыть Все
Save	Сохранить (С)
Save As...	Сохранить Как... (К)
Save All	Сохранить Все
Delete	Удалить (У)
Page Setup	Параметры Страницы (А)
Print	Печать (П)
Print Preview	Предварительный Просмотр (Д)
Printer Setup	Выбор Принтера (В)
Exit	Выход (Ы)
Exit and Return to	Выход и Возвращение в
Update	Обновить
Edit menu	Редактирование (Р)
Undo	Отменить (О)
Repeat	Повторить
Cut	Вырезать (В)
Copy	Копировать (К)
Copy Special	Специальная Копия
Paste	Вставить (А)
Paste Link	Установить Связь (У)
Paste Special	Специальная Вставка (С)
Clear	Очистить
Clear All	Очистить Все
Find...	Найти... (Н)
Search...	Поиск... (П)
Replace...	Замена... (З)
Go To...	Перейти к... (К)

ENGLISH	RUSSIAN
Delete...	Удалить...
Insert...	Поместить...
Object...	Объект... (Б)
Insert Object	Поместить Объект (М)
Options menu	Параметры (П)
Preferences	Предпочтения (П)
Full Menus	Полные Меню
Short Menus	Краткие Меню
Format menu	Формат
Character...	Символ... (И)
Paragraph...	Абзац... (Б)
Section...	Раздел...
Document...	Документ... (Д)
Number...	Число...
Alignment...	Выравнивание...
Utilities menu	Утилиты
Tools menu	Инструменты
Customize	Адаптировать
Macro menu	Макросы
Record...	Записать... (З)
Run...	Выполнить... (В)
Edit	Редактировать
Assign to Key	Присвоить Клавише
Assign to Menu	Присвоить Меню
Window menu	Окно (О)
New Window	Новое Окно (Н)
Cascade	Каскад (К)
Tile	Мозаика (М)
Next Window	Следующее Окно
Arrange All	Упорядочить Все
Hide	Спрятать
Unhide...	Показать...
Split	Разбить
Freeze Panes	Зафиксировать Подокна
Remove Split	Убрать Разбивку
Unfreeze Panes	Разфиксировать Подокна /
	Отменить Фиксацию
	Подокон
Zoom...	Фокус...
Help menu	Справка (С)
Contents	Содержание (С)
How to use Help	Использование Справки (И)
Search for Help on	Поиск Справки о (П)
Active Window	Активное Окно
Keyboard	Клавиатура (К)
Mouse	Мышь (М)
Tutorial	Учебник (У)
About	О Программе (О)

ENGLISH	RUSSIAN
Device menu	Устройство (У)
Scale menu	Шкала (Ш)
MIDI Sequencer...	Секвенсер MIDI...
Sound...	Звук... (З)
Time	Время (В)
Tracks	Фонограммы (Ф)
Effects menu	Эффекты
Revert...	Исходное Состояние... (И)
Insert File...	Поместить Файл... (Ф)
Mix with File...	Микшировать с
	Файлом... (И)
Delete Before Current Position	Удалить До Текущей
	Позиции (Д)
Delete After Current Position	Удалить После Текущей
	Позиции (П)
Increase Volume (by 25%)	Увеличить Громкость
	(на 25%) (В)
Decrease Volume	Уменьшить Громкость (М)
Increase Speed (by 100%)	Увеличить Скорость
	(на 100%) (У)
Decrease Speed	Уменьшить Скорость (С)
Add Echo	Реверберация (Е)
Reverse	Реверс (Р)

Help application

File menu	
Open	Файл (Ф)
Print Topic	Открыть (О)
Print Setup...	Печать Темы (П)
Exit	Выбор Принтера... (В)
	Выход (Ы)
Edit menu	
Copy...	Редактирование (Р)
Annotate...	Копировать... (К)
	Примечание.../Сноска...
Bookmark menu	
Define	Закладка (З)
	Определить... (О)
Help menu	
How to use Help	Справка (С)
Always on Top	Использование Справки (И)
About Help...	Всегда Впереди (Г)
	О Программе... (О)

Buttons

Contents	Содержание
Search	Поиск
Back	Назад
History	История
Glossary	Словарь

DIALOG BOXES

dialog box	диалоговое окно
wildcard	подстановочные символы

ENGLISH	RUSSIAN	ENGLISH	RUSSIAN
Dialog box elements		**Dialog box labels**	
button	кнопка	All	Все (Е)
check box	флажок проверки	Collate copies	Сличать Копии (Л)
chevrons	шевроны	Copies	Копии (К)
combo box	комбинированное окно	Direction	Направление
command button	кнопка команды	Directories	Каталоги (К)
dialog box title	заголовок диалогового окна	Down	Вниз (Н)
drop-down combo box	раскрывающееся	Drives	Устройства (У)
	комбинированное окно	File Name	Имя Файла (И)
drop-down list box	раскрывающееся окно	Find Next	Повторить Поиск (П)
	списка	Find What	Что Найти (Ч)
Goto/Gosub button	кнопка Перейти к	Font	Шрифт (Ш)
group box	окно/поле группы	Font Style	Вид Шрифта (Т)
label	метка	From	От / С
linked text and list box	связанное окно	Landscape	Ландшафт (Л)
	редактирования и списка	List Files of Type	Список Файлов Типа (Т)
list box	окно/поле списка	Match Case	Сравнивать
option button	флажок опции / кнопка		Строчные/Прописные
	опции		Буквы (С)
progress indicator	индикатор процесса	Match Whole Word Only	Должно Совпадать Все
push button	нажимаемая кнопка		Слово (Д)
radio button	кнопка опции	Orientation	Ориентация
slider	слайдер	Pages	Страницы (Т)
slider indicator	индикатор слайдера	Paper Size	Размер Бумаги (Р)
spin box	поле счетчика	Portrait	Портрет (П)
text box	окно текста / текстовое	Printer	Принтер
	поле	Print Quality	Качество Печати (Ч)
value set	набор значений	Print Range	Область Печати
		Print to File	Печать в Файл (Ф)
Dialog box buttons		Read Only	Только для Чтения (Ч)
Add	Добавить	Replace All	Заменить Все (С)
Apply	Применить	Replace With	Заменить на (Н)
Cancel	Отмена	Sample	Образец (О)
Change	Изменить	Save File as Type	Тип Сохраняемого
Create	Создать		Файла (Т)
Default	По Умолчанию	Scaling	Масштаб(-ирование) (М)
Define	Определить	Selection	Выбор
Done	Сделано	Size (font size)	Размер (размер шрифта) (Р)
Go To	Перейти к	Source (paper)	Источник (бумаги) (И)
Help	Справка	To	По
More	Дополнительно	Up	Вверх (В)
No	Нет		
OK	ОК		
Options	Параметры / Опции	**MESSAGE BOXES**	
Quit	Завершить	critical message	критическое сообщение
Redo	Переделать	message	информационное сообщение
Reset	Сброс	message box	окно сообщения
Resume	Восстановить	message line	строка сообщений
Retry	Повторить	warning message	предупреждающее
Search	Поиск		сообщение
Set	Задать		
Setup	Установка		
Switch to	Переключиться в		
Yes	Да		

ENGLISH	RUSSIAN	ENGLISH	RUSSIAN
OTHER GUI SCREEN ELEMENTS		HOME	HOME
Graphical options		INS	INSERT (INS)
gallery	галерея	LEFT ARROW	СТРЕЛКА ВЛЕВО
palette	палитра	NUM LOCK	NUM LOCK
text frame	рамка текста	PAUSE	PAUSE
toolbox	инструменты / панель	PG DN	PAGE DOWN (PG DN)
	инструментов	PG UP	PAGE UP (PG UP)
		PRINT SCREEN	PRINT SCREEN
		RIGHT ARROW	СТРЕЛКА ВПРАВО
Status bar abbreviations		SCROLL LOCK	SCROLL LOCK
Caps Lock on (CAPS)	CAPS	SHIFT	SHIFT
Column (Col)	здесь - Колонка (Клн)	SPACEBAR	ПРОБЕЛ
Extend selection on (EXT)	Расширить Выбор (РВ)	SYS RQ	SYS RQ
Line (Ln)	Строка (Ст)	TAB	TAB
Macro Recorder on (REC)	Макрокоманды (МАК)	UP ARROW	СТРЕЛКА ВВЕРХ
Num Lock on (NUM)	NUM		
Overtype on (OVR)	Замещать (ЗМЩ)	**USER ACTIONS**	
Page (Pg)	Страница (Стр)	**Keyboard actions**	
Scroll Lock on (SCRL)	SCRL	enter	ввести
Section (Sec)	Раздел (Раз)	press and hold down	нажать и держать нажатой
		type	набрать / ввести
Character formats			
bold	полужирный (ж)	**Mouse actions**	
double underline	двойное подчеркивание (д)	click	щелчок
italic	курсив (к)	double-click	двойной щелчок
small capitals	маленькие заглавные (з)	drag	перстаскивать
underline	подчеркивание (п)	drag-and-drop	перетащить и опустить
		drop	опустить
Paragraph formats		point	указать на
centered	центрированный (ц)		
justified	выравненный (в)	**Manipulating window appearance**	
left aligned	выравненный по левому	arrange	упорядочить
	краю (л)	close	закрыть
right aligned	выравненный по правому	freeze	зафиксировать
	краю (п)	hide	спрятать
		move	переместить
		resize	изменить размер
KEYS		restore	восстановить
Keynames		select	выбрать
(keypad) *	NUMPAD *	size	размер
(keypad) +	NUMPAD +	split	разбить
(keypad) -	NUMPAD -	switch	переключить
(keypad) /	NUMPAD /	unfreeze	разфиксировать / отменить
ALT	ALT		фиксацию
ALT GR	ALT GR		
BACKSPACE	BACKSPACE	**Selecting options or content**	
BREAK	BREAK	cancel	отменить
CAPS LOCK	CAPS LOCK	check	отметить
CTRL	CTRL	choose	выбрать
DEL	DELETE (DEL)	clear (undo Select)	очистить (отменить Выбор)
DOWN ARROW	СТРЕЛКА ВНИЗ	extend selection	расширить выбор
END	END		
ENTER	ENTER		
ENTER (keypad)	NUMPAD ENTER		
ESC	ESC		

ENGLISH	RUSSIAN
reduce selection	сжать выбор
select	выбрать
select (check box, option button)	установить (флажок проверки) выбрать (флажок опции)
select (data)	выбрать (данные)
select (drop-down menu)	выбрать (раскрывающееся меню)
select (list box)	выбрать (окно списка)

Viewing content

autoscroll	автопрокрутка
browse	пролистать
collapse	скрыть
expand	показать
scroll	прокрутить
view	просмотреть
zoom in	приблизить
zoom out	отодвинуть

Removing content

clear	очистить
copy	копировать
cut	вырезать
delete	удалить
paste	вставить

Manipulating objects

arrange	упорядочить
automatic link	автоматическая связь
Clipboard	Буфер Обмена
container application	несущее приложение
container document	несущий документ
copy	копировать
crop	(по-)стричь
destination application	принимающее приложение
destination document	документ-получатель, принимающий документ
drag-and-drop	перетащить и опустить
embed	внедрить
embedded object	внедренный объект
group	группа, группировать
link	связь / установить связь
linked object	связанный объект
main application	главное приложение
main document	главный документ

ENGLISH	RUSSIAN
manual link	ручная связь
object	объект
object linking & embedding (OLE)	связь и внедрение объектов (СВО)
OLE (object linking & embedding)	СВО (связь и внедрение объектов)
OLE application	приложение СВО
package	пакет
paste	вставить
scale	масштаб(-ировать)
size	размер
source application	приложение-источник
source document	документ-источник
update	обновить

APPLICATIONS FOR MICROSOFT WINDOWS

Accessories	Реквизиты
Applications	Приложения
Calculator	Калькулятор
Calendar	Календарь
Cardfile	Картотека
Character Map	Таблица Символов
Clipboard Viewer	Окно Буфера Обмена
Clock	Часы
Control Panel	Панель Управления
File Manager	Диспетчер Файлов
Games	Игры
Main	Главная
Media Player	Медиаплеер
MS-DOS Prompt	Режим MS-DOS / Приглашение MS-DOS
Notepad	Блокнот
Object Packager	Упаковщик Объектов
PIF Editor	Редактор PIF
Print Manager	Диспетчер Печати
Program Manager	Диспетчер Программ
Recorder	Запись Макрокоманд / Запись Макросов
Sound Recorder	Звукозапись
StartUp	Группа Запуска
Terminal	Терминал
Windows Setup	Windows Setup / Установка Windows

Terminology by Alphabet

Notes:
1. All terms formatted in **bold** refer to menu names or command names.
2. All characters between parentheses are preferred access keys.

ENGLISH	RUSSIAN	ENGLISH	RUSSIAN
(keypad) *	NUMPAD *	Cancel	Отмена
(keypad) +	NUMPAD +	cancel	отменить
(keypad) -	NUMPAD -	CAPS LOCK	CAPS LOCK
(keypad) /	NUMPAD /	Caps Lock on (CAPS)	CAPS
About	**О Программе (О)**	Cardfile	Картотека
About Help...	**О Программе... (О)**	**Cascade**	**Каскад (К)**
access key	клавиша доступа	cascading menu	меню каскад
Accessories	Реквизиты	cascading windows	окна каскадом
active window	активное окно	centered	центрированный (ц)
Active Window	**Активное Окно**	Change	Изменить
Add	Добавить	**Character...**	**Символ... (И)**
Add Echo	**Реверберация (Е)**	Character Map	Таблица Символов
Alignment...	**Выравнивание...**	check	отметить
All	Все (Е)	check box	флажок проверки
ALT	ALT	checked command	отмеченная команда
ALT GR	ALT GR	check mark	галочка
Always on Top	**Всегда Впереди (Г)**	chevrons	шевроны
Annotate...	**Примечание.../Спска...**	choose	выбрать
application icon	значок приложения /	**Clear**	**Очистить**
	значок прикладной	clear	очистить
	программы	**Clear All**	**Очистить Все**
Applications	Приложения	clear (undo Select)	очистить (отменить Выбор)
application window	окно приложения	click	щелчок
Apply	Применить	Clipboard	Буфер Обмена
arrange	упорядочить	Clipboard Viewer	Окно Буфера Обмена
Arrange All	**Упорядочить Все**	Clock	Часы
arrow	стрелка	**Close**	**Закрыть (З)**
arrow pointer	указатель стрелка	close	закрыть
Assign to Key	**Присвоить Клавише**	**Close All**	**Закрыть Все**
Assign to Menu	**Присвоить Меню**	collapse	скрыть
automatic link	автоматическая связь	Collate copies	Сличать Копии (Л)
autoscroll	автопрокрутка	Column (Col)	здесь - Колонка (Клн)
Back	Назад	combo box	комбинированное окно
BACKSPACE	BACKSPACE	command	команда
bold	полужирный (ж)	command button	кнопка команды
Bookmark menu	**Закладка (З)**	command separator	разделитель команд
border	граница	container application	несущее приложение
bottom window border	нижняя граница окна	container document	несущий документ
BREAK	BREAK	**Contents**	**Содержание (С)**
browse	пролистать	Contents	Содержание
button	кнопка	**Control menu**	**Системное меню**
Calculator	Калькулятор	Control-menu box	кнопка Системного меню
Calendar	Календарь	Control Panel	Панель Управления

ENGLISH	RUSSIAN
Copies	Копии (К)
Copy	**Копировать (К)**
copy	копировать
Copy...	**Копировать... (К)**
Copy Special	**Специальная Копия**
Create	Создать
critical message	критическое сообщение
crop	(по-)стричь
cross-hair pointer	указатель прицел
CTRL	CTRL
Customize	**Адаптировать**
Cut	**Вырезать (В)**
cut	вырезать
Decrease Speed	**Уменьшить Скорость (С)**
Decrease Volume	**Уменьшить Громкость (М)**
Default	По Умолчанию
Define	Определить
Define...	**Определить... (О)**
DEL	DELETE (DEL)
Delete	**Удалить (У)**
delete	удалить
Delete...	**Удалить...**
Delete After Current Position	**Удалить После Текущей Позиции (П)**
Delete Before Current Position	**Удалить До Текущей Позиции (Д)**
desktop	оформление
destination application	принимающее приложение
destination document	документ-получатель, принимающий документ
Device menu	**Устройство (У)**
dialog box	диалоговое окно
dialog box title	заголовок диалогового окна
Direction	Направление
Directories	Каталоги (К)
directory icon	значок каталога
disk icon	значок диска
Document...	**Документ... (Д)**
document file icon	значок файла документа
document icon	значок документа
document window	окно документа
Done	Сделано
double-click	двойной щелчок
double underline	двойное подчеркивание (д)
Down	Вниз (Н)
DOWN ARROW	СТРЕЛКА ВНИЗ
down scroll arrow	стрелка прокрутки вниз
drag	перетаскивать
drag-and-drop	перетащить и опустить
drive icon	значок устройства
Drives	Устройства (У)
drop	опустить

ENGLISH	RUSSIAN
drop-down combo box	раскрывающееся комбинированное окно
drop-down list box	раскрывающееся окно списка
drop-down menu	раскрывающееся меню
Edit	**Редактировать**
Edit menu	**Редактирование (Р)**
Effects menu	**Эффекты**
ellipsis	многоточие
embed	внедрить
embedded object	внедренный объект
END	END
ENTER	ENTER
enter	ввести
ENTER (keypad)	NUMPAD ENTER
ESC	ESC
Exit	**Выход (Ы)**
Exit and Return to	**Выход и Возвращение в**
expand	показать
extend selection	расширить выбор
Extend selection on (EXT)	Расширить Выбор (РВ)
File Manager	Диспетчер Файлов
File menu	**Файл (Ф)**
File Name	Имя Файла (И)
Find...	**Найти... (Н)**
Find Next	Повторить Поиск (П)
Find What	Что Найти (Ч)
font	шрифт
Font	Шрифт (Ш)
Font Style	Вид Шрифта (Т)
Format menu	**Формат**
freeze	зафиксировать
Freeze Panes	**Зафиксировать Подокна**
From	От / С
Full Menus	**Полные Меню**
gallery	галерея
Games	Игры
Glossary	Словарь
Go To	Перейти к
Go To...	**Перейти к... (К)**
Goto/Gosub button	кнопка Перейти к
group	группа, группировать
group box	окно/поле группы
group icon	значок группы
group window	окно группы
Help	Справка
Help menu	**Справка (С)**
Help window	окно справки
Hide	**Спрятать**
hide	спрятать
History	История
HOME	HOME

ENGLISH	RUSSIAN	ENGLISH	RUSSIAN
horizontal scroll bar	горизонтальная линейка просмотра	menu command	команда меню
horizontal split bar	горизонтальная линия разбиения	menu name	имя меню
		message	информационное сообщение
hourglass pointer	указатель песочные часы	message box	окно сообщения
How to use Help	Использование Справки (И)	message line	строка сообщений
		MIDI Sequencer...	Секвенсер MIDI...
I-beam pointer	указатель луч	Minimize	Свернуть (С)
icon	значок	Minimize button	кнопка Свернуть
inactive window	неактивное окно	Mix with File...	Микшировать с Файлом... (И)
Increase Speed (by 100%)	Увеличить Скорость (на 100%) (У)	More	Дополнительно
Increase Volume (by 25%)	Увеличить Громкость (на 25%) (В)	Mouse	Мышь (М)
		mouse pointer	указатель мыши
INS	INSERT (INS)	Move	Переместить (П)
Insert...	Поместить...	move	переместить
Insert File...	Поместить Файл... (Ф)	MS-DOS Prompt	Режим MS-DOS / Приглашение MS-DOS
insertion point	место ввода / позиция ввода		
Insert menu	Поместить	New...	Создать... (З)
Insert Object...	Поместить Объект... (М)	New Window	Новое Окно (Н)
italic	курсив (к)	Next	Следующий (Л)
justified	выравненный (в)	Next Window	Следующее Окно
Keyboard	Клавиатура (К)	No	Нет
label	метка	Notepad	Блокнот
Landscape	Ландшафт (Л)	Number...	Число...
left aligned	выравненный по левому краю (л)	NUM LOCK	NUM LOCK
		Num Lock on (NUM)	NUM
LEFT ARROW	СТРЕЛКА ВЛЕВО	object	объект
left scroll arrow	стрелка прокрутки влево	Object...	Объект... (Б)
left window border	левая граница окна	object linking & embedding (OLE)	связь и внедрение объектов (СВО)
Line (Ln)	Строка (Ст)	Object Packager	Упаковщик Объектов
link	связь / установить связь	OK	OK
linked object	связанный объект	OLE application	приложение СВО
linked text and list box	связанное окно редактирования и списка	OLE (object linking & embedding)	СВО (связь и внедрение объектов)
list box	окно/поле списка	Open	Открыть (О)
List Files of Type	Список Файлов Типа (Т)	option button	флажок опции / кнопка опции
Macro menu	Макросы		
Macro Recorder on (REC)	Макрокоманды (МАК)	Options	Параметры / Опции
Main	Главная	Options menu	Параметры (П)
main application	главное приложение	Orientation	Ориентация
main document	главный документ	Overtype on (OVR)	Замещать (ЗМЩ)
manual link	ручная связь	package	пакет
Match Case	Сравнивать Строчные/Прописные Буквы (С)	Page (Pg)	Страница (Стр)
		Pages	Страницы (Т)
Match Whole Word Only	Должно Совпадать Все Слово (Д)	Page Setup	Параметры Страницы (А)
Maximize	Развернуть (А)	palette	палитра
Maximize button	кнопка Развернуть	pane	подокно
Media Player	Медиаплеер	Paper Size	Размер Бумаги (Р)
menu	меню	Paragraph...	Абзац... (Б)
menu bar	строка меню	Paste	Вставить (А)

ENGLISH	RUSSIAN	ENGLISH	RUSSIAN
paste	вставить	**Revert...**	**Исходное**
Paste Link	**Установить Связь (У)**		**Состояние... (И)**
Paste Special	**Специальная**	right aligned	выравненный по правому
	Вставка (С)		краю (п)
PAUSE	PAUSE	RIGHT ARROW	СТРЕЛКА ВПРАВО
PG DN	PAGE DOWN (PG DN)	right scroll arrow	стрелка прокрутки вправо
PG UP	PAGE UP (PG UP)	right window border	правая граница окна
PIF Editor	Редактор PIF	ruler	линейка
point	указать на	**Run...**	**Выполнить...**
pointer	указатель	**Run...**	**Выполнить... (В)**
Portrait	Портрет (П)	Sample	Образец (О)
Preferences	**Предпочтения (П)**	**Save**	**Сохранить (С)**
press and hold down	нажать и держать нажатой	**Save All**	**Сохранить Все**
Print	**Печать (П)**	**Save As...**	**Сохранить Как... (К)**
Printer	Принтер	Save File as Type	Тип Сохраняемого
Printer Setup	**Выбор Принтера (В)**		Файла (Т)
Print Manager	Диспетчер Печати	scale	масштаб(-ировать)
Print Preview	**Предварительный**	**Scale menu**	**Шкала (Ш)**
	Просмотр (Д)	Scaling	Масштаб(-ирование) (М)
Print Quality	Качество Печати (Ч)	scroll	прокрутить
Print Range	Область Печати	scroll arrow	стрелка прокрутки
PRINT SCREEN	PRINT SCREEN	scroll bar	линейка просмотра
Print Setup...	**Выбор Принтера... (В)**	scroll box	бегунок
Print to File	Печать в Файл (Ф)	SCROLL LOCK	SCROLL LOCK
Print Topic	**Печать Темы (П)**	Scroll Lock on (SCRL)	SCRL
program group	группа программ	Search	Поиск
program item	программный элемент	**Search...**	**Поиск... (П)**
program-item icon	значок программного	**Search for Help on**	**Поиск Справки о (П)**
	элемента	**Section...**	**Раздел...**
Program Manager	Диспетчер Программ	Section (Sec)	Раздел (Раз)
progress indicator	индикатор процесса	select	выбрать
push button	нажимаемая кнопка	select	выбрать
Quit	Завершить	select (check box, option	установить (флажок
radio button	кнопка опции	button)	проверки) выбрать
Read Only	Только для Чтения (Ч)		(флажок опции)
Record...	**Записать... (З)**	select (data)	выбрать (данные)
Recorder	Запись Макрокоманд /	select (drop-down menu)	выбрать (раскрывающееся
	Запись Макросов		меню)
Redo	Переделать	selected command	выбранная команда
reduce selection	сжать выбор	Selection	Выбор
Remove Split	**Убрать Разбивку**	selection cursor	курсор выбора
Repeat	**Повторить**	select (list box)	выбрать (окно списка)
Replace...	**Замена... (З)**	Set	Задать
Replace All	Заменить Все (С)	Setup	Установка
Replace With	Заменить на (Н)	SHIFT	SHIFT
Reset	Сброс	shortcut key	быстрая клавиша
resize	изменить размер	**Short Menus**	**Краткие Меню**
Restore	**Восстановить (В)**	**Size**	**Размер (Р)**
restore	восстановить	size	размер
Restore button	кнопка Восстановить	Size (font size)	Размер (размер шрифта) (Р)
Resume	Восстановить	sizing handle	ручка изменения размера
Retry	Повторить	slider	слайдер
Reverse	**Реверс (Р)**	slider indicator	индикатор слайдера

ENGLISH	RUSSIAN	ENGLISH	RUSSIAN
small capitals	маленькие заглавные (з)	unavailable command	недоступная команда
Sound...	**Звук... (З)**	underline	подчеркивание (п)
Sound Recorder	Звукозапись	**Undo**	**Отменить (О)**
source application	приложение-источник	unfreeze	разфиксировать / отменить
source document	документ-источник		фиксацию
Source (paper)	Источник (бумаги) (И)	**Unfreeze Panes**	**Разфиксировать Подокна/**
SPACEBAR	ПРОБЕЛ		**Отменить Фиксацию**
spin box	поле счетчика		**Подокон**
Split	**Разбить (Б)**	**Unhide...**	**Показать...**
Split	**Разбить**	Up	Вверх (В)
split	разбить	UP ARROW	СТРЕЛКА ВВЕРХ
split bar	линия разбиения	up scroll arrow	стрелка прокрутки вверх
split box	маркер разбиения	**Update**	**Обновить**
StartUp	Группа Запуска	update	обновить
status bar	строка состояния	**Utilities menu**	**Утилиты**
status-bar indicator	индикатор строки	value set	набор значений
	состояния	vertical scroll bar	вертикальная линейка
submenu	подменю		просмотра
switch	переключить	vertical split bar	вертикальная линия
Switch to	Переключиться в		разбиения
Switch To...	**Переключиться в... (Е)**	view	просмотреть
SYS RQ	SYS RQ	**View menu**	**Просмотр**
TAB	TAB	wallpaper	обои
Terminal	Терминал	warning message	предупреждающее
text box	окно текста / текстовое		сообщение
	поле	wildcard	подстановочные символы
text frame	рамка текста	window	окно
Tile	**Мозаика (М)**	window background	фон окна
tiled windows	окна мозаикой	window border	граница окна
Time	**Время (В)**	window corner	угол окна
title bar	строка заголовка	window frame	рамка окна
To	По	**Window menu**	**Окно (О)**
tool	инструмент	window size	размер окна
toolbar	панель инструментов	window title	заголовок окна
toolbox	инструменты / панель	Windows Setup	Windows Setup / Установка
	инструментов		Windows
Tools menu	**Инструменты**	workspace	рабочая область
top window border	верхняя граница окна	Yes	Да
Tracks	**Фонограммы (Ф)**	**Zoom...**	**Фокус...**
Tutorial	**Учебник (У)**	zoom in	приблизить
type	набрать / ввести	zoom out	отодвинуть

C H A P T E R   2 0

Spanish

This chapter lists the Spanish translations of all terms formatted in *italic* in Part 1. Terminology is listed in two ways: by category and in alphabetical order. The first section includes translations in the following categories: Window Elements, Menus, Dialog Boxes, Message Boxes, Other GUI Screen Elements, Keys, User Actions, and Applications For Microsoft Windows.

Terminology by Category

ENGLISH	SPANISH	ENGLISH	SPANISH
WINDOW ELEMENTS		window frame	marco de la ventana
Main window elements		window size	tamaño de la ventana
active window	ventana activa	window title	título de la ventana
application window	ventana de la aplicación	workspace	área de trabajo
border	bordes		
bottom window border	borde inferior de la ventana	**Window controls**	
cascading windows	ventanas en cascada	Control-menu box	cuadro de Menú de control
desktop	escritorio	down scroll arrow	flecha de desplazamiento abajo
document window	ventana de documento	horizontal scroll bar	Barra de desplazamiento
group window	ventana de grupo		horizontal
Help window	ventana de Ayuda	horizontal split bar	Barra de división horizontal
inactive window	ventana inactiva	left scroll arrow	flecha de desplazamiento a la
left window border	borde izquierdo de la ventana		izquierda
menu bar	barra de menús	Maximize button	botón Maximizar
pane	sección	Minimize button	botón Minimizar
right window border	borde derecho de la ventana	Restore button	botón Restablecer
ruler	Regla	right scroll arrow	flecha de desplazamiento a la
status bar	Barra de estado		derecha
tiled windows	ventanas en mosaico	scroll arrow	flecha de desplazamiento
title bar	Barra de títulos	scroll bar	Barra de desplazamiento
toolbar	Barra de herramientas	scroll box	cuadro de desplazamiento
top window border	borde superior de la ventana	split bar	Barra de división
wallpaper	papel tapiz	split box	cuadro de división
window	ventana	up scroll arrow	flecha de desplazamiento arriba
window background	fondo de la ventana		
window border	borde de la ventana		
window corner	esquina de la ventana		

ENGLISH	SPANISH	ENGLISH	SPANISH
vertical scroll bar	Barra de desplazamiento vertical	**Menus and commands**	
		View menu	Ver (v)
vertical split bar	Barra de división vertical	Insert menu	Insertar (i)
Pointers		Control menu	Menú Control
arrow	flecha	Restore	Restaurar (r)
arrow pointer	puntero de flecha	Move	Mover (m)
cross-hair pointer	cursor en cruz	Size	Tamaño (t)
hourglass pointer	reloj de arena	Minimize	Minimizar (n)
I-beam pointer	cursor en I	Maximize	Maximizar (x)
insertion point	punto de inserción	Next	Siguiente (s)
mouse pointer	puntero del Mouse	Close	Cerrar (c)
pointer	puntero	Run...	Ejecutar... (e)
selection cursor	cursor de selección	Switch to...	Cambiar a... (b)
		Split	Dividir (d)
Icons			
application icon	icono de aplicación	File menu	Archivo (a)
directory icon	icono de directorio	New...	Nuevo... (n)
disk icon	icono de disco	Open	Abrir (a)
document file icon	icono de archivo de documento	Close	Cerrar (c)
		Close All	Cerrar todo (t)
document icon	icono de documento	Save	Guardar (g)
drive icon	icono de unidad	Save As...	Guardar como... (o)
group icon	icono de grupo	Save All	Guardar todo (t)
icon	icono	Delete	Eliminar (l)
program-item icon	icono de programa	Page Setup	Preparar página (p)
		Print	Imprimir (i)
General terms		Print Preview	Presentación preliminar (p)
access key	tecla de acceso	Printer Setup	Especificar impresora (e)
check mark	marca de verificación	Exit	Salir (s)
ellipsis	puntos suspensivos	Exit and Return to	Salir y volver a (s)
font	fuente	Update	Actualizar (a)
object	objeto		
program group	grupo de programas	Edit menu	Edición (e)
program item	elemento de programa	Undo	Deshacer (z)
shortcut key	método abreviado	Repeat	Repetir (r)
sizing handle	cuadro de tamaño	Cut	Cortar (x)
status-bar indicator	indicador de la barra de estado	Copy	Copiar (c)
tool	herramienta	Copy Special	Copia especial (o)
unavailable command	comando no disponible	Paste	Pegar (v)
		Paste Link	Pegar vínculo
MENUS		Paste Special	Pegado especial (s)
		Clear	Borrar (b)
Menu elements		Clear All	Borrar todo (t)
cascading menu	menú en cascada	Find...	Buscar...(b)
checked command	comando activado	Search...	Buscar... (b)
command	comando	Replace...	Reemplazar... (r)
command separator	separador de comandos	Go To...	Ir a... (i)
drop-down menu	menú desplegable	Delete...	Eliminar... (e)
menu	menú	Insert...	Insertar... (i)
menu command	comando de menú	Object...	Objeto... (o)
menu name	nombre de menú	Insert Object...	Insertar objeto... (o)
selected command	comando activo		
submenu	submenú	Options menu	Opciones (o)
		Preferences	Preferencias (p)

ENGLISH	SPANISH	ENGLISH	SPANISH
Full Menus	Menús completos (m)	Insert File...	Insertar archivo... (i)
Short Menus	Menús cortos (m)	Mix with File...	Combinar con archivo... (o)
		Delete Before Current Position	Eliminar antes de la posición
Format menu	Formato (f)		actual (m)
Character...	Carácter... (c)	Delete After Current Position	Eliminar después de la
Paragraph...	Párrafo... (p)		posición actual (l)
Section...	Sección... (s)	Increase Volume (by 25%)	Subir volumen (25%) (s)
Document...	Documento... (d)	Decrease Volume	Bajar volumen (b)
Number...	Número... (n)	Increase Speed (by 100%)	Aumentar velocidad
Alignment...	Alineación... (a)		(100%) (a)
		Decrease Speed	Reducir velocidad (r)
Utilities menu	Utilidades (u)	Add Echo	Agregar eco (e)
Tools menu	Herramientas (h)	Reverse	Inverso (v)
Customize	Personalizar (p)		
		Help application	
Macro menu	Macro (femenino) (m)	File menu	Archivo (a)
Record...	Grabar... (g)	Open	Abrir (a)
Run...	Ejecutar... (j)	Print Topic	Imprimir tema (i)
Edit	Editar (e)	Print Setup...	Especificar impresora... (i)
Assign to Key	Asignar a una tecla (t)	Exit	Salir (s)
Assign to Menu	Asignar a un menú (m)		
		Edit menu	Edición (e)
Window menu	Ventana (v)	Copy...	Copiar... (c)
New Window	Nueva ventana (n)	Annotate...	Anotar... (a)
Cascade	Cascada (c)		
Tile	Mosaico (m)	Bookmark menu	Marcador (m)
Next Window	Siguiente ventana (s)	Define...	Definir... (d)
Arrange All	Organizar todo (t)		
Hide	Ocultar (o)	Help menu	?
Unhide...	Mostrar... (m)	How to use Help	Uso de la Ayuda (u)
Split	Dividir (d)	Always on Top	Siempre visible (s)
Freeze Panes	Inmovilizar secciones (v)	About Help...	Acerca de... (a)
Remove Split	Anular división (d)		
Unfreeze Panes	Movilizar secciones (v)	**Buttons**	
Zoom...	Zoom... (z)	Contents	Indice (i)
		Search	Buscar (b)
Help menu	Ayuda (u)	Back	Atrás (t)
Contents	Indice (i)	History	Historial (h)
How to use Help	Uso de la ayuda (u)	Glossary	Glosario (g)
Search for Help on	Buscar ayuda sobre (b)		
Active Window	Ventana activa (v)	**DIALOG BOXES**	
Keyboard	Teclado (t)	dialog box	cuadro de diálogo
Mouse	Mouse (cursiva e inicial en	wildcard	comodín
	mayúscula) (m)		
Tutorial	Tutorial (u)	**Dialog box elements**	
About	Acerca de (a)	button	botón
		check box	casilla de verificación
Device menu	Dispositivo (d)	chevrons	comillas angulares
Scale menu	Escala (e)	combo box	cuadro combinado
MIDI Sequencer...	Secuenciador MIDI...	command button	botón de comando
Sound...	Sonido... (s)	dialog box title	título de cuadro de diálogo
Time	Tiempo (t)	drop-down combo box	cuadro combinado desplegable
Tracks	Pistas (p)	drop-down list box	cuadro de lista desplegable
		Goto/Gosub button	botón Ir a/ Ir a sub
Effects menu	Efectos (c)	group box	cuadro de grupo
Revert...	Volver... (v)		

ENGLISH	SPANISH
label	etiqueta
linked text and list box	cuadro de edición/lista vinculados
list box	cuadro de lista
option button	botón de opción
progress indicator	indicador de progreso
push button	botón de comando
radio button	botón de radio
slider	dispositivo deslizante
slider indicator	indicador de deslizamiento
spin box	cuadro de giro
text box	cuadro de texto
value set	asignar valor

Dialog box buttons

Add	Agregar
Apply	Aplicar
Cancel	Cancelar
Change	Cambiar
Create	Crear
Default	Predeterminado
Define	Definir
Done	Terminado
Go To	Ir a (i)
Help	Ayuda
More	Más
No	No
OK	Aceptar
Options	Opciones
Quit	Salir
Redo	Repetir
Reset	Restablecer
Resume	Reanudar
Retry	Reintentar
Search	Buscar (b)
Set	Establecer
Setup	Instalar
Switch to	Pasar a
Yes	Sí

Dialog box labels

All	Todo (t)
Collate Copies	Pegar copias (p)
Copies	Copias (c)
Direction	Dirección
Directories	Directorios (d)
Down	Abajo (a)
Drives	Unidades (u)
File Name	Nombre de archivo (a)
Find Next	Buscar siguiente (u)
Find What	Buscar (b)
Font	Fuente (f)
Font Style	Estilo de fuente (e)
From	Desde/De (d)
Landscape	Horizontal (h)
List Files of Type	Mostrar archivos de tipo (m)

ENGLISH	SPANISH
Match Case	Mayúsculas/minúsculas (m)
Match Whole Word Only	Palabra completa solamente (p)
Orientation	Orientación (o)
Pages	Páginas (p)
Paper Size	Tamaño del papel (m)
Portrait	Vertical (v)
Printer	Impresora (i)
Print Quality	Calidad de la impresión (i)
Print Range	Campo de impresión
Print to File	Imprimir en un archivo (m)
Read Only	Sólo lectura (s)
Replace All	Reemplazar todo (t)
Replace With	Reemplazar con (r)
Sample	Muestra (m)
Save File as Type	Guardar como archivo tipo (g)
Scaling	Proporción (p)
Selection	Selección (s)
Size (font size)	Tamaño (fuente) (t)
Source (paper)	Origen (papel) (r)
To	Hasta/A (h)
Up	Arriba (r)

MESSAGE BOXES

critical message	mensaje crítico
message	mensaje informativo
message box	cuadro de mensajes
message line	línea de mensajes
warning message	mensaje de advertencia

OTHER GUI SCREEN ELEMENTS

Graphical options

gallery	galería
palette	paleta
text frame	cuadro de texto
toolbox	caja de herramientas

Status bar abbreviations

Caps Lock on (CAPS)	MAYÚS
Column (Col)	Col
Extend selection on (EXT)	EX
Line (Ln)	Lín
Macro Recorder on (REC)	GM
Num Lock on (NUM)	NÚM
Overtype on (OVR)	SO
Page (Pg)	Pág
Scroll Lock on (SCRL)	BD
Section (Sec)	Sec

Character formats

bold	negrita (n)
double underline	subrayado doble (b)
italic	cursiva (k)

ENGLISH	SPANISH
small capitals	versales (l)
underline	subrayado (s)

Paragraph formats

centered	centrado (e)
justified	justificado (j)
left aligned	alineado a la izquierda (i)
right aligned	alineado a la derecha (d)

KEYS

Shortcut keys

CTRL+B (Bold)	CTRL+N
CTRL+C (Copy)	CTRL+C
CTRL+D (Double underline)	CTRL+B
CTRL+E (Center)	CTRL+E
CTRL+I (Italics)	CTRL+K
CTRL+J (Justify)	CTRL+J
CTRL+L (Left align)	CTRL+I
CTRL+R (Right align)	CTRL+D
CTRL+U (Underline)	CTRL+S
CTRL+V (Paste)	CTRL+V
CTRL+W (Word underline)	CTRL+P
CTRL+X (Cut)	CTRL+X
CTRL+Z (Undo)	CTRL+Z
DEL (Clear)	DEL

Keynames

(keypad) *	MULTIPLICACIÓN NUMÉRICO (* NUM)
(keypad) +	MÁS NUMÉRICO (+NUM)
(keypad) -	MENOS NUMERICO (- NUM)
(keypad) /	DIVISIÓN NUMÉRICO (/ NUM)
ALT	ALT
ALT GR	ALT GR
BACKSPACE	RETROCESO (RET)
BREAK	INTERRUMPIR (INTER)
CAPS LOCK	BLOQUEA MAYÚSCULAS (BLOQ MAYÚS)
CTRL	CONTROL (CTRL)
DEL	SUPRIMIR (SUPR)
DOWN ARROW	FLECHA ABAJO (ABAJO)
END	FIN (FIN)
ENTER	ENTRAR (ENTRAR)
ENTER (keypad)	ENTRAR NUMÉRICO (ENT NUM)
ESC	ESCAPE (ESC)
HOME	INICIO (INICIO)
INS	INSERTAR (INS)
LEFT ARROW	FLECHA IZQUIERDA (IZDA.)
NUM LOCK	BLOQUEO NUMÉRICO (BLOQ NUM)
PAUSE	PAUSA

ENGLISH	SPANISH
PG DN	AVANZAR PÁGINA (AV PÁG)
PG UP	RETROCEDER PÁGINA (RE PÁG)
PRINT SCREEN	IMPRIMIR PANTALLA (IMP PANT)
RIGHT ARROW	FLECHA DERECHA (DCHA)
SCROLL LOCK	BLOQUEO DE DESPLAZAMIENTO (BLOQ DESPL)
SHIFT	MAYÚSCULAS (MAYÚS)
SPACEBAR	BARRA ESPACIADORA (ESPACIO)
SYS RQ	PETICIÓN DEL SISTEMA (PET SIS)
TAB	TABULADOR (TAB)
UP ARROW	FLECHA ARRIBA (ARRIBA)

USER ACTIONS

Keyboard actions

enter	introducir
press and hold down	mantener presionado
type	escribir

Mouse actions

click	hacer clic
double-click	hacer doble clic
drag	arrastrar
drag-and-drop	arrastrar y colocar
drop	colocar
point	señalar

Manipulating window appearance

arrange	organizar
close	cerrar
freeze	inmovilizar
hide	ocultar
move	mover
resize	ajustar tamaño
restore	restaurar
select	seleccionar
size	tamaño
split	dividir
switch	cambiar
unfreeze	movilizar

Selecting options or content

cancel	cancelar
check	verificar
choose	escoger
clear (undo Select)	borrar
extend selection	extender selección
reduce selection	comprimir selección

ENGLISH	SPANISH
select	seleccionar
select (check box, option button)	seleccionar (casilla de verificación, botón de opción)
select (data)	seleccionar (datos)
select (drop-down menu)	seleccionar (menús desplegables)
select (list box)	seleccionar (cuadro de lista)

Viewing content

autoscroll	desplazamiento automático
browse	examinar
collapse	contraer
expand	expandir
scroll	desplazar
view	ver
zoom in	zoom para acercar
zoom out	zoom para alejar

Removing content

clear	borrar
copy	copiar
cut	cortar
delete	eliminar
paste	pegar

Manipulating objects

arrange	organizar
automatic link	vículo automático
Clipboard	Portapapeles
container application	aplicación contenedora
container document	documento contenedor
copy	copiar
crop	recortar
destination application	aplicación destino
destination document	documento destino
drag-and-drop	arrastrar y colocar
embed	incrustar
embedded object	objeto incrustado
group	agrupar (v) / grupo (n)
link	vincular
linked object	objeto vinculado
main application	aplicación principal

ENGLISH	SPANISH
main document	documento principal
manual link	vínculo manual
object	objeto
object linking & embedding (OLE)	incrustación y vinculación de objetos (OLE)
OLE (object linking & embedding)	OLE (incrustación y vinculación de objetos)
OLE application	aplicación OLE
package	paquete
paste	pegar
scale	graduar
size	ajustar tamaño
source application	aplicación origen
source document	documento origen
update	actualizar

APPLICATIONS FOR MICROSOFT WINDOWS

Accessories	Accesorios
Applications	Aplicaciones
Calculator	Calculadora
Calendar	Calendario
Cardfile	Fichero
Character Map	Mapa de caracteres
Clipboard Viewer	Visor del Portapapeles
Clock	Reloj
Control Panel	Panel de control
File Manager	Administrador de archivos
Games	Juegos
Main	Principal
Media Player	Transmisor de medios
MS-DOS Prompt	Símbolo del sistema
Notepad	Bloc de notas
Object Packager	Empaquetador de objetos
PIF Editor	Editor PIF
Print Manager	Administrador de impresión
Program Manager	Administrador de programas
Recorder	Grabadora
Sound Recorder	Grabadora de sonidos
StartUp	Iniciar
Terminal	Terminal
Windows Setup	Instalar Windows

Terminology by Alphabet

Notes:
1. All terms formatted in **bold** refer to menu names or command names.
2. All characters between parentheses are preferred access keys.

ENGLISH	SPANISH	ENGLISH	SPANISH
(keypad) *	MULTIPLICACIÓN NUMÉRICO (* NUM)	cancel	cancelar
		CAPS LOCK	BLOQUEA MAYÚSCULAS (BLOQ MAYÚS)
(keypad) +	MÁS NUMÉRICO (+NUM)		
(keypad) -	MENOS NUMERICO (- NUM)	Caps Lock on (CAPS)	MAYÚS
		Cardfile	Fichero
(keypad) /	DIVISIÓN NUMÉRICO (/ NUM)	**Cascade**	**Cascada (c)**
About	**Acerca de (a)**	cascading menu	menú en cascada
About Help...	**Acerca de... (a)**	cascading windows	ventanas en cascada
access key	tecla de acceso	centered	centrado (e)
Accessories	Accesorios	Change	Cambiar
active window	ventana activa	**Character...**	**Carácter... (c)**
Active Window	**Ventana activa (v)**	Character Map	Mapa de caracteres
Add	Agregar	check	verificar
Add Echo	**Agregar eco (e)**	check box	casilla de verificación
Alignment...	**Alineación... (a)**	checked command	comando activado
All	Todo (t)	check mark	marca de verificación
ALT	ALT	chevrons	comillas angulares
ALT GR	ALT GR	choose	escoger
Always on Top	**Siempre visible (s)**	**Clear**	**Borrar (b)**
Annotate...	**Anotar... (a)**	clear	borrar
application icon	icono de aplicación	**Clear All**	**Borrar todo (t)**
Applications	Aplicaciones	clear (undo Select)	borrar
application window	ventana de la aplicación	click	hacer clic
Apply	Aplicar	Clipboard	Portapapeles
arrange	organizar	Clipboard Viewer	Visor del Portapapeles
Arrange All	**Organizar todo (t)**	Clock	Reloj
arrow	flecha	**Close**	**Cerrar (c)**
arrow pointer	puntero de flecha	close	cerrar
Assign to Key	**Asignar a una tecla (t)**	**Close All**	**Cerrar todo (t)**
Assign to Menu	**Asignar a un menú (m)**	collapse	contraer
automatic link	vículo automático	Collate Copies	Pegar copias (p)
autoscroll	desplazamiento automático	Column (Col)	Col
Back	Atrás (t)	combo box	cuadro combinado
BACKSPACE	RETROCESO (RET)	command	comando
bold	negrita (n)	command button	botón de comando
Bookmark menu	**Marcador (m)**	command separator	separador de comandos
border	bordes	container application	aplicación contenedora
bottom window border	borde inferior de la ventana	container document	documento contenedor
BREAK	INTERRUMPIR (INTER)	**Contents**	**Indice (i)**
browse	examinar	Contents	Indice (i)
button	botón	**Control menu**	**Menú Control**
Calculator	Calculadora	Control-menu box	cuadro de Menú de control
Calendar	Calendario	Control Panel	Panel de control
Cancel	Cancelar	Copies	Copias (c)
		Copy	**Copiar (c)**

ENGLISH	SPANISH	ENGLISH	SPANISH
copy	copiar	Down	Abajo (a)
Copy...	**Copiar... (c)**	DOWN ARROW	FLECHA ABAJO (ABAJO)
Copy Special	**Copia especial (o)**	down scroll arrow	flecha de desplazamiento abajo
Create	Crear		
critical message	mensaje crítico	drag	arrastrar
crop	recortar	drag-and-drop	arrastrar y colocar
cross-hair pointer	cursor en cruz	drive icon	icono de unidad
CTRL	CONTROL (CTRL)	Drives	Unidades (u)
CTRL+B (Bold)	CTRL+N	drop	colocar
CTRL+C (Copy)	CTRL+C	drop-down combo box	cuadro combinado desplegable
CTRL+D (Double underline)	CTRL+B	drop-down list box	cuadro de lista desplegable
CTRL+E (Center)	CTRL+E	drop-down menu	menú desplegable
CTRL+I (Italics)	CTRL+K	**Edit**	**Editar (e)**
CTRL+J (Justify)	CTRL+J	**Edit menu**	**Edición (e)**
CTRL+L (Left align)	CTRL+I	**Effects menu**	**Efectos (c)**
CTRL+R (Right align)	CTRL+D	ellipsis	puntos suspensivos
CTRL+U (Underline)	CTRL+S	embed	incrustar
CTRL+V (Paste)	CTRL+V	embedded object	objeto incrustado
CTRL+W (Word underline)	CTRL+P	END	FIN (FIN)
CTRL+X (Cut)	CTRL+X	ENTER	ENTRAR (ENTRAR)
CTRL+Z (Undo)	CTRL+Z	enter	introducir
Customize	**Personalizar (p)**	ENTER (keypad)	ENTRAR NUMÉRICO (ENT NUM)
Cut	**Cortar (x)**		
cut	cortar	ESC	ESCAPE (ESC)
Decrease Speed	**Reducir velocidad (r)**	**Exit**	**Salir (s)**
Decrease Volume	**Bajar volumen (b)**	**Exit and Return to**	**Salir y volver a (s)**
Default	Predeterminado	expand	expandir
Define	Definir	extend selection	extender selección
Define...	**Definir... (d)**	Extend selection on (EXT)	EX
DEL	SUPRIMIR (SUPR)	File Manager	Administrador de archivos
DEL (Clear)	DEL	**File menu**	**Archivo (a)**
Delete	**Eliminar (l)**	File Name	Nombre de archivo (a)
delete	eliminar	**Find...**	**Buscar...(b)**
Delete...	**Eliminar... (e)**	Find Next	Buscar siguiente (u)
Delete After Current Position	**Eliminar después de la posición actual (l)**	Find What	Buscar (b)
		font	fuente
Delete Before Current Position	**Eliminar antes de la posición actual (m)**	Font	Fuente (f)
		Font Style	Estilo de fuente (e)
desktop	escritorio	**Format menu**	**Formato (f)**
destination application	aplicación destino	freeze	inmovilizar
destination document	documento destino	**Freeze Panes**	**Inmovilizar secciones (v)**
Device menu	**Dispositivo (d)**	From	Desde/De (d)
dialog box	cuadro de diálogo	**Full Menus**	**Menús completos (m)**
dialog box title	título de cuadro de diálogo	gallery	galería
Direction	Dirección	Games	Juegos
Directories	Directorios (d)	Glossary	Glosario (g)
directory icon	icono de directorio	Go To	Ir a (i)
disk icon	icono de disco	**Go To...**	**Ir a... (i)**
Document...	**Documento... (d)**	Goto/Gosub button	botón Ir a/ Ir a sub
document file icon	icono de archivo de documento	group	agrupar (v) / grupo (n)
		group box	cuadro de grupo
document icon	icono de documento	group icon	icono de grupo
document window	ventana de documento	group window	ventana de grupo
Done	Terminado	Help	Ayuda
double-click	hacer doble clic	**Help menu**	**?**
double underline	subrayado doble (b)	Help window	ventana de Ayuda

ENGLISH	SPANISH	ENGLISH	SPANISH
Hide	**Ocultar (o)**	message box	cuadro de mensajes
hide	ocultar	message line	línea de mensajes
History	Historial (h)	**MIDI Sequencer...**	**Secuenciador MIDI...**
HOME	INICIO (INICIO)	**Minimize**	**Minimizar (n)**
horizontal scroll bar	Barra de desplazamiento	Minimize button	botón Minimizar
	horizontal	**Mix with File...**	**Combinar con archivo... (o)**
horizontal split bar	Barra de división horizontal	More	Más
hourglass pointer	reloj de arena	**Mouse**	**Mouse (cursiva e inicial**
How to use Help	**Uso de la Ayuda (u)**		**en mayúscula) (m)**
I-beam pointer	cursor en I	mouse pointer	puntero del Mouse
icon	icono	**Move**	**Mover (m)**
inactive window	ventana inactiva	move	mover
Increase Speed (by 100%)	**Aumentar velocidad**	MS-DOS Prompt	Símbolo del sistema
	(100%) (a)	**New...**	**Nuevo... (n)**
Increase Volume (by 25%)	**Subir volumen (25%) (s)**	**New Window**	**Nueva ventana (n)**
INS	INSERTAR (INS)	**Next**	**Siguiente (s)**
Insert...	**Insertar... (i)**	**Next Window**	**Siguiente ventana (s)**
Insert File...	**Insertar archivo... (i)**	No	No
insertion point	punto de inserción	Notepad	Bloc de notas
Insert menu	**Insertar (i)**	**Number...**	**Número... (n)**
Insert Object...	**Insertar objeto... (o)**	NUM LOCK	BLOQUEO NUMÉRICO
italic	cursiva (k)		(BLOQ NUM)
justified	justificado (j)	Num Lock on (NUM)	NÚM
Keyboard	**Teclado (t)**	object	objeto
label	etiqueta	**Object...**	**Objeto... (o)**
Landscape	Horizontal (h)	object linking & embedding	incrustación y vinculación de
left aligned	alineado a la izquierda (i)	(OLE)	objetos (OLE)
LEFT ARROW	FLECHA IZQUIERDA	Object Packager	Empaquetador de objetos
	(IZDA.)	OK	Aceptar
left scroll arrow	flecha de desplazamiento a la	OLE application	aplicación OLE
	izquierda	OLE (object linking &	OLE (incrustación y
left window border	borde izquierdo de la ventana	embedding)	vinculación de objetos)
Line (Ln)	Lín	Open	Abrir (a)
link	vincular	**Open**	**Abrir (a)**
linked object	objeto vinculado	option button	botón de opción
linked text and list box	cuadro de edición/lista	Options	Opciones
	vinculados	**Options menu**	**Opciones (o)**
list box	cuadro de lista	Orientation	Orientación (o)
List Files of Type	Mostrar archivos de tipo (m)	Overtype on (OVR)	SO
Macro menu	**Macro (femenino) (m)**	package	paquete
Macro Recorder on (REC)	GM	Page (Pg)	Pág
Main	Principal	Pages	Páginas (p)
main application	aplicación principal	**Page Setup**	**Preparar página (p)**
main document	documento principal	palette	paleta
manual link	vínculo manual	pane	sección
Match Case	Mayúsculas/minúsculas (m)	Paper Size	Tamaño del papel (m)
Match Whole Word Only	Palabra completa	**Paragraph...**	**Párrafo... (p)**
	solamente (p)	Paste	Pegar (v)
Maximize	**Maximizar (x)**	paste	pegar
Maximize button	botón Maximizar	**Paste Link**	**Pegar vínculo**
Media Player	Transmisor de medios	**Paste Special**	**Pegado especial (s)**
menu	menú	PAUSE	PAUSA
menu bar	barra de menús	PG DN	AVANZAR PÁGINA
menu command	comando de menú		(AV PÁG)
menu name	nombre de menú	PG UP	RETROCEDER PÁGINA
message	mensaje informativo		(RE PÁG)

ENGLISH	SPANISH
PIF Editor	Editor PIF
point	señalar
pointer	puntero
Portrait	Vertical (v)
Preferences	**Preferencias (p)**
press and hold down	mantener presionado
Print	**Imprimir (i)**
Printer	Impresora (i)
Printer Setup	**Especificar impresora (e)**
Print Manager	Administrador de impresión
Print Preview	**Presentación preliminar (p)**
Print Quality	Calidad de la impresión (i)
Print Range	Campo de impresión
PRINT SCREEN	IMPRIMIR PANTALLA (IMP PANT)
Print Setup...	**Especificar impresora... (i)**
Print to File	Imprimir en un archivo (m)
Print Topic	**Imprimir tema (i)**
program group	grupo de programas
program item	elemento de programa
program-item icon	icono de programa
Program Manager	Administrador de programas
progress indicator	indicador de progreso
push button	botón de comando
Quit	Salir
radio button	botón de radio
Read Only	Sólo lectura (s)
Record...	**Grabar... (g)**
Recorder	Grabadora
Redo	Repetir
reduce selection	comprimir selección
Remove Split	**Anular división (d)**
Repeat	**Repetir (r)**
Replace...	**Reemplazar... (r)**
Replace All	Reemplazar todo (t)
Replace With	Reemplazar con (r)
Reset	Restablecer
resize	ajustar tamaño
Restore	**Restaurar (r)**
restore	restaurar
Restore button	botón Restablecer
Resume	Reanudar
Retry	Reintentar
Reverse	**Inverso (v)**
Revert...	**Volver... (v)**
right aligned	alineado a la derecha (d)
RIGHT ARROW	FLECHA DERECHA (DCHA)
right scroll arrow	flecha de desplazamiento a la derecha
right window border	borde derecho de la ventana
ruler	Regla
Run...	**Ejecutar... (e)**
Run...	**Ejecutar... (j)**
Sample	Muestra (m)
Save	**Guardar (g)**

ENGLISH	SPANISH
Save All	**Guardar todo (t)**
Save As...	**Guardar como... (o)**
Save File as Type	Guardar como archivo tipo (g)
scale	graduar
Scale menu	**Escala (e)**
Scaling	Proporción (p)
scroll	desplazar
scroll arrow	flecha de desplazamiento
scroll bar	Barra de desplazamiento
scroll box	cuadro de desplazamiento
SCROLL LOCK	BLOQUEO DE DESPLAZAMIENTO (BLOQ DESPL)
Scroll Lock on (SCRL)	BD
Search	Buscar (b)
Search...	**Buscar... (b)**
Search for Help on	**Buscar ayuda sobre (b)**
Section...	**Sección... (s)**
Section (Sec)	Sec
select	seleccionar
select (check box, option button)	seleccionar (casilla de verificación, botón de opción)
select (data)	seleccionar (datos)
select (drop-down menu)	seleccionar (menús desplegables)
selected command	comando activo
Selection	Selección (s)
selection cursor	cursor de selección
select (list box)	seleccionar (cuadro de lista)
Set	Establecer
Setup	Instalar
SHIFT	MAYÚSCULAS (MAYÚS)
shortcut key	método abreviado
Short Menus	**Menús cortos (m)**
Size	**Tamaño (t)**
size	tamaño
size	ajustar tamaño
Size (font size)	Tamaño (fuente) (t)
sizing handle	cuadro de tamaño
slider	dispositivo deslizante
slider indicator	indicador de deslizamiento
small capitals	versales (l)
Sound...	**Sonido... (s)**
Sound Recorder	Grabadora de sonidos
source application	aplicación origen
source document	documento origen
Source (paper)	Origen (papel) (r)
SPACEBAR	BARRA ESPACIADORA (ESPACIO)
spin box	cuadro de giro
Split	**Dividir (d)**
split	dividir
split bar	Barra de división
split box	cuadro de división
StartUp	Iniciar

ENGLISH	SPANISH	ENGLISH	SPANISH
status bar	Barra de estado	Up	Arriba (r)
status-bar indicator	indicador de la barra de estado	UP ARROW	FLECHA ARRIBA (ARRIBA)
submenu	submenú	up scroll arrow	flecha de desplazamiento
switch	cambiar		arriba
Switch to	Pasar a	**Update**	**Actualizar (a)**
Switch to...	**Cambiar a... (b)**	update	actualizar
SYS RQ	PETICIÓN DEL SISTEMA	**Utilities menu**	**Utilidades (u)**
	(PET SIS)	value set	asignar valor
TAB	TABULADOR (TAB)	vertical scroll bar	Barra de desplazamiento
Terminal	Terminal		vertical
text box	cuadro de texto	vertical split bar	Barra de división vertical
text frame	cuadro de texto	view	ver
Tile	**Mosaico (m)**	**View menu**	**Ver (v)**
tiled windows	ventanas en mosaico	wallpaper	papel tapiz
Time	**Tiempo (t)**	warning message	mensaje de advertencia
title bar	Barra de títulos	wildcard	comodín
To	Hasta/A (h)	window	ventana
tool	herramienta	window background	fondo de la ventana
toolbar	Barra de herramientas	window border	borde de la ventana
toolbox	caja de herramientas	window corner	esquina de la ventana
Tools menu	**Herramientas (h)**	window frame	marco de la ventana
top window border	borde superior de la ventana	**Window menu**	**Ventana (v)**
Tracks	**Pistas (p)**	window size	tamaño de la ventana
Tutorial	**Tutorial (u)**	window title	título de la ventana
type	escribir	Windows Setup	Instalar Windows
unavailable command	comando no disponible	workspace	área de trabajo
underline	subrayado (s)	Yes	Sí
Undo	**Deshacer (z)**	**Zoom...**	**Zoom... (z)**
unfreeze	movilizar	zoom in	zoom para acercar
Unfreeze Panes	**Movilizar secciones (v)**	zoom out	zoom para alejar
Unhide...	**Mostrar... (m)**		

CHAPTER 21

Swedish

This chapter lists the Swedish translations of all terms formatted in *italic* in Part 1. Terminology is listed in two ways: by category and in alphabetical order. The first section includes translations in the following categories: Window Elements, Menus, Dialog Boxes, Message Boxes, Other GUI Screen Elements, Keys, User Actions, and Applications For Microsoft Windows.

Terminology by Category

ENGLISH	SWEDISH	ENGLISH	SWEDISH
WINDOW ELEMENTS		window corner	fönsterhörn
Main window elements		window frame	fönsterram
active window	aktivt fönster	window size	fönsterstorlek
application window	programfönster	window title	fönsternamn
border	kantlinje	workspace	arbetsyta
bottom window border	nedre fönsterkant		
cascading windows	överlappande fönster	**Window controls**	
desktop	skrivbord	Control-menu box	systemmenyruta
document window	dokumentfönster	down scroll arrow	rullningspil (ned)
group window	gruppfönster	horizontal scroll bar	vågrät rullningslist
Help window	hjälpfönster	horizontal split bar	vågrät delningslist
inactive window	inaktivt fönster	left scroll arrow	rullningspil (vänster)
left window border	vänster fönsterkant	Maximize button	maximeringsknapp
menu bar	menyrad	Minimize button	minimeringsknapp
pane	fönsterruta	Restore button	återställningsknapp
right window border	höger fönsterkant	right scroll arrow	rullningspil (höger)
ruler	linjal	scroll arrow	rullningspil
status bar	statusfält	scroll bar	rullningslist
tiled windows	fönster sida vid sida	scroll box	rullningsruta
title bar	namnlist	split bar	delningslist
toolbar	verktygsfält	split box	delningsruta
top window border	övre fönsterkant	up scroll arrow	rullningspil (upp)
wallpaper	bakgrund	vertical scroll bar	lodrät rullningslist
window	fönster	vertical split bar	lodrät delningslist
window background	fönsterbakgrund		
window border	fönsterkant		

ENGLISH	SWEDISH	ENGLISH	SWEDISH
Pointers		Move	Flytta (f)
arrow	pil	Size	Ändra storlek (ä)
arrow pointer	korspil	Minimize	Minimera (m)
cross-hair pointer	hårkors	Maximize	Maximera (x)
hourglass pointer	timglas	Next	Nästa (n)
I-beam pointer	textmarkör	Close	Stäng (s)
insertion point	insättningspunkt	Run...	Kör... (k)
mouse pointer	muspekare	Switch To...	Aktiva sessioner... (a)
pointer	pekare	Split	Dela (d)
selection cursor	markör		
		File menu	Arkiv (a)
Icons		New...	Ny(tt)... (n)
application icon	programikon	Open	Öppna (ö)
directory icon	katalogikon	Close	Stäng (s)
disk icon	diskikon	Close All	Stäng alla (s)
document file icon	dokumentfilsikon	Save	Spara (p)
document icon	dokumentikon	Save As...	Spara som... (m)
drive icon	enhetsikon	Save All	Spara allt/alla (r)
group icon	gruppikon	Delete	Ta bort fil (t)
icon	ikon	Page Setup	Utskriftsformat (f)
program-item icon	programobjektsikon	Print	Skriv ut (u)
		Print Preview	Förhandsgranska (g)
General terms		Printer Setup	Skrivarinställning (i)
access key	snabbtangent	Exit	Avsluta (a)
check mark	bock	Exit and Return to	Avsluta och gå till (a)
ellipsis	punkter	Update	Uppdatera (u)
font	teckensnitt		
object	objekt	Edit menu	Redigera (r)
program group	programgrupp	Undo	Ångra (å)
program item	programobjekt	Repeat	Upprepa (u)
shortcut key	kortkommando	Cut	Klipp ut (k)
sizing handle	storlekshandtag	Copy	Kopiera (p)
status-bar indicator	statusfältsindikator	Copy Special	Kopiera special (o)
tool	verktyg	Paste	Klistra in (l)
unavailable command	spärrat kommando	Paste Link	Klistra in länk (ä)
		Paste Special	Klistra in special (c)
MENUS		Clear	Radera (r)
Menu elements		Clear All	Radera allt/alla (r)
cascading menu	undermeny	Find...	Sök... (s)
checked command	förbockat kommando	Search...	Sök... (s)
command	kommando	Replace...	Ersätt... (e)
command separator	kommandoavgränsare	Go To...	Gå till... (g)
drop-down menu	meny	Delete...	Ta bort... (t)
menu	meny	Insert...	Infoga... (i)
menu command	menykommando	Object...	Objekt...(o)
menu name	menynamn	Insert Object...	Infoga objekt... (o/g)
selected command	markerat kommando		
submenu	undermeny	Options menu	Alternativ (v)
		Preferences	Inställningar (i)
Menus and commands		Full Menus	Långa menyer (m)
View menu	Visa (s)	Short Menus	Korta menyer (m)
Insert menu	Infoga (i)		
		Format menu	Format (t)
Control menu	systemmenyn	Character...	Tecken... (e)
Restore	Återställ (å)	Paragraph...	Stycke... (s)

ENGLISH	SWEDISH
Section...	Avsnitt... (a)
Document...	Dokument... (d)
Number...	Tal... (t)
Alignment...	Justering... (j)
Utilities menu	Extra (x)
Tools menu	Verktyg (g)
Customize	Anpassa (a)
Macro menu	Makro (m)
Record...	Spela in... (i)
Run...	Kör... (k)
Edit	Redigera (r)
Assign to Key	Koppla till tangent (t)
Assign to Menu	Koppla till meny (m)
Window menu	Fönster (ö)
New Window	Nytt fönster (n)
Cascade	Överlappande (ö)
Tile	Sida vid sida (s)
Next Window	Nästa fönster (ä)
Arrange All	Ordna alla (o)
Hide	Dölj (d)
Unhide...	Ta fram... (f)
Split	Dela (d)
Freeze Panes	Lås fönsterrutor (l)
Remove Split	Ta bort delning (d)
Unfreeze Panes	Lås upp fönsterrutor (l)
Zoom...	Zooma... (z)
Help menu	?
Contents	Innehåll (i)
How to use Help	Använda Hjälp (h)
Search for Help on	Sök hjälp om (s)
Active Window	Aktivt fönster (f)
Keyboard	Tangentbord (t)
Mouse	Mus (m)
Tutorial	Självstudier (u)
About	Om (o)
Device menu	Enhet (e)
Scale menu	Skala (s)
MIDI Sequencer...	MIDI-sequencer...
Sound...	Ljud... (l)
Time	Tid (t)
Tracks	Spår (s)
Effects menu	Effekter (f)
Revert...	Återställ... (å)
Insert File...	Infoga ljud... (i)
Mix with File...	Mixa med ljud... (m)
Delete Before Current Position	Ta bort före aktuell position (f)
Delete After Current Position	Ta bort efter aktuell position (e)
Increase Volume (by 25%)	Öka volymen (med 25%) (ö)

ENGLISH	SWEDISH
Decrease Volume	Minska volymen (m)
Increase Speed (by 100%)	Öka hastigheten (med 100%) (k)
Decrease Speed	Minska hastigheten (i)
Add Echo	Lägg till eko (e)
Reverse	Baklänges (b)
Help application	
File menu	Arkiv (a)
Open	Öppna (ö)
Print Topic	Skriv ut avsnitt (u)
Print Setup...	Skrivarinställning... (i)
Exit	Avsluta (a)
Edit menu	Redigera (r)
Copy...	Kopiera... (p)
Annotate...	Anteckning... (a)
Bookmark menu	Bokmärke (m)
Define...	Definiera... (d)
Help menu	?
How to use Help	Använda Hjälp (h)
Always on Top	Alltid överst (ö)
About Help...	Om... (o)
Buttons	
Contents	Innehåll (i)
Search	Sök (s)
Back	Bakåt (b)
History	Tidigare (t)
Glossary	Ordlista (o)
DIALOG BOXES	
dialog box	dialogruta
wildcard	jokertecken
Dialog box elements	
button	knapp
check box	kryssruta
chevrons	«-tecken
combo box	kombinationsruta
command button	kommandoknapp
dialog box title	namn på dialogruta
drop-down combo box	kombinationsruta
drop-down list box	listruta
Goto/Gosub button	dialogknapp
group box	gruppruta
label	etikett
linked text and list box	länkad skriv-/listruta
list box	listruta
option button	alternativknapp
progress indicator	förloppsindikator
push button	kommandoknapp
radio button	alternativknapp

ENGLISH	SWEDISH	ENGLISH	SWEDISH
slider	skjutreglage	Print Quality	Utskriftskvalitet (u)
slider indicator	regel	Print Range	Skriv ut
spin box	rotationsruta	Print to File	Skriv till fil (v)
text box	textruta	Read Only	Skrivskydd (r)
value set	möjliga värden	Replace All	Ersätt alla
		Replace With	Ersätt med (t)
Dialog box buttons		Sample	Exempel
Add	Lägg till	Save File as Type	Filformat (f)
Apply	Använd	Scaling	Skalning (k)
Cancel	Avbryt	Selection	Markerat (m)
Change	Ändra	Size (font size)	Storlek (k)
Create	Skapa	Source (paper)	Källa (ä)
Default	Standard	To	Till (t)
Define	Definiera	Up	Uppåt (u)
Done	OK		
Go To	Gå till		
Help	Hjälp	**MESSAGE BOXES**	
More	Fler	critical message	meddelande om allvarligt fel
No	Nej	message	meddelande
OK	OK	message box	meddelanderuta
Options	Alternativ	message line	meddelanderad
Quit	Avsluta	warning message	varningsmeddelande
Redo	Gör om		
Reset	Återställ		
Resume	Fortsätt	**OTHER GUI SCREEN**	
Retry	Försök igen	**ELEMENTS**	
Search	Sök	**Graphical options**	
Set	Välj	gallery	galleri
Setup	Inställningar	palette	palett
Switch to	Växla till	text frame	textram
Yes	Ja	toolbox	verktygslåda
Dialog box labels		**Status bar abbreviations**	
All	Allt (a)	Caps Lock on (CAPS)	CAPS
Collate copies	Sortera kopior (r)	Column (Col)	Kol
Copies	Kopior (k)	Extend selection on (EXT)	UTV
Direction	Riktning	Line (Ln)	Ra
Directories	Kataloger (k)	Macro Recorder on (REC)	INSP
Down	Nedåt (n)	Num Lock on (NUM)	NUM
Drives	Enheter (e)	Overtype on (OVR)	ÖVER
File Name	Filnamn (n)	Page (Pg)	Si
Find Next	Sök nästa (n)	Scroll Lock on (SCRL)	SCRL
Find What	Sök efter (e)	Section (Sec)	Avs
Font	Teckensnitt (t)		
Font Style	Stil (s)	**Character formats**	
From	Från (f)	bold	fet (f)
Landscape	Liggande (l)	double underline	dubbelt understruken (d)
List Files of Type	Filformat (f)	italic	kursiv (k)
Match Case	Matcha gemener/	small capitals	kapitäler (p)
	VERSALER (m)	underline	understruken (u)
Match Whole Word Only	Matcha hela ord (o)		
Orientation	Orientering	**Paragraph formats**	
Pages	Sidor (s)	centered	centrerat (c)
Paper Size	Storlek (k)	justified	justerat (j)
Portrait	Stående (t)	left aligned	vänsterställt (v)
Printer	Skrivare	right aligned	högerställt (h)

ENGLISH	SWEDISH
KEYS	
Shortcut keys	
CTRL+B (Bold)	CTRL+F
CTRL+C (Copy)	CTRL+C
CTRL+D (Double underline)	CTRL+D
CTRL+E (Center)	CTRL+E
CTRL+I (Italics)	CTRL+K
CTRL+J (Justify)	CTRL+J
CTRL+L (Left align)	CTRL+L
CTRL+R (Right align)	CTRL+R
CTRL+U (Underline)	CTRL+U
CTRL+V (Paste)	CTRL+V
CTRL+W (Word underline)	CTRL+W
CTRL+X (Cut)	CTRL+X
CTRL+Z (Undo)	CTRL+Z
DEL (Clear)	DEL
Keynames	
(keypad) *	NUM *
(keypad) +	NUM +
(keypad) -	NUM -
(keypad) /	NUM /
ALT	ALT
ALT GR	ALT GR
BACKSPACE	BACKSTEG
BREAK	BREAK
CAPS LOCK	CAPS LOCK
CTRL	CTRL
DEL	DEL
DOWN ARROW	NEDPIL
END	END
ENTER	RETUR
ENTER (keypad)	NUM RETUR
ESC	ESC
HOME	HOME
INS	INS
LEFT ARROW	VÄNSTERPIL
NUM LOCK	NUM LOCK
PAUSE	PAUSE
PG DN	PGDN
PG UP	PGUP
PRINT SCREEN	PRINTSCRN
RIGHT ARROW	HÖGERPIL
SCROLL LOCK	SCROLL LOCK
SHIFT	SKIFT
SPACEBAR	BLANKSTEG
SYS RQ	SYS RQ
TAB	TAB
UP ARROW	UPPIL
USER ACTIONS	
Keyboard actions	
enter	skriva
press and hold down	hålla ned
type	skriva

ENGLISH	SWEDISH
Mouse actions	
click	klicka på (ett objekt)
double-click	dubbelklicka på (ett objekt)
drag	dra
drag-and-drop	dra och släpp
drop	släppa
point	peka på
Manipulating window appearance	
arrange	ordna
close	stänga
freeze	låsa
hide	dölja
move	flytta
resize	ändra storlek
restore	återställa
select	markera
size	ändra storlek
split	dela
switch	växla till
unfreeze	låsa upp
Selecting options or content	
cancel	avbryta
check	markera/bocka för
choose	välja
clear (undo Select)	avmarkera
extend selection	utvidga markering
reduce selection	krympa markering
select	markera
select (check box, option button)	markera (kryssruta, alternativknapp)
select (data)	markera
select (drop-down menu)	välja
select (list box)	välja
Viewing content	
autoscroll	automatisk rullning
browse	bläddra
collapse	komprimera
expand	expandera
scroll	rulla
view	visa
zoom in	zooma in
zoom out	zooma ut
Removing content	
clear	radera/rensa
copy	kopiera
cut	klippa ut
delete	ta bort
paste	klistra in

ENGLISH	SWEDISH
Manipulating objects	
arrange	ordna
automatic link	automatisk länk
Clipboard	Urklipp
container application	målprogram
container document	måldokument
copy	kopiera
crop	beskära
destination application	målprogram
destination document	måldokument
drag-and-drop	dra och släpp
embed	bädda in
embedded object	inbäddat objekt
group	gruppera
link	länka
linked object	länkat objekt
main application	huvudprogram
main document	huvuddokument
manual link	manuell länk
object	objekt
object linking & embedding (OLE)	objektlänkning och inbäddning (OLE)
OLE (object linking & embedding)	OLE (Object Linking & Embedding)
OLE application	OLE-program
package	paket
paste	klistra in
scale	skala
size	ändra storlek
source application	källprogram

ENGLISH	SWEDISH
source document	källdokument
update	uppdatera
APPLICATIONS FOR MICROSOFT WINDOWS	
Accessories	Tillbehör
Applications	Program
Calculator	Kalkylatorn
Calendar	Kalendern
Cardfile	Kartoteket
Character Map	Teckenuppsättning
Clipboard Viewer	Urklipp
Clock	Klockan
Control Panel	Kontrollpanelen
File Manager	Filhanteraren
Games	Spel
Main	Huvudgrupp
Media Player	Mediaspelaren
MS-DOS Prompt	MS-DOS-prompt
Notepad	Anteckningar
Object Packager	Paketeraren
PIF Editor	PIF-editorn
Print Manager	Utskriftshanteraren
Program Manager	Programhanteraren
Recorder	Inspelaren
Sound Recorder	Ljudinspelaren
StartUp	Autostart
Terminal	Terminalen
Windows Setup	Windows installationsprogram

Terminology by Alphabet

Notes:
1. All terms formatted in **bold** refer to menu names or command names.
2. All characters between parentheses are preferred access keys.

ENGLISH	SWEDISH	ENGLISH	SWEDISH
(keypad) *	NUM *	Cardfile	Kartoteket
(keypad) +	NUM +	**Cascade**	**Överlappande (ö)**
(keypad) -	NUM -	cascading menu	undermeny
(keypad) /	NUM /	cascading windows	överlappande fönster
About	**Om (o)**	centered	centrerat (c)
About Help...	**Om... (o)**	Change	Ändra
access key	snabbtangent	**Character...**	**Tecken... (e)**
Accessories	Tillbehör	Character Map	Teckenuppsättning
active window	aktivt fönster	check	markera/bocka för
Active Window	**Aktivt fönster (f)**	check box	kryssruta
Add	Lägg till	checked command	förbockat kommando
Add Echo	**Lägg till eko (e)**	check mark	bock
Alignment...	**Justering... (j)**	chevrons	«-tecken
All	Allt (a)	choose	välja
ALT	ALT	**Clear**	**Radera (r)**
ALT GR	ALT GR	clear	radera/rensa
Always on Top	**Alltid överst (ö)**	**Clear All**	**Radera allt/alla (r)**
Annotate...	**Anteckning... (a)**	clear (undo Select)	avmarkera
application icon	programikon	click	klicka på (ett objekt)
application window	programfönster	Clipboard	Urklipp
Applications	Program	Clipboard Viewer	Urklipp
Apply	Använd	Clock	Klockan
arrange	ordna	Close	Stäng (s)
Arrange All	**Ordna alla (o)**	close	stänga
arrow	pil	**Close All**	**Stäng alla (s)**
arrow pointer	korspil	collapse	komprimera
Assign to Key	**Koppla till tangent (t)**	Collate copies	Sortera kopior (r)
Assign to Menu	**Koppla till meny (m)**	Column (Col)	Kol
automatic link	automatisk länk	combo box	kombinationsruta
autoscroll	automatisk rullning	command	kommando
Back	Bakåt (b)	command button	kommandoknapp
BACKSPACE	BACKSTEG	command separator	kommandoavgränsare
bold	fet (f)	container application	målprogram
Bookmark menu	**Bokmärke (m)**	container document	måldokument
border	kantlinje	**Contents**	**Innehåll (i)**
bottom window border	nedre fönsterkant	Contents	Innehåll (i)
BREAK	BREAK	**Control menu**	**systemmenyn**
browse	bläddra	Control-menu box	systemmenyruta
button	knapp	Control Panel	Kontrollpanelen
Calculator	Kalkylatorn	Copies	Kopior (k)
Calendar	Kalendern	**Copy**	**Kopiera (p)**
Cancel	Avbryt	copy	kopiera
cancel	avbryta	**Copy...**	**Kopiera... (p)**
CAPS LOCK	CAPS LOCK	**Copy Special**	**Kopiera special (o)**
Caps Lock on (CAPS)	CAPS	Create	Skapa

ENGLISH	SWEDISH	ENGLISH	SWEDISH
critical message	meddelande om allvarligt fel	drive icon	enhetsikon
crop	beskära	Drives	Enheter (e)
cross-hair pointer	hårkors	drop	släppa
CTRL	CTRL	drop-down combo box	kombinationsruta
CTRL+B (Bold)	CTRL+F	drop-down list box	listruta
CTRL+C (Copy)	CTRL+C	drop-down menu	meny
CTRL+D (Double underline)	CTRL+D	Edit	Redigera (r)
CTRL+E (Center)	CTRL+E	**Edit menu**	**Redigera (r)**
CTRL+I (Italics)	CTRL+K	**Effects menu**	**Effekter (f)**
CTRL+J (Justify)	CTRL+J	ellipsis	punkter
CTRL+L (Left align)	CTRL+L	embed	bädda in
CTRL+R (Right align)	CTRL+R	embedded object	inbäddat objekt
CTRL+U (Underline)	CTRL+U	END	END
CTRL+V (Paste)	CTRL+V	enter	skriva
CTRL+W (Word underline)	CTRL+W	ENTER	RETUR
CTRL+X (Cut)	CTRL+X	ENTER (keypad)	NUM RETUR
CTRL+Z (Undo)	CTRL+Z	ESC	ESC
Customize	**Anpassa (a)**	**Exit**	**Avsluta (a)**
Cut	**Klipp ut (k)**	**Exit and Return to**	**Avsluta och gå till (a)**
cut	klippa ut	expand	expandera
Decrease Speed	**Minska hastigheten (i)**	extend selection	utvidga markering
Decrease Volume	**Minska volymen (m)**	Extend selection on (EXT)	UTV
Default	Standard	File Manager	Filhanteraren
Define	Definiera	**File menu**	**Arkiv (a)**
Define...	**Definiera... (d)**	File Name	Filnamn (n)
DEL	DEL	**Find...**	**Sök... (s)**
DEL (Clear)	DEL	Find Next	Sök nästa (n)
Delete	**Ta bort fil (t)**	Find What	Sök efter (e)
delete	ta bort	font	teckensnitt
Delete...	**Ta bort... (t)**	Font	Teckensnitt (t)
Delete After Current Position	**Ta bort efter aktuell position (e)**	Font Style	Stil (s)
Delete Before Current Position	**Ta bort före aktuell position (f)**	**Format menu**	**Format (t)**
		freeze	låsa
desktop	skrivbord	**Freeze Panes**	**Lås fönsterrutor (l)**
destination application	målprogram	From	Från (f)
destination document	måldokument	**Full Menus**	**Långa menyer (m)**
Device menu	**Enhet (e)**	gallery	galleri
dialog box	dialogruta	Games	Spel
dialog box title	namn på dialogruta	Glossary	Ordlista (o)
Direction	Riktning	Go To	Gå till
Directories	Kataloger (k)	**Go To...**	**Gå till... (g)**
directory icon	katalogikon	Goto/Gosub button	dialogknapp
disk icon	diskikon	group	gruppera
Document...	**Dokument... (d)**	group box	gruppruta
document file icon	dokumentfilsikon	group icon	gruppikon
document icon	dokumentikon	group window	gruppfönster
document window	dokumentfönster	Help	Hjälp
Done	OK	**Help menu**	**?**
double-click	dubbelklicka på (ett objekt)	Help window	hjälpfönster
double underline	dubbelt understruken (d)	**Hide**	**Dölj (d)**
Down	Nedåt (n)	hide	dölja
DOWN ARROW	NEDPIL	History	Tidigare (t)
down scroll arrow	rullningspil (ned)	HOME	HOME
drag	dra	horizontal scroll bar	vågrät rullningslist
drag-and-drop	dra och släpp	horizontal split bar	vågrät delningslist
		hourglass pointer	timglas

ENGLISH	SWEDISH	ENGLISH	SWEDISH
How to use Help	Använda Hjälp (h)	MS-DOS Prompt	MS-DOS-prompt
I-beam pointer	textmarkör	New...	Ny(tt)... (n)
icon	ikon	New Window	Nytt fönster (n)
inactive window	inaktivt fönster	Next	Nästa (n)
Increase Speed (by 100%)	Öka hastigheten (med 100%) (k)	Next Window	Nästa fönster (ä)
Increase Volume (by 25%)	Öka volymen (med 25%) (ö)	No	Nej
INS	INS	Notepad	Anteckningar
Insert...	Infoga... (i)	Number...	Tal... (t)
Insert File...	Infoga ljud... (i)	NUM LOCK	NUM LOCK
insertion point	insättningspunkt	Num Lock on (NUM)	NUM
Insert menu	Infoga (i)	object	objekt
Insert Object...	Infoga objekt... (o/g)	Object...	Objekt...(o)
italic	kursiv (k)	object linking & embedding (OLE)	objektlänkning och inbäddning (OLE)
justified	justerat (j)	Object Packager	Paketeraren
Keyboard	Tangentbord (t)	OK	OK
label	etikett	OLE application	OLE-program
Landscape	Liggande (l)	OLE (object linking & embedding)	OLE (Object Linking & Embedding)
left aligned	vänsterställt (v)	Open	Öppna (ö)
LEFT ARROW	VÄNSTERPIL	option button	alternativknapp
left scroll arrow	rullningspil (vänster)	Options	Alternativ
left window border	vänster fönsterkant	Options menu	Alternativ (v)
Line (Ln)	Ra	Orientation	Orientering
link	länka	Overtype on (OVR)	ÖVER
linked object	länkat objekt	package	paket
linked text and list box	länkad skriv-/listruta	Page (Pg)	Si
list box	listruta	Pages	Sidor (s)
List Files of Type	Filformat (f)	Page Setup	Utskriftsformat (f)
Macro menu	Makro (m)	palette	palett
Macro Recorder on (REC)	INSP	pane	fönsterruta
Main	Huvudgrupp	Paper Size	Storlek (k)
main application	huvudprogram	Paragraph...	Stycke... (s)
main document	huvuddokument	Paste	Klistra in (l)
manual link	manuell länk	paste	klistra in
Match Case	Matcha gemener/ VERSALER (m)	Paste Link	Klistra in länk (ä)
		Paste Special	Klistra in special (c)
Match Whole Word Only	Matcha hela ord (o)	PAUSE	PAUSE
Maximize	Maximera (x)	PG DN	PGDN
Maximize button	maximeringsknapp	PG UP	PGUP
Media Player	Mediaspelaren	PIF Editor	PIF-editorn
menu	meny	point	peka på
menu bar	menyrad	pointer	pekare
menu command	menykommando	Portrait	Stående (t)
menu name	menynamn	Preferences	Inställningar (i)
message	meddelande	press and hold down	hålla ned
message box	meddelanderuta	Print	Skriv ut (u)
message line	meddelanderad	Printer	Skrivare
MIDI Sequencer...	MIDI-sequencer...	Printer Setup	Skrivarinställning (i)
Minimize	Minimera (m)	Print Manager	Utskriftshanteraren
Minimize button	minimeringsknapp	Print Preview	Förhandsgranska (g)
Mix with File...	Mixa med ljud... (m)	Print Quality	Utskriftskvalitet (u)
More	Fler	Print Range	Skriv ut
Mouse	Mus (m)	PRINT SCREEN	PRINTSCRN
mouse pointer	muspekare	Print Setup...	Skrivarinställning... (i)
Move	Flytta (f)	Print to File	Skriv till fil (v)
move	flytta		

ENGLISH	SWEDISH	ENGLISH	SWEDISH
Print Topic	**Skriv ut avsnitt (u)**	select (check box,	markera (kryssruta,
program group	programgrupp	option button)	alternativknapp)
program item	programobjekt	select (data)	markera
program-item icon	programobjektsikon	select (drop-down menu)	välja
Program Manager	Programhanteraren	selected command	markerat kommando
progress indicator	förloppsindikator	Selection	Markerat (m)
push button	kommandoknapp	selection cursor	markör
Quit	Avsluta	select (list box)	välja
radio button	alternativknapp	Set	Välj
Read Only	Skrivskydd (r)	Setup	Inställningar
Record...	**Spela in... (i)**	SHIFT	SKIFT
Recorder	Inspelaren	shortcut key	kortkommando
Redo	Gör om	**Short Menus**	**Korta menyer (m)**
reduce selection	krympa markering	**Size**	**Ändra storlek (ä)**
Remove Split	**Ta bort delning (d)**	size	ändra storlek
Repeat	**Upprepa (u)**	Size (font size)	Storlek (k)
Replace...	**Ersätt... (e)**	sizing handle	storlekshandtag
Replace All	Ersätt alla	slider	skjutreglage
Replace With	Ersätt med (t)	slider indicator	regel
Reset	Återställ	small capitals	kapitäler (p)
resize	ändra storlek	**Sound...**	**Ljud... (l)**
Restore	**Återställ (å)**	Sound Recorder	Ljudinspelaren
restore	återställa	source application	källprogram
Restore button	återställningsknapp	source document	källdokument
Resume	Fortsätt	Source (paper)	Källa (ä)
Retry	Försök igen	SPACEBAR	BLANKSTEG
Reverse	**Baklänges (b)**	spin box	rotationsruta
Revert...	**Återställ... (å)**	**Split**	**Dela (d)**
right aligned	högerställt (h)	split	dela
RIGHT ARROW	HÖGERPIL	split bar	delningslist
right scroll arrow	rullningspil (höger)	split box	delningsruta
right window border	höger fönsterkant	StartUp	Autostart
ruler	linjal	status bar	statusfält
Run...	**Kör... (k)**	status-bar indicator	statusfältsindikator
Sample	Exempel	submenu	undermeny
Save	**Spara (p)**	switch	växla till
Save All	**Spara allt/alla (r)**	Switch to	Växla till
Save As...	**Spara som... (m)**	**Switch To...**	**Aktiva sessioner... (a)**
Save File as Type	Filformat (f)	SYS RQ	SYS RQ
scale	skala	TAB	TAB
Scale menu	**Skala (s)**	Terminal	Terminalen
Scaling	Skalning (k)	text box	textruta
scroll	rulla	text frame	textram
scroll arrow	rullningspil	**Tile**	**Sida vid sida (s)**
scroll bar	rullningslist	tiled windows	fönster sida vid sida
scroll box	rullningsruta	**Time**	**Tid (t)**
SCROLL LOCK	SCROLL LOCK	title bar	namnlist
Scroll Lock on (SCRL)	SCRL	To	Till (t)
Search	Sök (s)	tool	verktyg
Search	Sök	toolbar	verktygsfält
Search...	**Sök... (s)**	toolbox	verktygslåda
Search for Help on	**Sök hjälp om (s)**	**Tools menu**	**Verktyg (g)**
Section...	**Avsnitt... (a)**	top window border	övre fönsterkant
Section (Sec)	Avs	**Tracks**	**Spår (s)**
select	markera	**Tutorial**	**Självstudier (u)**

ENGLISH	SWEDISH	ENGLISH	SWEDISH
type	skriva	wallpaper	bakgrund
unavailable command	spärrat kommando	warning message	varningsmeddelande
underline	understruken (u)	wildcard	jokertecken
Undo	**Ångra (å)**	window	fönster
unfreeze	låsa upp	window background	fönsterbakgrund
Unfreeze Panes	**Lås upp fönsterrutor (l)**	window border	fönsterkant
Unhide...	**Ta fram... (f)**	window corner	fönsterhörn
Up	Uppåt (u)	window frame	fönsterram
UP ARROW	UPPIL	**Window menu**	**Fönster (ö)**
up scroll arrow	rullningspil (upp)	window size	fönsterstorlek
Update	**Uppdatera (u)**	window title	fönsternamn
update	uppdatera	Windows Setup	Windows installationsprogram
Utilities menu	**Extra (x)**	workspace	arbetsyta
value set	möjliga värden	Yes	Ja
vertical scroll bar	lodrät rullningslist	**Zoom...**	**Zooma... (z)**
vertical split bar	lodrät delningslist	zoom in	zooma in
view	visa	zoom out	zooma ut
View menu	**Visa (s)**		

Appendixes

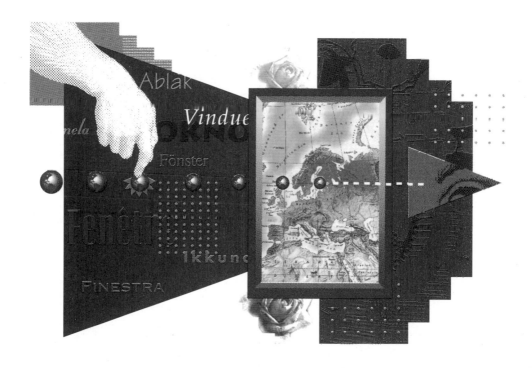

APPENDIX A

Keyboards

This appendix lists the IBM Enhanced keyboards for the languages covered in Part 2.

Czechoslovakia/Czech

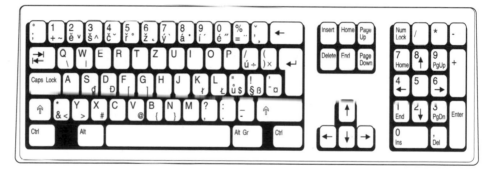

Czechoslavakia/Slovak

Denmark

France

Germany

Hungary

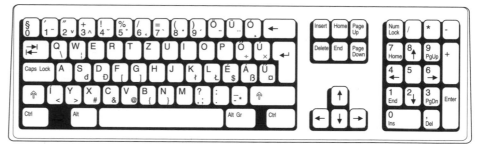

Italy

Netherlands

Norway

Poland

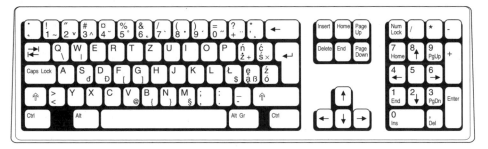

Portugal

Russia

Spain

Sweden/Finland

Switzerland

United Kingdom

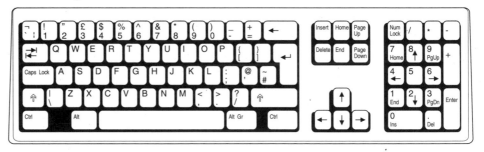

United States

A P P E N D I X   B

National Standards

This appendix lists formats used for time, dates, numbers, and currency in the countries where the fourteen languages covered in Part 2 are spoken.

Austria (German)

Description	Format	Example
Country	Country code: 43 Country abbreviation: AT	
Time	24-hour clock; hours and minutes separated by colon Leading zero before hours: Yes	21:59 09:59
Date	Short date order: DMY, separated by period Leading zero days: No Leading zero months: No Century indication: No Long date format: dddd, d. MMMM yyyy	9.9.99 Dienstag, 9. September 1999
Numerical	Thousand separator: Period Decimal separator: Comma	1.234,56
Currency	Currency symbol: S, precedes amount Space between symbol and amount Two decimal digits Negative currency: Minus sign precedes amount	S 1.234,56 -S 1.234,56
Other	List separator: Semicolon	A;B;1;2;3

Belgium (Dutch)

Description	Format	Example
Country	Country code: 32 Country abbreviation: BE	
Time	24-hour clock; hours and minutes separated by colon Leading zero before hours: No	21:59 9:59
Date	Short date order: DMY, separated by slash Leading zero days: No Leading zero months: Yes Century indication: No Long date format: dddd d MMMM yyyy	9/09/99 zaterdag 9 september 1999
Numerical	Thousands separator: Period Decimal separator: Comma	1.234,56
Currency	Currency symbol: BF, follows amount Space between symbol and amount Two decimal digits Negative currency: Minus sign precedes amount	1.234,56 BF -1.234,56 BF
Other	List separator: Semicolon	A;B;1;2;3

Belgium (French)

Description	Format	Example
Country	Country code: 32 Country abbreviation: BE	
Time	24-hour clock; hours and minutes separated by colon Leading zero before hours: No	21:59 9:59
Date	Short date order: DMY, separated by slash Leading zero days: No Leading zero months: Yes Century indication: No Long date format: dddd d MMMM yyyy	9/09/99 mardi le 9 septembre 1999
Numerical	Thousands separator: Period Decimal separator: Comma	1.234,56
Currency	Currency symbol: FB, follows amount Space between symbol and amount Two decimal digits Negative currency: Minus sign precedes amount	1.234,56 FB -1.234,56 FB
Other	List separator: Semicolon	A;B;1;2;3

Czechoslovakia (Czech and Slovak)

Description	Format	Example
Country	Country code: 42 Country abbreviation: CS	
Time	24-hour clock; hours and minutes separated by colon Leading zero before hours: No	21:59 9:59
Date	Short date order: DMY, separated by period Leading zero days: No Leading zero months: No Century indication: Yes Long date format: d. MMMM yyyy	9.9.1999 9. září 1999
Numerical	Thousands separator: Space Decimal separator: Comma	1 234,56
Currency	Currency symbol: Kčs, follows amount Space between symbol and amount Two decimal digits Negative currency: Minus sign precedes amount	1 234,56 Kčs -1 234,56 Kčs
Other	List separator: Semicolon	A;B;1;2;3

Denmark (Danish)

Description	Format	Example
Country	Country code: 45 Country abbreviation: DK	
Time	24-hour clock; hours and minutes separated by period Leading zero before hours: Yes	21.59 09.59
Date	Short date order: DMY, separated by dash Leading zero days: Yes Leading zero months: Yes Century indication: No Long date format: d. MMMM yyyy	09-09-99 9. september 1999
Numerical	Thousands separator: Period Decimal separator: Comma	1.234,56
Currency	Currency symbol: kr, precedes amount Space between symbol and amount Two decimal digits Negative currency: Minus sign precedes amount	kr 1.234,56 kr -1.234,56
Other	List separator: Semicolon	A;B;1;2;3

Finland (Finnish)

Description	Format	Example
Country	Country code: 358 Country abbreviation: FI	
Time	24-hour clock; hours and minutes separated by period Leading zero before hours: No	21.59 9.59
Date	Short date order: DMY, separated by period Leading zero days: No Leading zero months: No Century indication: Yes Long date format: d. MMMM'ta yyyy	9.9.1999 9. syyskuuta 1999
Numerical	Thousands separator: Space Decimal separator: Comma	1 234,56
Currency	Currency symbol: mk, follows amount Space between symbol and amount Two decimal digits Negative currency: Minus sign precedes amount	1 234,56 mk -1 234,56 mk
Other	List separator: Semicolon	A;B;1;2;3

France (French)

Description	Format	Example
Country	Country code: 33 Country abbreviation: FR	
Time	24-hour clock; hours and minutes separated by colon Leading zero before hours: Yes	21:59 09:59
Date	Short date order: DMY, separated by period Leading zero days: Yes Leading zero months: Yes Century indication: Yes Long date format: dddd d MMMM yyyy	09.09.1999 mardi le 9 septembre 1999
Numerical	Thousands separator: Space Decimal separator: Comma	1 234,56
Currency	Currency symbol: F, follows amount Space between symbol and amount Two decimal digits Negative currency: Minus sign precedes amount	1 234,56 F -1 234,56 F
Other	List separator: Semicolon	A;B;1;2;3

Germany (German)

Description	Format	Example
Country	Country code: 49 Country abbreviation: DE	
Time	24-hour clock; hours and minutes separated by colon Leading zero before hours: Yes	21:59 09:59
Date	Short date order: DMY, separated by period Leading zero days: No Leading zero months: No Century indication: No Long date format: dddd, d. MMMM yyyy	9.9.99 Dienstag, 9. September 1999
Numerical	Thousands separator: Period Decimal separator: Comma	1.234,56
Currency	Currency symbol: DM, follows amount Space between symbol and amount Two decimal digits Negative currency: Minus sign precedes amount	1.234,56 DM -1.234,56 DM
Other	List separator: Semicolon	A;B;1;2;3

Hungary (Hungarian)

Description	Format	Example
Country	Country code: 36 Country abbreviation: HU	
Time	24-hour clock; hours and minutes separated by period Leading zero before hours: No	21.59 9.59
Date	Short date order: YMD, separated by period Leading zero days: Yes Leading zero months: Yes Century indication: Yes Long date format: yyyy. MMMM d.	1999.09.09 1999. szeptember 9.
Numerical	Thousands separator: Space Decimal separator: Comma	1 234,56
Currency	Currency symbol: Ft, follows amount Space between symbol and amount Two decimal digits Negative currency: Minus sign precedes amount	1 234,56 Ft -1 234,56 Ft
Other	List separator: Semicolon	A;B;1;2;3

Iceland (Icelandic)

Description	Format	Example
Country	Country code: 354 Country abbreviation: IS	
Time	24-hour clock; hours and minutes separated by colon Leading zero before hours: Yes	21:59 09:59
Date	Short date order: YMD, separated by dash Leading zero days: Yes Leading zero months: Yes Century indication: Yes Long date format: d. MMMM yyyy	1999-09-09 9. september 1999
Numerical	Thousands separator: Space Decimal separator: Comma	1 234,56
Currency	Currency symbol: kr, follows amount Thousands separator: Period Space between symbol and amount Zero decimal digits Negative currency: Minus sign precedes amount	1.234 kr -1.234 kr
Other	List separator: Semicolon	A;B;1;2;3

Italy (Italian)

Description	Format	Example
Country	Country code: 39 Country abbreviation: IT	
Time	24-hour clock; hours and minutes separated by period Leading zero before hours: No	21.59 9.59
Date	Short date order: DMY, separated by slash Leading zero days: Yes Leading zero months: Yes Century indication: No Long date format: dddd d MMMM yyyy	09/09/99 Venerdì 9 settembre 1999
Numerical	Thousands separator: Period Decimal separator: Comma	1.234,56
Currency	Currency symbol: L., precedes amount Space between symbol and amount Zero decimal digits Negative currency: Minus sign precedes amount	L. 1.234 -L. 1.234
Other	List separator: Semicolon	A;B;1;2;3

Netherlands (Dutch)

Description	Format	Example
Country	Country code: 31 Country abbreviation: NL	
Time	24-hour clock; hours and minutes separated by colon Leading zero before hours: No	21:59 9:59
Date	Short date order: DMY, separated by dash Leading zero days: No Leading zero months: Yes Century indication: No Long date format: dddd d MMMM yyyy	9-09-99 zaterdag 9 september 1999
Numerical	Thousands separator: Period Decimal separator: Comma	1.234,56
Currency	Currency symbol: F, precedes amount Space between symbol and amount Two decimal digits Negative currency: Minus sign follows amount	F 1.234,56 F 1.234,56-
Other	List separator: Semicolon	A;B;1;2;3

Norway (Norwegian)

Description	Format	Example
Country	Country code: 47 Country abbreviation: NO	
Time	24-hour clock; hours and minutes separated by colon Leading zero before hours: Yes	21:59 09:59
Date	Short date order: DMY, separated by period Leading zero days: Yes Leading zero months: Yes Century indication: No Long date format: d. MMMM yyyy	09.09.99 9. september 1999
Numerical	Thousands separator: Space Decimal separator: Comma	1 234,56
Currency	Currency symbol: kr, precedes amount Space between symbol and amount Two decimal digits Negative currency: Minus sign precedes amount	kr 1 234,56 kr -1 234,56
Other	List separator: Semicolon	A;B;1;2;3

Poland (Polish)

Description	Format	Example
Country	Country code: 48 Country abbreviation: PL	
Time	24-hour clock; hours and minutes separated by colon Leading zero before hours: Yes	21:59 09:59
Date	Short date order: YMD, separated by dash Leading zero days: Yes Leading zero months: Yes Century indication: No Long date format: dddd d MMMM yyyy	99-09-09 Piątek 9 września 1999 roku
Numerical	Thousands separator: Space Decimal separator: Comma	1 234,56
Currency	Currency symbol: zł, follows amount Space between symbol and amount Two decimal digits Negative currency: Minus sign precedes amount	1 234,56 zł -1 234,56 zł
Other	List separator: Semicolon	A;B;1;2;3

Portugal (Portuguese)

Description	Format	Example
Country	Country code: 351 Country abbreviation: PT	
Time	24-hour clock; hours and minutes separated by colon Leading zero before hours: No	21:59 9:59
Date	Short date order: DMY, separated by dash Leading zero days: Yes Leading zero months: Yes Century indication: Yes Long date format: d MMMM yyyy	09-09-1999 9 de setembro de 1999
Numerical	Thousands separator: Period Decimal separator: Comma	1.234,56
Currency	Currency symbol: Esc., follows amount Decimal separator: $ Space between symbol and amount Two decimal digits Negative currency: Minus sign precedes amount	1.234$56 Esc. -1.234$56 Esc.
Other	List separator: Semicolon	A;B;1;2;3

Russia (Russian)

Description	Format	Example
Country	Country code: 07 Country abbreviation: RUS	
Time	24-hour clock: hours and minutes separated by colon Leading zero before hours: No	21:59 9:59
Date	Short date order: DMY, separated by slash Leading zero days: No Leading zero months: Yes Century indication: No Long date format: dd MMMM yyyy	9/09/99 09 июня 1999
Numerical	Thousands separator: Space Decimal separator: Period	1 234.56
Currency	Currency symbol: руб., follows amount Space between symbol and amount Two decimal digits Negative currency: Minus sign precedes amount	1 234.56 руб. -1 234.56 руб.
Other	List separator: Comma	A,B,1,2,3

Spain (Spanish)

Description	Format	Example
Country	Country code: 34 Country abbreviation: ES	
Time	24-hour clock; hours and minutes separated by colon Leading zero before hours: No	21:59 9:59
Date	Short date order: DMY, separated by slash Leading zero days: No Leading zero months: Yes Century indication: No Long date format: d dddd MMMM yyyy	9/09/99 9 de setiembre de 1999
Numerical	Thousands separator: Period Decimal separator: Comma	1.234,56
Currency	Currency symbol: Pts, follows amount Space between symbol and amount Zero decimal digits Negative currency: Minus sign precedes amount	1.234 Pts -1.234 Pts
Other	List separator: Semicolon	A;B;1;2;3

Sweden (Swedish)

Description	Format	Example
Country	Country code: 46 Country abbreviation: SE	
Time	24-hour clock; hours and minutes separated by period Leading zero before hours: Yes	21.59 09.59
Date	Short date order: YMD, separated by dash Leading zero days: Yes Leading zero months: Yes Century indication: Yes Long date format: d MMMM yyyy	1999-09-09 den 9 september 1999
Numerical	Thousands separator: Space Decimal separator: Comma	1 234,56
Currency	Currency symbol: kr, follows amount Space between symbol and amount Two decimal digits Negative currency: Minus sign precedes amount	1 234,56 kr -1 234,56 kr
Other	List separator: Semicolon	A;B;1;2;3

Switzerland (French)

Description	Format	Example
Country	Country code: 41 Country abbreviation: CH	
Time	24-hour clock; hours and minutes separated by period Leading zero before hours: Yes	21.59 09.59
Date	Short date order: DMY, separated by period Leading zero days: No Leading zero months: Yes Century indication: No Long date format: dd. MMMM yyyy	9.09.99 le 09. septembre 1999
Numerical	Thousands separator: Apostrophe Decimal separator: Comma	1'234,56
Currency	Currency symbol: Fr., precedes amount Space between symbol and amount Two decimal digits Negative currency: Minus sign precedes amount	Fr. 1'234,56 Fr. -1'234,56
Other	List separator: Semicolon	A;B;1;2;3

Switzerland (German)

Description	Format	Example
Country	Country code: 41 Country abbreviation: CH	
Time	24-hour clock; hours and minutes separated by period Leading zero before hours: Yes	21.59 09.59
Date	Short date order: DMY, separated by period Leading zero days: No Leading zero months: No Century indication: No Long date format: dddd, d. MMMM yyyy	9.9.99 Dienstag, 9. September 1999
Numerical	Thousands separator: Apostrophe Decimal separator: Period	1'234.56
Currency	Currency symbol: sFr., precedes amount Space between symbol and amount Two decimal digits Negative currency: Minus sign precedes amount	sFr. 1'234.56 sFr. -1'234.56
Other	List separator: Semicolon	A;B;1;2;3

Switzerland (Italian)

Description	Format	Example
Country	Country code: 41 Country abbreviation: CH	
Time	24-hour clock; hours and minutes separated by period Leading zero before hours: Yes	21.59 09.59
Date	Short date order: DMY, separated by period Leading zero days: No Leading zero months: Yes Century indication: No Long date format: dddd, dd. MMMM yyyy	9.09.99 Venerdì, 09. Settembre 1999
Numerical	Thousands separator: Apostrophe Decimal separator: Period	1'234.56
Currency	Currency symbol: Fr., precedes amount Space between symbol and amount Two decimal digits Negative currency: Minus sign precedes amount	Fr. 1'234.56 Fr. -1'234.56
Other	List separator: Semicolon	A;B;1;2;3

United Kingdom (English)

Description	Format	Example
Country	Country code: 44 Country abbreviation: GB	
Time	24-hour clock; hours and minutes separated by colon Leading zero before hours: Yes	21:59 09:59
Date	Short date order: DMY, separated by slash Leading zero days: Yes Leading zero months: Yes Century indication: No Long date format: dd MMMM yyyy	09/09/99 09 September 1999
Numerical	Thousands separator: Comma Decimal separator: Period	1,234.56
Currency	Currency symbol: £, precedes amount No space between symbol and amount Two decimal digits Negative currency: Minus sign precedes amount	£1,234.56 -£1,234.56
Other	List separator: Comma	A,B,1,2,3

United States (English)

Description	Format	Example
Country	Country code: 1 Country abbreviation: US	
Time	12-hour clock; hours and minutes separated by colon Leading zero before hours: No	9:59 AM 9:59 AM
Date	Short date order: MDY, separated by slash Leading zero days: No Leading zero months: Yes Century indication: No Long date format: dddd, MMMM dd, yyyy	09/9/99 Friday, September 09, 1999
Numerical	Thousands separator: Comma Decimal separator: Period	1,234.56
Currency	Currency symbol: $, precedes amount No space between symbol and amount Two decimal digits Negative currency: Minus sign precedes amount	$1,234.56 -$1,234.56
Other	List separator: Comma	A,B,1,2,3

APPENDIX C

Character Sets

On the following pages, you will find the appropriate Windows character sets for the European Latin-character languages (code pages 1252, 1250) and the Windows character set for Cyrillic-character languages (code page 1251).

Code Page 1252

Char	Code	Char	Code	Char	Code	Char	Code	Char	Code	Char	Code	Char	Code
	(00)	%	(037)	J	(074)	o	(0111)	"	(0148)	¹	(0185)	Þ	(0222)
	(01)	&	(038)	K	(075)	p	(0112)	•	(0149)	º	(0186)	ß	(0223)
	(02)	'	(039)	L	(076)	q	(0113)	—	(0150)	»	(0187)	à	(0224)
	(03)	(	(040)	M	(077)	r	(0114)	–	(0151)	¼	(0188)	á	(0225)
	(04)	)	(041)	N	(078)	s	(0115)		(0152)	½	(0189)	â	(0226)
	(05)	*	(042)	O	(079)	t	(0116)	™	(0153)	¾	(0190)	ã	(0227)
	(06)	+	(043)	P	(080)	u	(0117)	š	(0154)	¿	(0191)	ä	(0228)
	(07)	,	(044)	Q	(081)	v	(0118)	›	(0155)	À	(0192)	å	(0229)
	(08)	-	(045)	R	(082)	w	(0119)	œ	(0156)	Á	(0193)	æ	(0230)
	(09)	.	(046)	S	(083)	x	(0120)		(0157)	Â	(0194)	ç	(0231)
	(010)	/	(047)	T	(084)	y	(0121)		(0158)	Ã	(0195)	è	(0232)
	(011)	0	(048)	U	(085)	z	(0122)	Ÿ	(0159)	Ä	(0196)	é	(0233)
	(012)	1	(049)	V	(086)	{	(0123)		(0160)	Å	(0197)	ê	(0234)
	(013)	2	(050)	W	(087)	|	(0124)	¡	(0161)	Æ	(0198)	ë	(0235)
	(014)	3	(051)	X	(088)	}	(0125)	¢	(0162)	Ç	(0199)	ì	(0236)
	(015)	4	(052)	Y	(089)	~	(0126)	£	(0163)	È	(0200)	í	(0237)
	(016)	5	(053)	Z	(090)		(0127)	¤	(0164)	É	(0201)	î	(0238)
	(017)	6	(054)	[	(091)		(0128)	¥	(0165)	Ê	(0202)	ï	(0239)
	(018)	7	(055)	\	(092)		(0129)	¦	(0166)	Ë	(0203)	ð	(0240)
	(019)	8	(056)	]	(093)	‚	(0130)	§	(0167)	Ì	(0204)	ñ	(0241)
	(020)	9	(057)	^	(094)	ƒ	(0131)	¨	(0168)	Í	(0205)	ò	(0242)
	(021)	:	(058)	_	(095)	„	(0132)	©	(0169)	Î	(0206)	ó	(0243)
	(022)	;	(059)	`	(096)	…	(0133)	ª	(0170)	Ï	(0207)	ô	(0244)
	(023)	<	(060)	a	(097)	†	(0134)	«	(0171)	Ð	(0208)	õ	(0245)
	(024)	=	(061)	b	(098)	‡	(0135)	¬	(0172)	Ñ	(0209)	ö	(0246)
	(025)	>	(062)	c	(099)	ˆ	(0136)	-	(0173)	Ò	(0210)	÷	(0247)
	(026)	?	(063)	d	(0100)	‰	(0137)	®	(0174)	Ó	(0211)	ø	(0248)
	(027)	@	(064)	e	(0101)	Š	(0138)	¯	(0175)	Ô	(0212)	ù	(0249)
	(028)	A	(065)	f	(0102)	‹	(0139)	°	(0176)	Õ	(0213)	ú	(0250)
	(029)	B	(066)	g	(0103)	Œ	(0140)	±	(0177)	Ö	(0214)	û	(0251)
	(030)	C	(067)	h	(0104)		(0141)	²	(0178)	×	(0215)	ü	(0252)
	(031)	D	(068)	i	(0105)		(0142)	³	(0179)	Ø	(0216)	ý	(0253)
	(032)	E	(069)	j	(0106)		(0143)	´	(0180)	Ù	(0217)	þ	(0254)
!	(033)	F	(070)	k	(0107)		(0144)	µ	(0181)	Ú	(0218)	ÿ	(0255)
"	(034)	G	(071)	l	(0108)	'	(0145)	¶	(0182)	Û	(0219)		
#	(035)	H	(072)	m	(0109)	'	(0146)	·	(0183)	Ü	(0220)		
$	(036)	I	(073)	n	(0110)	"	(0147)	¸	(0184)	Ý	(0221)		

Notes:

Character 032 represents a space. Character 0160 represents a non-breaking space. Extended characters can be created by holding down the ALT key while typing on the numeric keypad the number shown between parentheses.

Code Page 1250

(00)	% (037)	J (074)	o (0111)	” (0148)	ą (0185)	Ţ (0222)
(01)	& (038)	K (075)	p (0112)	• (0149)	ş (0186)	ß (0223)
(02)	' (039)	L (076)	q (0113)	— (0150)	» (0187)	ŕ (0224)
(03)	((040)	M (077)	r (0114)	– (0151)	Ľ (0188)	á (0225)
(04)	) (041)	N (078)	s (0115)	(0152)	” (0189)	â (0226)
(05)	* (042)	O (079)	t (0116)	™ (0153)	ĺ (0190)	ă (0227)
(06)	+ (043)	P (080)	u (0117)	š (0154)	ż (0191)	ä (0228)
(07)	, (044)	Q (081)	v (0118)	› (0155)	Ŕ (0192)	Í (0229)
(08)	- (045)	R (082)	w (0119)	ś (0156)	Á (0193)	ć (0230)
(09)	. (046)	S (083)	x (0120)	ť (0157)	Â (0194)	ç (0231)
(010)	/ (047)	T (084)	y (0121)	ž (0158)	Ă (0195)	č (0232)
(011)	0 (048)	U (085)	z (0122)	ź (0159)	Ä (0196)	é (0233)
(012)	1 (049)	V (086)	{ (0123)	° (0160)	Ĺ (0197)	ę (0234)
(013)	2 (050)	W (087)	| (0124)	ˇ (0161)	Ć (0198)	ë (0235)
(014)	3 (051)	X (088)	} (0125)	˘ (0162)	Ç (0199)	ě (0236)
(015)	4 (052)	Y (089)	~ (0126)	Ł (0163)	Č (0200)	í (0237)
(016)	5 (053)	Z (090)	(0127)	¤ (0164)	É (0201)	î (0238)
(017)	6 (054)	[(091)	(0128)	Ą (0165)	Ę (0202)	ď (0239)
(018)	7 (055)	\ (092)	(0129)	¦ (0166)	Ë (0203)	đ (0240)
(019)	8 (056)	] (093)	‚ (0130)	§ (0167)	Ě (0204)	ń (0241)
(020)	9 (057)	^ (094)	(0131)	¨ (0168)	Í (0205)	ň (0242)
(021)	: (058)	_ (095)	„ (0132)	© (0169)	Î (0206)	ó (0243)
(022)	, (059)	` (096)	… (0133)	Ş (0170)	Ď (0207)	ô (0244)
(023)	< (060)	a (097)	† (0134)	« (0171)	Đ (0208)	ő (0245)
(024)	= (061)	b (098)	‡ (0135)	¬ (0172)	Ń (0209)	ö (0246)
(025)	> (062)	c (099)	(0136)	- (0173)	Ň (0210)	÷ (0247)
(026)	? (063)	d (0100)	‰ (0137)	® (0174)	Ó (0211)	ř (0248)
(027)	@ (064)	e (0101)	Š (0138)	Ż (0175)	Ô (0212)	ů (0249)
(028)	A (065)	f (0102)	‹ (0139)	° (0176)	Ő (0213)	ú (0250)
(029)	B (066)	g (0103)	Ś (0140)	⊥ (0177)	Ö (0214)	ű (0251)
- (030)	C (067)	h (0104)	Ť (0141)	¸ (0178)	× (0215)	ü (0252)
(031)	D (068)	i (0105)	Ž (0142)	ł (0179)	Ř (0216)	ý (0253)
(032)	E (069)	j (0106)	Ź (0143)	´ (0180)	Ů (0217)	ţ (0254)
! (033)	F (070)	k (0107)	(0144)	µ (0181)	Ú (0218)	˙ (0255)
" (034)	G (071)	l (0108)	' (0145)	¶ (0182)	Ű (0219)	
# (035)	H (072)	m (0109)	' (0146)	· (0183)	Ü (0220)	
$ (036)	I (073)	n (0110)	" (0147)	¸ (0184)	Ý (0221)	

Notes:

Character 032 represents a space. Character 0160 represents a non-breaking space. Extended characters can be created by holding down the ALT key while typing on the numeric keypad the number shown between parentheses.

Code Page 1251

	(00)	%	(037)	J	(074)	o	(0111)	"	(0148)	№	(0185)	Ю	(0222)
	(01)	&	(038)	K	(075)	p	(0112)	•	(0149)	є	(0186)	Я	(0223)
	(02)	'	(039)	L	(076)	q	(0113)	—	(0150)	»	(0187)	а	(0224)
	(03)	(	(040)	M	(077)	r	(0114)	–	(0151)	ј	(0188)	б	(0225)
	(04)	)	(041)	N	(078)	s	(0115)		(0152)	Ѕ	(0189)	в	(0226)
	(05)	*	(042)	O	(079)	t	(0116)	™	(0153)	ѕ	(0190)	г	(0227)
	(06)	+	(043)	P	(080)	u	(0117)	љ	(0154)	ї	(0191)	д	(0228)
	(07)	,	(044)	Q	(081)	v	(0118)	›	(0155)	А	(0192)	е	(0229)
	(08)	-	(045)	R	(082)	w	(0119)	њ	(0156)	Б	(0193)	ж	(0230)
	(09)	.	(046)	S	(083)	x	(0120)	ќ	(0157)	В	(0194)	з	(0231)
	(010)	/	(047)	T	(084)	y	(0121)	ћ	(0158)	Г	(0195)	и	(0232)
	(011)	0	(048)	U	(085)	z	(0122)	џ	(0159)	Д	(0196)	й	(0233)
	(012)	1	(049)	V	(086)	{	(0123)		(0160)	Е	(0197)	к	(0234)
	(013)	2	(050)	W	(087)	|	(0124)	Ў	(0161)	Ж	(0198)	л	(0235)
	(014)	3	(051)	X	(088)	}	(0125)	ў	(0162)	З	(0199)	м	(0236)
	(015)	4	(052)	Y	(089)	~	(0126)	Ј	(0163)	И	(0200)	н	(0237)
	(016)	5	(053)	Z	(090)		(0127)	¤	(0164)	Й	(0201)	о	(0238)
	(017)	6	(054)	[	(091)	Ђ	(0128)	Ґ	(0165)	К	(0202)	п	(0239)
	(018)	7	(055)	\	(092)	Ѓ	(0129)	¦	(0166)	Л	(0203)	р	(0240)
	(019)	8	(056)	]	(093)	,	(0130)	§	(0167)	М	(0204)	с	(0241)
	(020)	9	(057)	^	(094)	ѓ	(0131)	Ё	(0168)	Н	(0205)	т	(0242)
	(021)	:	(058)	_	(095)	„	(0132)	©	(0169)	О	(0206)	у	(0243)
	(022)	;	(059)	`	(096)	…	(0133)	Є	(0170)	П	(0207)	ф	(0244)
	(023)	<	(060)	a	(097)	†	(0134)	«	(0171)	Р	(0208)	х	(0245)
	(024)	=	(061)	b	(098)	‡	(0135)	¬	(0172)	С	(0209)	ц	(0246)
	(025)	>	(062)	c	(099)		(0136)		(0173)	Т	(0210)	ч	(0247)
	(026)	?	(063)	d	(0100)	‰	(0137)	®	(0174)	У	(0211)	ш	(0248)
	(027)	@	(064)	e	(0101)	Љ	(0138)	Ї	(0175)	Ф	(0212)	щ	(0249)
	(028)	A	(065)	f	(0102)	‹	(0139)	°	(0176)	Х	(0213)	ъ	(0250)
	(029)	B	(066)	g	(0103)	Њ	(0140)	±	(0177)	Ц	(0214)	ы	(0251)
	(030)	C	(067)	h	(0104)	Ќ	(0141)	І	(0178)	Ч	(0215)	ь	(0252)
	(031)	D	(068)	i	(0105)	Ћ	(0142)	і	(0179)	Ш	(0216)	э	(0253)
	(032)	E	(069)	j	(0106)	Џ	(0143)	ґ	(0180)	Щ	(0217)	ю	(0254)
!	(033)	F	(070)	k	(0107)	ђ	(0144)	µ	(0181)	Ъ	(0218)	я	(0255)
"	(034)	G	(071)	l	(0108)	'	(0145)	¶	(0182)	Ы	(0219)		
#	(035)	H	(072)	m	(0109)	'	(0146)	·	(0183)	Ь	(0220)		
$	(036)	I	(073)	n	(0110)	"	(0147)	ё	(0184)	Э	(0221)		

Notes:

Character 032 represents a space. Character 0160 represents a non-breaking space. Extended characters can be created by holding down the ALT key while typing on the numeric keypad the number shown between parentheses.

Bibliography

Additional information on the theory and practice of user interface design may be found in the following works. The bibliographies of these works provide many additional references to the large literature on user interface design.

Apple Computer. *Human Interface Guidelines: The Apple Desktop Interface*. Reading, MA: Addison-Wesley, 1987.

Brown, C. M. *Human-Computer Interface Design Guidelines*. Norwood, NJ: Ablex Publishing Corp., 1988.

Chew, J. C., & Whiteside, J., eds. *Empowering People: CHI '90 Conference Proceedings*. ACM Press, 1990.

Hewlett-Packard. *HP New Wave Environment: User Interface Design Rules*. [Manual Part No. D1701-90003.] Santa Clara, CA: Hewlett Packard, 1988.

IBM. *Common User Access: Advanced Interface Design Guide*. Boca Raton, FL: IBM, 1989.

Johnson, J. et al. "The Xerox Star: A Retrospective". *Computer*, September 1989: 11-26.

Laurel, B., ed. *The Art of Human-Computer Interface Design*. Reading, MA: Addison-Wesley, 1990.

Liddle, D. E. *What Makes a Desktop Different*.

Microsoft Corporation. *The Windows Interface: An Application Design Guide*. Redmond, WA: Microsoft Press, 1992.

Nielsen, J., ed. *Coordinating User Interfaces for Consistency*. Boston: Academic Press, 1989.

Norman, D. A. *The Psychology of Everyday Things*. New York: Basic Books, 1988.

Open Software Foundation. *OSF/Motif Style Guide: Revision 1.1*. Cambridge, MA: Open Software Foundation, 1990.

Robertson, S. P., Olson, G. M., & Olson, J. S., eds. *Reaching Through Technology: CHI '91 Conference Proceedings*. Addison-Wesley, 1991.

Shneiderman, B. *Designing the User Interface: Strategies for Effective Human-Computer Interaction.* Reading, MA: Addison-Wesley, 1987.

Sun Microsystems. *OPEN LOOK Graphical User Interface Application Style Guidelines.* Reading, MA: Addison-Wesley, 1990.

Sun Microsystems. *OPEN LOOK Graphical User Interface Functional Specification.* Reading, MA: Addison-Wesley, 1989.

Index

Symbol

A

B

C

Great Programming Resources from Microsoft Press

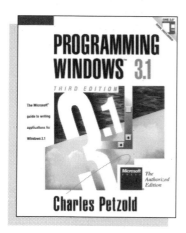

Programming Windows™ 3.1

Charles Petzold

"Broad in scope and omitting little, this book is a must for anyone serious about Windows." **BYTE**

A valuable resource for both new Windows 3.1 programmers and owners of the previous edition. "The Petzold Book" has become the book Windows programmers depend on—packed with indispensable reference data, tested programming advice, keen insight, and page after page of new sample programs. The most authoritative, thorough resource available for anyone seeking information on the dynamics and structure of Windows. Includes one 1.44-MB 3.5-inch disk.

ISBN 1-55615-395-3   1008 pages $49.95 ($67.95 Canada)

The Microsoft® Guide to C++ Programming

Kaare Christian

Valuable insights, information, sample code, and analysis with detailed discussions of the C++ object-oriented paradigm—ideal for the professional C programmer eager to start programming in C++. This three-part book contains a thorough and accessible introduction to object-oriented concepts and C++, source code examples in Microsoft C/C++ version 7, and a hands-on guide to the Microsoft Foundation Class (MFC) Library for Windows. No matter what implementation of C++ you use, this book will be indispensable.

ISBN 1-55615-394-5   496 pages $27.95 ($37.95 Canada)

Microsoft® Windows™ 3.1 Developer's Workshop

Microsoft Corporation

This is a winning collection of articles on significant Windows 3.1 programming issues—from the best programming minds in the business. The book covers internationalizing software for Windows ■ programming Windows for Pen Computing ■ the GDI device transform ■ NetBIOS programming ■ developing virtual device drivers ■ Visual Basic as a professional tool. Includes one 1.44-MB 3.5-inch disk containing all the source code and executable (EXE) files in the book.

ISBN 1-55615-480-1   350 pages $34.95 ($47.95 Canada)

The Windows™ Interface:
An Application Design Guide

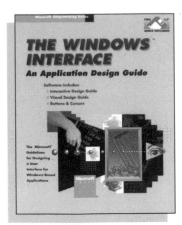

Microsoft Corporation
248 pages, softcover with two 1.44-MB 3.5-inch disks
ISBN 1-55615-439-9
$39.95*   ($54.95 Canada)

This book contains the Microsoft guidelines for creating well-designed, consistent user interfaces for applications that run on the Microsoft Windows version 3.1 operating system. It's an essential reference for all programmers and designers working on applications for Windows, regardless of experience level or development tool used.

Beginning with the basic principles of user interface design, the book moves from discussions of mouse and keyboard input elements to detailed information on the major elements of the user interface. The concluding chapters cover Windows for Pen Computing and several other important topics, such as adding Help systems and providing ways for users to customize the interface. If you're developing applications for Microsoft Windows, this book will be a key resource.

Bundled with the book is a set of companion disks.
They include the following materials:

Interactive Design Guide

A demonstration application that incorporates the ideas and recommendations presented in *The Windows Interface*. It also includes an online version of this book's contents with powerful, full-text searching capabilities for instant access to all areas the user is interested in locating.

Visual Design Guide

This online reference complements *The Windows Interface*. It focuses on artistic considerations, such as how to use color effectively, how to design icons, and how to make buttons look raised, depressed, or inactive. It also contains examples of visuals, including toolbars, icons, and different types of buttons.

Buttons and Cursors

This is a collection of images that developers can incorporate directly into their applications. The disk also comes with a dynamic link library (DLL) that can create all states of a button from a bit map of the button's surface area. The disk includes a license agreement, allowing developers to use the images and the DLL in their products royalty-free.

Register Today!

Return *The GUI Guide* registration form for:

✔ Microsoft Press catalogs featuring books on related Microsoft software
✔ exclusive offers on specially priced books

Please mail the completed form to:

Microsoft Press Registration
The GUI Guide
PO Box 3019
Bothell, WA   98041-9910

or by fax to:

Microsoft Press
Attn: Marketing Department
Fax #: 206-936-7329

The GUI Guide Registration Form

NAME

COMPANY

ADDRESS

CITY   STATE   ZIP

1-55615-538-7A   Type: A1I

IMPORTANT—READ CAREFULLY BEFORE OPENING SOFTWARE PACKET(S). By opening the sealed packet(s) containing the software, you indicate your acceptance of the following Microsoft License Agreement.

MICROSOFT LICENSE AGREEMENT

(Book Companion Disks)

This is a legal agreement between you (either an individual or an entity) and Microsoft Corporation. By opening the sealed software packet(s) you are agreeing to be bound by the terms of this agreement. If you do not agree to the terms of this agreement, promptly return the unopened software packet(s) and any accompanying written materials to the place you obtained them for a full refund.

MICROSOFT SOFTWARE LICENSE

1. GRANT OF LICENSE. Microsoft grants to you the right to use for reference purposes one copy of the Microsoft software files included with this book (the "SOFTWARE") on a single terminal connected to a single computer. The SOFTWARE is in "use" on a computer when it is loaded into temporary memory (i.e., RAM) or installed into permanent memory (e.g., hard disk, CD-ROM, or other storage device) of that computer. You may not network the SOFTWARE or otherwise use it on more than one computer or computer terminal at the same time.

2. COPYRIGHT. The SOFTWARE is owned by Microsoft or its suppliers and is protected by United States copyright laws and international treaty provisions. Therefore, you must treat the SOFTWARE like any other copyrighted material (e.g., a book or musical recording) except that you may either (a) make one copy of the SOFTWARE solely for backup or archival purposes, or (b) transfer the SOFTWARE to a single hard disk provided you keep the original solely for backup or archival purposes. You may not modify, adapt, distribute or create derivative works of the SOFTWARE. You may not copy the written materials accompanying the SOFTWARE. All rights not granted to you herein are reserved by Microsoft.

3. OTHER RESTRICTIONS. You may not rent or lease the SOFTWARE, but you may transfer the SOFTWARE and accompanying written materials on a permanent basis provided you retain no copies and the recipient agrees to the terms of this Agreement. You may not reverse engineer, decompile, or disassemble the SOFTWARE. If the SOFTWARE is an update or has been updated, any transfer must include the most recent update and all prior versions.

4. DUAL MEDIA SOFTWARE. If the SOFTWARE package contains both 3.5" and 5.25" disks, then you may use only the disks appropriate for your single-user computer. You may not use the other disks on another computer or loan, rent, lease, or transfer them to another user except as part of the permanent transfer (as provided above) of all SOFTWARE and written materials.

DISCLAIMER OF WARRANTY

THE SOFTWARE (including instructions for its use) is provided "AS IS" WITHOUT WARRANTY OF ANY KIND. MICROSOFT FURTHER DISCLAIMS ALL IMPLIED WARRANTIES INCLUDING WITHOUT LIMITATION ANY IMPLIED WARRANTIES OF MERCHANT-ABILITY OR OF FITNESS FOR A PARTICULAR PURPOSE. THE ENTIRE RISK ARISING OUT OF THE USE OR PERFORMANCE OF THE SOFTWARE AND DOCUMENTATION REMAINS WITH YOU.

IN NO EVENT SHALL MICROSOFT, ITS AUTHORS, OR ANYONE ELSE INVOLVED IN THE CREATION, PRODUCTION, OR DELIVERY OF THE SOFTWARE BE LIABLE FOR ANY DAMAGES WHATSOEVER (INCLUDING, WITHOUT LIMITATION, DAMAGES FOR LOSS OF BUSINESS PROFITS, BUSINESS INTERRUPTION, LOSS OF BUSINESS INFORMATION, OR OTHER PECUNIARY LOSS) ARISING OUT OF THE USE OF OR INABILITY TO USE THE SOFTWARE OR DOCUMENTATION, EVEN IF MICROSOFT HAS BEEN ADVISED OF THE POSSIBILITY OF SUCH DAMAGES. BECAUSE SOME STATES/COUNTRIES DO NOT ALLOW THE EXCLUSION OR LIMITATION OF LIABILITY FOR CONSEQUENTIAL OR INCIDENTAL DAMAGES, THE ABOVE LIMITATION MAY NOT APPLY TO YOU.

U.S. GOVERNMENT RESTRICTED RIGHTS

The SOFTWARE and documentation are provided with RESTRICTED RIGHTS. Use, duplication, or disclosure by the Government is subject to restrictions as set forth in subparagraph (c)(1)(ii) of The Rights in Technical Data and Computer Software clause at DFARS 252.227-7013 or subparagraphs (c)(1) and (2) of the Commercial Computer Software — Restricted Rights 48 CFR 52.227-19, as applicable. Manufacturer is Microsoft Corporation/One Microsoft Way/Redmond, WA 98052-6399.

If you acquired this product in the United States, this Agreement is governed by the laws of the State of Washington.

Should you have any questions concerning this Agreement, or if you desire to contact Microsoft Press for any reason, please write: Microsoft Press/One Microsoft Way/Redmond, WA 98052-6399.

5.25-inch disk for The GUI Guide

You can order the enclosed disk in 5.25-inch format—free of charge. Include only shipping charges of $5.00 per disk set. To order, request item number **097-000-825**. Send your name and address (no P.O. Boxes please), and daytime phone number along with your check or money order for shipping (U.S. funds only) to: Microsoft Press, Attn: The GUI Guide, P.O. Box 3011, Bothell, WA 98041-3011. Allow 2–3 weeks for delivery. Offer valid in the U.S. only.